Flying High in Travel

Flying High in Travel

A Complete Guide to Careers in the Travel Industry

New Expanded Edition

KAREN RUBIN

John Wiley & Sons, Inc.

New York • Chichester • Brisbane • Toronto • Singapore

In recognition of the importance of preserving what has been written, it is a policy of John Wiley & Sons, Inc., to have books of enduring value published in the United States printed on acid-free paper, and we exert our best efforts to that end.

Library of Congress Cataloging-in-Publication Data:

Rubin, Karen, 1951-
Flying high in travel: a complete guide to careers in the travel industry/ Karen Rubin.—expanded ed.
p. cm.
Includes index.
ISBN 0-471-55173-2 (pbk.)
1. Travel agents—Vocational guidance. I. Title.
G154.R82 1992
338.4'79102373—dc20 91-26084

Printed in the United States of America

10 9 8 7 6 5

To my parents, for their unbridled support,
my husband and sons, for their unbounded inspiration,
and to Eric Friedheim, who helped me help myself.

May each become
all that he or she can be
and humankind realize its humanity.

Preface

As in the first edition of *Flying High in Travel: A Complete Guide to Careers in the Travel Industry,* my goal is to speak personally and arm you with as much information as possible to conduct a realistic and effective job search leading to a career in the travel industry.

My approach differs from the careers-in-travel books that take a simplistic view, dwelling on specific (and obvious) job functions such as travel agent, airline pilot, and tour escort and from the scholarly references that tend to confine career information to a chapter or an appendix. In contrast, I take a business approach, categorizing topics based on specific industry segments such as hospitality, tour operations, and cruise lines.

This format takes into account the fact that most travel businesses have similar job functions (sales and marketing, operations, etc.), but that each segment has its particular personality and offers a different set of opportunities. Moreover, this approach demonstrates how the various segments interact with one another and how jobs are part of a career path—important perspectives for job-seekers, particularly the growing legions of those attempting to move from one part of the industry to another.

Flying High is a guidebook in the truest sense. It is an effort to provide a Grand Tour of the travel industry, a $350 billion mega-industry that employs more than 6 million people in scores of different segments. But any guidebook must necessarily be a snapshot, freezing a fleeting moment in an ever-changing landscape.

When *Flying High* was first published, the effects of deregulation were just taking hold, transforming business fundamentals and literally shaking the foundation of many travel enterprises. Things have changed dramatically since then: Companies that had been in business for generations have folded, merged, or consolidated. An industry that had been castigated for its stability and predictability (three times a year, airlines would, in lock step, raise fares)—one in which individuals would spend an entire career in a single company or part of the industry—is now in a constant state of flux due to deregulation, demographic and economic shifts, and globalization. People find themselves moving on within only a few years or even a few months.

More has changed in the last five years in the travel industry than had changed in the prior 50 years. A microcosm of socio-political-economic forces, major world events such as the end of the Cold War and the Persian Gulf War have dramatically changed the makeup and mandate of companies, and with them, their needs for travel professionals.

This new edition addresses these changes and gives more emphasis to segments and aspects of the industry that had not been covered before, such as the ski industry, the theme parks and attractions industry (a sizeable employer), and emerging professions in technology and security.

Each year, tens of thousands of people search for a job in the travel industry. Many are lured by the glamour and excitement of travel and are guided by false impressions and unrealistic expectations. They typically cram themselves into a few well-known, highly visible occupations, neglecting the vast opportunities in lesser known travel fields that might offer greater personal satisfaction.

The travel industry draws people of all ages and backgrounds. There are those just leaving high school (this is one of the few fields in which people with only a high school diploma can still rise to the top of their profession). More and more people are coming to the travel industry from colleges, and hundreds of schools around the country have opened travel and tourism departments. There also are significant numbers of career changers–particularly teachers, nurses, and businessmen–and retirees who seek to start over in travel, many of whom start off with a vocational school program.

For decades, the travel industry has shown an uncanny ability to grow, despite economic downturns and political unrest. However, 1990 brought an unprecedented combination of events: recession and war combined with an ongoing trend of consolidation and restructuring. For the first time in anyone's memory, the industry virtually stopped moving forward. Major companies folded up while many others laid off workers.

The tens of thousands of out-of-work travel professionals caught up in the maelstrom of consolidations and bankruptcies have made for an extremely competitive job climate. There is a glut of middle and senior management people all looking for jobs. However, there should be a correction by the middle of the decade and a return to swelling demand for travel professionals as the industry emerges as the world's largest by the year 2000.

Though initially the going will be tough, there are still job opportunities; but you have to be savvy. You have to research, know what to look for and where to look. You need to know about alternatives–different facets of the travel industry and different job functions–in order to expand the opportunities available to you and improve your chances of success.

Since *Flying High* was first published, I have launched Travel Executive Search, a recruitment company specializing in the travel industry. This role, combined with nearly 20 years as a journalist specializing in the travel industry, has enabled me to incorporate into this new edition more specific, first-hand information and insights into travel careers and career paths, salaries, what employers look for, and where the opportunities lie in the travel industry.

Remember: There are 6 million people employed in some 500,000 travel and tourism businesses. You are looking for just one job. It may take time, but if you are persistent and know who to approach and how to market yourself, you will be successful.

I would like to express my thanks to my editor at Wiley, Claire Thompson, for encouraging me to tackle this topic again, and Eric Friedheim, who once again has been a catalyst to my career.

KAREN RUBIN

Great Neck, New York
February 1992

Contents

Landing a Job

1

Introduction and Overview

Fulfilling the Dream

A Dynamic and Challenging Career

Most people dream of working at something that they find to be interesting, challenging, and fun – something that they enjoy doing even after work hours are over. Travel is such an activity. For many travel is a dream of a lifetime and working at a job that makes it possible to travel can be a dream come true. This book is about fulfilling this dream.

But it is first necessary to dispel the illusions that surround travel careers. A career in travel is considered very glamorous and adventurous. Once inside the industry, however, some people find that the reality of hard work, long hours, and low pay dulls the glow.

Most people who have not simply fallen into a career in travel seek it because they love to travel. If this is your main reason for entering the business, you are better off staying in some other field where you are likely to earn 20 to 40 percent more in salary and have three or four weeks of paid vacation a year to travel as you wish. For you are not apt to travel as frequently, as cheaply, or as spontaneously as you might expect in the travel industry – especially now since free and reduced-rate travel are becoming more restricted and the federal government is hoping to tax free trips as fringe benefits. Also, most people in the industry who travel do so for business purposes to the point where traveling can become too much of a good thing, bringing more stress than satisfaction.

You *should* pursue a career in travel because of the *business* and the *product* itself, namely, travel. Travel and tourism is one of the most dynamic industries anywhere, offering extraordinary opportunities for mobility, creativity, and personal satisfaction. Having a role in the betterment of society and contributing to world peace are not just ideals, they are integral to an endeavor that brings disparate peoples and ideas together.

In many ways, the travel industry is a business like any other, with many of the same concerns and problems that arise in selling groceries, making women's shoes, or designing office buildings. There are the same concerns for profit and loss and for accounts receivables and payables; there are the same problems of productivity, market share, and high cost of investment capital that affect most industries. But people who have had an opportunity to experience other occupations find something special in the travel industry–energy, creativity, fast pace, diversity, challenge, and growth–that they had not found elsewhere. In fact, so often in this book, people refer to their particular part of travel as "fun" and "showtime." And when for one reason or another, people are forced to leave the industry, many feel a sense of withdrawal.

The industry's product–travel–is like no other. Travel becomes addictive; it is for good reason that people say they have been bitten by the "travel bug." Travel is "a life-changing, life-enhancing experience," explained travel agent Richard Dixon. Working in and with "travel" brings an excitement to the job that airline people feel even if they work miles away from the airport and that travel agents feel as they sit for hours on end searching the computer display for schedules and fares. There is a sense of sharing in some marvelous adventure.

Travel is very much a "people" business. No matter how sophisticated airplanes or computer reservations systems or videotext systems become, there is no getting away from the fact that the business is all about servicing people. The industry attracts "people-people," individuals who are energetic and open to new experiences, ideas, and, most of all, people. Because people tend to stay in the industry, even if they move from one area of work to another, a close camaraderie usually develops even among those who work for competitors.

In some respects, travel is a service; in others, it is a commodity, just as any item you buy off a shelf if the price is right. Yet, unlike most other commodities, travel–a seat on an airplane or a room in a hotel–cannot be stored away. The high perishability makes for high risk, challenging industry professionals to be brilliant forecasters and marketers, to excel at information management, and to be efficient operators.

On the other hand, the potential for the industry is unlimited, for unlike a VCR, which you might buy once and have for many years, travel is an experience that has to be renewed each time, and each time will be different.

Moreover, there are unlimited possibilities in the style of travel. The same customer might take one trip or a dozen trips in a year, traveling for business, vacations, and weekends, to visit family and friends or to take part in an event. And people travel differently during the course of a lifetime: as a college student backpacking through Europe; a single, young professional looking for sun or snow; a newlywed; a professional couple; a family with young children; a chief executive officer on an expense account; the couple whose children have left the "nest"; a retiree; a widow or widower.

The customers for travel are not confined to any particular stratum of society. A passenger on a $6,000 trek of the Himalayas might be a secretary or a mailman as easily as a stockbroker.

The travel industry is expanding and changing constantly, and new job titles and specialties are being created all the time. Few industries provide as much opportunity for someone with limited formal education to rise as quickly through the ranks to positions of enormous responsibility and prestige; to be an entrepreneur; to work for some of the largest or smallest companies; and to see almost instant results from an innovation. Few industries provide as much mobility–moving up in an organization or to other companies or other fields and even to live and work virtually anywhere in the world.

A Vital and Necessary Service

The term *tourism* may conjure up stereotypical images of paunchy, balding men in Bermuda shorts and blue-haired grannies in tennis shoes, disembarking from a tour bus with instant cameras in hand. In this context, travel and tourism seems frivolous and nonessential. Nothing could be further from the truth. Travel and tourism forms a complex network of vital and necessary services that touches virtually every individual and every business in the world. Leisure travel – vacations for rest and relaxation, cultural pursuits, adventure, or visits with friends and relatives – is only half of what the travel and tourism industry does, but even these seeming luxuries have become necessities of modern life. Nonetheless, the same airplanes, hotels, car rentals, and trains that are in place to serve the tourist also transport and house the businessperson negotiating deals, the diplomat, the politician, and the artist. The travel and tourism industry makes commerce, diplomacy, and exchanges of ideas and cultures possible. Face-to-face contacts between people at any distance whatsoever could not take place without the diverse services provided by travel and tourism.

"The world is becoming a global village," Pope John Paul II told a private audience of 7,000 travel professionals in 1985, "in which people of different continents are made to feel like neighbors. Modern transportation has removed the obstacles of distance, enabling people to appreciate each other, engage in the exchange of ideas and commerce. Tourism can help overcome real prejudices and foster bonds. Tourism can be a real force of world peace."

Travel and tourism plays a critical role in the economies of tiny villages and huge countries. In countries like Mexico, Jamaica, and Spain, tourism is the linchpin for the economy. For countries lacking valuable resources or heavy industry, tourism represents hope in breaking a spiral of poverty and misery. Closer to home, there are countless examples of communities where tourism is the base for the economy, including Orlando, Atlantic City, and Las Vegas.

In a world where so many make their living by selling people what they do not want or should not want or could care less about, most travel industry professionals derive tremendous satisfaction from selling people a "good time." They sense that what they do is important and that they are contributing in a real way to the betterment of society through facilitating people-to-people contacts. In short, people feel good about working in the travel industry and promoting tourism.

Many are fond of saying that travel dates back to Noah or Moses or the Pilgrims. The travel industry, however, is a phenomenon of the Industrial Revolution, with its social revolution of minimum wages and paid vacations, coupled with the technological revolution that made for buses, jet planes, elevators, and air conditioning. Mass travel and the annual vacation ritual only date from the end of World War II, with the jet plane and the packaged tour; in polls, travel ranks just after a home and an insurance policy as a necessary expense.

Travel has not only changed from a luxury to a necessity in the American lifestyle, but the trend toward greater affluence, the effect of more leisure time, and the maturing of the Baby Boomers into their peak earnings (and travel) years all prompt forecasters to predict fantastic growth for the industry in years to come. Indeed, many expect travel and tourism to become the single largest industry in the world by the year 2000–and not just in dollars, but in jobs.

All of this bodes extremely well for the jobs outlook in the travel and tourism industry. Indeed, despite all the technological developments, travel and tourism remains a business of serving people, so is people-intensive. Six million Americans already make their living in the industry. Another two million are employed in related fields. The travel and tourism industry has shown an uncanny ability to generate new jobs even when the rest of the economy is in the doldrums, and the industry is expected to show some of the strongest growth rates in new jobs in the future.

It is not just the quantity of jobs that is appealing, but the quality and diversity. Travel and tourism is so diversified that it entails virtually every kind of activity and employs almost every kind of worker. It is common to think of the industry in terms of "travel agent," "flight attendant," "airline pilot," "tour escort," and "front-desk clerk." People readily recognize airlines, hotels, car rentals, and tour companies as travel and tourism businesses. But the industry is also real estate, ecology, urban planning, architecture, interior design, engineering, computer science, politics, public relations, marketing, personnel, publishing, telecommunications, finance, law, and scores of other fields. Travel and tourism employs archaeologists, sociologists, lawyers, doctors, teachers, computer specialists, artists, writers, marine scientists, actors, musicians, and countless other professionals. Indeed, the industry offers an alternate path to fulfill any number of professional dreams.

Moreover, industry leaders express concern about a shortage of workers during this decade. "We will have to be more flexible in establishing split time and flex time for our employees," said a hotel industry executive, "and exert a recruiting effort beyond anything we have seen before, because if we can't service that market, we will lose it."

Overcoming the Catch-22

Ironically, the tremendous demand for workers will not make getting into the travel business any easier; if anything, getting in will be tougher. Already, there are about 100 applicants for every job. In the travel agency business, newcomers are having such a difficult time that they are offering to work for free in exchange for the training and experience. The demand for new employees is concentrated among the experienced, or middle-management layers, while the increased reliance on sophisticated computer systems, the extraordinary pace, and the low profit margins have made it difficult for companies to retain their on-the-job training programs. Helping you get around the catch-22 of needing experience to get experience is the aim of this book.

In the end, it does not matter whether there are thousands of jobs or only a few; all you want is one. Succeeding in getting one requires a strategy. You need to be able to focus in and target your objectives and to convince a potential employer that even if you do not actually have industry experience, you understand the fundamentals and are motivated to learn.

There are no sure-fire methods of landing a job. It comes down to personalities and the philosophy of the person doing the hiring. You will get an idea of how varied the career paths can be from the people interviewed in this book.

Each of the chapters on an industry segment describes how the industry is structured, what key issues it faces, and what the future is likely to hold. The information is intended to give you the fundamentals so that you can demonstrate to a potential employer some understanding of the business. It will also give you a better handle on whether a field is right for you. It will show you that there is more than one way of accomplishing your primary goals. This book will also give you a better idea of what employers are looking for so that you can make a more convincing presentation during an interview.

Indeed, a career is more than any one job; it is a series of steps up a ladder, and a job is only one rung. In travel, especially, you may start off in the hotel business and wind up in airlines or car rentals or travel agencies. The travel industry is expanding so rapidly that in most instances the objective is just to get into a field or a company any way that you can—as a reservationist, a receptionist, a secretary, a clerk, or an accountant. This is particularly true if you are coming from another field to a similar job in travel. You will then be able to move up or move over extremely rapidly.

If there is one theme that is common to every facet of this fantastically fragmented industry, it is its growing professionalism. The industry is recognizing the need to prepare for middle management by creating more entry-level training and development programs. Indeed, it is likely that two distinct career paths to the top will emerge—one from within the ranks and one from vocational and academic programs.

So many people fall into their careers and live with frustration and discontentment until they are able to retire. After nearly 20 years as a journalist reporting on the travel industry and now as an executive recruiter for the travel industry, interacting with literally thousands of professionals and watching them rise in their careers, I can honestly say that I have never met so many people who love what they do. A career in travel is competitive, challenging, and frequently beyond control, but it is also fun. There is a certain giddy delight attached to working in travel.

This book is written for those who aspire to management or a profession in travel and tourism, for those who seek more than a job, but a career in travel. Let this be your guide to success.

Travel and Tourism Industry Overview

It took Marco Polo 12 years to journey from Italy to China, at great peril all along the way. People take for granted the size, scope, and complexity of the international network of facilities and services that make it possible to retrace Marco Polo's trek today in a matter of weeks.

It is extremely difficult to define precisely what the "travel and tourism" industry is. "[It] has been described, half facetiously, as a collection of diverse products sold by a fragmented industry to segmented markets through a complex distribution chain," noted the U.S. Travel Data Center (USTDC), the Washington, D.C.-based travel research affiliate of the Travel Industry Association of America, in its *Economic Review of Travel 1989–90.*

"It comprises the airline terminal in the suburbs, the restaurant in town, the highway motel, the travel agency down the block, and a host of other businesses that do not even recognize their dependence on tourism, since visitors are [often] indistinguishable from local customers."

The late futurist Herman Kahn projected that tourism would be the world's largest industry by the year 2000, and his forecast is being realized. Despite advancements in telecommunications—and sometimes because of them—physically traveling has become more important than ever. Indeed, Americans took a total of 1.3 billion person-trips (one person on a trip 100 miles or more from home) in 1990, according to the USTDC.

The travel and tourism industry is the third largest retail industry in business receipts after automotive dealers and food stores, according to the USTDC, which measures the economic impact of travel and tourism in the United States. Spending on travel services in the United States totaled about $350 billion and generated more than $42.8 billion in tax revenue.

To put these extraordinary figures into perspective, Americans spent more on travel than on clothing, accessories, jewelry, and personal care combined or on household utilities, including telephone service, the USTDC noted. Travel spending in this country averaged $959 million each day, $40 million each hour, $660,000 each minute, $11,000 each second.

Most of the money goes to airlines, car rentals, bus companies, cruiselines, the railroad, lodgings, restaurants, tour companies, travel agents, attractions and theme parks, sightseeing companies, and convention centers.

The travel and tourism industry is the country's second largest employer. With each $60,000 spent by travelers directly supporting one job, the $350 billion spent on travel in the United

States generated 5.8 million jobs totaling $73.5 billion in payroll income.

In 48 of the 50 states and in thousands of localities, tourism has become the leading employer. In many areas, tourism has brought renewed vitality to communities once dependent on smokestack industries.

Over the past decade, travel industry employment has grown 43 percent, more than twice the growth rate for all industries, the USTDC noted. And, since 1972, payroll jobs in travel-related businesses have more than doubled, while total U.S. payroll employment increased by less than 50 percent.

Few travel companies appeal to the entire spectrum of travelers; instead they gear their products or services to distinct markets. This is called *market segmentation.* For example, many marketers are looking at the fantastic growth among women business travelers. Many hotel companies have gone so far as to create "women-only" floors to cater to this market. The family market is another growth area, as the Baby Boomers (the huge population born between 1946 and 1960) become parents themselves. Club Med has responded by opening up "mini clubs" and "baby clubs" at some of its resorts; the cruise industry has provided child care centers on board ships. Some companies are targeting the 18-to-25-year old group because they tend to be single and have a lot of discretionary money; others eye the 25-to-34-year-old group of dual-income, childless couples, who have money, if not much time, to travel; still others target senior citizens, who control the biggest chunk of discretionary income and have the time and inclination to travel.

The phenomenon of market segmentation is most apparent in the hotel industry, where hotels are being divided by floors according to the services and pricing that would appeal to a particular market. Airlines, of course, have been offering first, business, and tourist classes for years.

Deregulation, Automation, and Professionalism

The 500,000 different businesses involved in travel have their special interests and concerns. But virtually every travel entity and everyone working in travel is affected by three key interrelated developments: (1) deregulation, (2) automation, and (3) increased professionalism. These are essential to understanding the dynamics of the travel industry.

Deregulation of the airline, motorcoach, and travel agency industries changed the whole economics and structure of the industry—the relationships of companies to one another. Though hotels, tour companies, car rental agencies, cruiselines, and others had always been deregulated, the deregulation of these key industry segments had enormous impact on their own businesses.

By replacing what had essentially been a franchise with free market competition, companies had to revamp their products, their pricing, and the manner in which they distributed to their customers. The path was open for innovation, new companies, new services, and new ways of doing business. Travel was always an industry of low profit margin, and deregulation put additional pressure on cost controls and maximizing productivity.

The plethora of products and services has made computerized information and reservations systems essential. Consider that there are some five million airfares, changing at the rate of 120,000 a week.

Though travel is not generally considered "high-tech," the industry is, in fact, on the leading edge of consumer applications of sophisticated computers, communications, and transportation modes, in distribution, marketing, and product services.

With the greater premium placed on productivity, as well as on the need for capital-intensive technology and expensive marketing, a third trend has developed—consolidation. Consolidation is most visible among airlines where mergers, acquisitions, and bankruptcies have whittled down the number to a few major carriers. Consolidation has brought retrenchment by companies in which whole tiers of middle and upper management have been eliminated.

Yet another trend has come about—globalization, the multinational ownership or alliances of airlines, hotels, travel management companies, and the like, in response to falling barriers and borders and a greater appreciation of the world as a global marketplace.

These trends—deregulation, consolidation, automation, and globalization—are revolutionizing how the travel business is conducted and changing the professional makeup of the industry.

New opportunities are opening up all the time. There is enormous demand for marketers, quality control coordinators, computer specialists, yield management experts, researchers, trainers, and people with international business and language skills. On the other hand, many entry-level jobs have been eliminated.

Regardless of the kind of travel entity, there are categories of activities that are common to almost every one:

Product Development

Operations

Sales and Marketing

Public Relations

Administration

Automation/Management Information Systems (MIS)

In the past, success was almost universally of the bottoms-up variety – rising up through the ranks. Now, a second career path is emerging, with a new breed of travel professionals coming out of colleges, universities, and vocational schools, as well as from other industries.

While the outlook for travel and tourism is extremely bright, there is great volatility within the industry. This year's hot spot may be next year's trouble spot. Changes in airfares, currency values, and political situation all affect interest in and access to destinations; weather, natural disasters, or strikes can also destroy a destination or a company.

This is not an industry to go into for security; it is an industry to go into for challenge, excitement, and responsibility.

In the subsequent chapters, we will look at the various entities that collectively make up the travel and tourism industry. Since this book looks at the people that make travel and tourism activity possible, we will not just look at the conventional categories. We will look instead at the entire system, including, for example, destination promotion, aviation management, and support services. For this book is aimed at helping you share in the incomparable experience that working in the travel and tourism industry affords.

Agents, Operators, Planners

2

Travel Agents and Travel Agencies

The Travel Agent: Fulfiller of Dreams

In the days when travel was a once-in-a-lifetime event, the travel agent was quite literally a "fulfiller of dreams" – the one who made such lifelong ambitions of traveling to exotic locales reality. Even today, when travel is more of an annual rite than an extraordinary event, most agents still see their function as fulfilling dreams for, in essence, agents sell an experience in order to satisfy client expectations.

To most people, the travel agent personifies the travel industry. The most visible segment of the industry, the agent is actually the last link in an intricate chain of facilities and services. To travel suppliers like airlines, hotels, car rental companies, tour operators, and the like, the agent is their retailer – their distribution system – to the public. The travel agency gives the suppliers local contact with the public that they could not afford on their own.

Many people confuse the "travel agent" with the "travel agency." The agent is essentially a counselor who deals directly with the prospective traveler (the client). In contrast, the agency is an entire business that performs various sales and marketing functions and administrative tasks. In small agencies, a single person can be the counselor as well as the owner/manager who also handles the business issues; the larger the agency, the more specialization. Some of the largest travel agencies that handle commercial travel (travel for business purposes) even employ a quality control coordinator, who acts as a liaison between client and agency.

The travel agent treads a fine line between supplier and client. While travel agencies are essentially (and legally) the "agent" acting on behalf of the travel suppliers (being paid a commission each time they sell a company's service), travel counselors see their role as providing an objective (nonbiased) referral service for their clients. Though there are often monetary incentives (in the form of override commissions) to book a certain airline, tour company, car rental firm, and so on, their primary concern is to recommend the one that will best satisfy their clients' price and service wants because, as agents, they depend so much on repeat and referral business. Unlike the real estate agency that sees its client once in five or ten years or a lifetime or the fast-food restaurant that sells a standardized product, the travel agent services (more than sells) a client once, twice, or perhaps ten times in a single year. Though today's travelers may be more sophisticated and experienced, there is still a lot of hand-holding by their travel agents, who become trusted professionals much like their doctors, lawyers, or accountants.

Agents generally feel a tremendous sense of responsibility about making everything go perfectly, by tying all the myriad details of a trip together. "There are times when I am at home at night and I go over in my mind all the details of the trip," said Daniela Kelly, a New York agent. "Sometimes I give my home number, like when one of my clients had a trip with 20 different flights."

A mistake like bringing the client back to the wrong airport or timing a connection badly can have disastrous consequences. Even if the agent performs perfectly, he or she is only an intermediary; the tour company or some other supplier can make a mistake and the client can still hold the agent accountable (and liable).

Travel agency work affords an opportunity to become a professional with little or no advanced schooling. The work involves considerable problem-solving ability as well as the ability to deal with details and organize them. People-contact (face-to-face and by telephone) is the essence of the job; in fact, contacts (with both clients and suppliers) are as important to professional success as product knowledge. Having contacts inside travel companies themselves enables the agent to free up space at a hotel that is "booked solid," upgrade an airline ticket, or get extra or special service for a VIP. Nor is the client contact merely casual. "You have to involve yourself with the customer," reflected Jaime Patxot, a New York–based agent. "You dig into their personal life in order to come up with appropriate recommendations. We are psychiatrists sometimes."

Though personal service is still the essence of the business, computers are becoming fundamental to operations. Well over 95 percent of the more than 32,000 appointed travel agencies are now automated with airline reservations systems.

No day is the same; each day presents new challenges. Indeed, deregulation (the lifting of government-imposed rules on business operations among airlines and agencies) has introduced an entirely new element to the business – negotiations with travel suppliers on rates and commissions and even services.

The travel agency business offers excellent career mobility. Getting into the business is extremely difficult because experience is at a premium and the pace, economics of the business, and reliance on computers no longer allow for apprenticeships. But once inside, even after only two years of experience, an individual will find that there is enormous opportunity to rise. Mobility is more limited in small agencies, but large agency organizations offer all the career paths of any big business.

The travel agency industry is still very entrepreneurial. Ambitious agents who reach their heights at a small agency frequently go out on their own or move into senior management at other agencies.

The smallest agencies generally have one to four people – owner, manager, counselor, and bookkeeper or clerk; there also may be some commissioned outside sales agents. Medium-sized agencies may have a groups specialist, a commercial department, and counselors who specialize in destinations (such as the Caribbean, or Europe) or in cruises. The largest agencies are organized much like other big businesses, with personnel, operations, and marketing and sales departments; there also may be a sophisticated mailing department, a resident computer specialist, and training and development experts. The largest agencies may have several different businesses, including retail travel, corporate travel, incentive travel, convention and meeting planning, group tours, wholesale travel, travel school, and even package express, and thus require many more clerical, secretarial, and other support people. Indeed, one "mega-agency" lists 130 different job titles.

The pace of work is usually hectic, sometimes frantic. "There are certain days when you have the feeling of 'burnout,' when you get ten people in a row rushing in asking for a 'deal' to Florida. It gets to you," reflected Kelly.

The daily rush is intensified whenever there is an airline strike, a natural disaster, or some other event that would necessitate changing travel arrangements.

While the travel agent primarily services a client, the agent also must be a salesperson; the sales inventory is represented by the brochures on the rack. "Eighty percent of the people who come in here already know what they want," commented Patxot. "You are just servicing them. But the rest, you do sell." Agents have to learn various techniques of discerning the client's true wants and needs in order to narrow down what part of the world and what type of trip to recommend. "I show the client the world; he buys one piece of it," he said.

There is increasing emphasis on sales techniques, particularly on how to "close" a sale (get the customer to commit to the trip and put down a deposit) because there is so much shopping around by consumers. Agents are also frequently encouraged by management to "sell up" to higher-priced programs or to push "preferred" suppliers because they pay higher commissions to the agency. Agents also act as salespeople by drawing new clients to an agency, but frequently agencies employ outside salespeople who work solely on commission to perform this function.

Not too long ago, agents knew the airlines and fares to popular destinations by heart because there were relatively few airlines and rates changed at specified times after being approved by the government. But with deregulation, the airlines serving an airport can change overnight, and there are literally tens of thousands of new fares daily. Sheer growth of the industry on the one hand, and deregulation on the other, have made it impossible for any agent to keep track of all the fast-changing products, prices, and rules necessary to properly advise clients and book their travel. Increasingly, the travel agent functions as an information provider, drawing to some extent on personal familiarity and experience with places, facilities, and companies, but relying increasingly on powerful computers, weighty references, and even video brochures.

Traveling Is Not So Free

Most people who become travel agents do so mainly because they expect to travel extensively for free. "You don't travel that much, and you don't make any money at all," quipped one 20-year veteran.

Familiarization trips, or "fams" as they are called, which agents take in order to get to know destinations and facilities, are only occasionally free. Usually, they cost the agents something. A working agent is generally entitled to reduced-rate travel on many airlines, but airlines are becoming more restrictive on the passes. The IRS now is looking to tax the trips as fringe benefits. Also, employers establish policy on whether fams are to be taken as vacation time and whether the agent pays for the trip out of his or her own pocket. Moreover, time on these trips is generally taken up with seminars and hotel inspections, leaving little free time.

Still, it is true that most travel agents travel considerably more than the average person. "Being a travel agent gives me the opportunity to live a lifestyle I couldn't otherwise afford," said Richard Dixon, owner/manager of The Travel Spot, Cranford, NJ. "I've been around the world six times. There's no place I haven't been."

Salaries Are Improving

Travel agencies have traditionally been very low paying. The glamour attached to travel and the opportunity to travel at reduced cost were considered benefits. The fact that the job is frequently a second income in a household (since most agents were women returning to work after raising their families), and the fact that not much educational or prior work experience is required also tended to keep wages down. While it is possible to make a fairly good income (even six figures for the most ambitious commissioned sales agents with an elite following or for a vice president of a large, multibranch agency), salaries are about 20 to 40 percent lower than in comparable positions in other industries.

According to a 1989 "Salary & Benefits Survey" by the American Society of Travel Agents (ASTA), an Alexandria, VA-based trade association, the average income for full-time inside sales agents is $15,610. Agents' earnings start at $11,000 for the entry-level sales agent; with one to two years, the agent earns $13,095; three to five years, $16,195; six to ten years, $19,035; and ten or more years, $21,655.

Agencies with a business-travel sales orientation generally pay more than those focused around leisure travel. The average income for a full-time corporate agent is $16,870–more than $2,000 over what a leisure agent earns.

Salaries are linked to agency volume: The average income earned by full-time inside sales agents in firms doing less than $1 million is $13,495, compared with more than $17,500 for agents employed in travel agencies doing more than $5 million in volume.

About two-thirds of all agencies compensate inside sales agents on a salary-only basis. Nearly one-fourth use a combination of salary and commission.

The average income for agency managers, according to the 1989 ASTA survey, is $22,270. Those with less than one year of experience earn $17,370; with one to two years of experience, they earn $18,510; three to five years, $20,595; six to ten years, $22,735, and more than ten years, $26,015. Again, agencies with a business-travel orientation pay managers more–an average of $24,300, or 15 percent more–than leisure agencies. Agency sales volume is also a factor: Managers of agencies doing less than $1 million earn an average of $18,200, or 31 percent less than managers of agencies doing more than $5 million in sales, who earn an average of $26,500. Most managers (72.1 percent) are compensated by salary only, but nearly one-fourth receive both salary and commission. About one-third of the agency sales force is on some sort of commission structure either exclusively (22 percent) or partly.

However, there is a category of outside sales agents (as distinguished from inside sales agents, who tend to work on salary), who almost always work exclusively on commission, which generally is a percentage of the net commission earned on the business they bring in. Most outside sales agents who do all their own work (sales as well as ticketing and documentation) earn 41 to 50 percent of the net commission; outside sales agents who rely on assistance from agency staff typically make 21 to 40 percent of the commission (net commission is about 10 percent of the sale). A commissioned sales agent may make only $2,500 in the first year, but an agent with many years of experience can earn $35,000, $50,000, and even more. How much a commissioned agent makes depends largely upon the type of clients that the agent brings in – corporate clients, independent leisure clients, or groups.

Salaries are generally a function of sales volume, number of staff managed, and size of the company. Large agencies have more specialization and more positions with management responsibility and thus pay considerably more than the typical travel agency. For example, an executive vice president of a $150-million regional company earns over $90,000; a regional vice president earns a base of $85,000; the president and chief executive officer of a large regional agency earns $100,000.

Other examples are as follows: account executive, $30,000 to $35,000; corporate sales manager, $30,000 to $60,000; branch manager, $25,000 to $40,000; general manager of a high-volume corporate agency, $60,000; corporate agent with five years of experience, $27,000; regional sales director, $35,000; director of MIS, $50,000 to $60,000; senior meeting planner, $35,000 to $40,000.

Salaries for agents are improving as well. Because of the complexity and sheer quantity of travel products and offerings and the computerized systems necessary for day-to-day functions, travel agents are just beginning to be appreciated as true professionals. Supply/demand balance has also shifted dramatically.

There are presently about 150,000 travel agents; by the year 2000, forecasts call for between 204,000 and 235,000, according to the Department of Labor, which lists travel agents as one of the fastest-growing professions for the decade. In all, industry experts estimate that there will be a need for 24,000 new travel agents each year throughout the decade to cover growth and attrition.

An experienced agent skilled in using an airline computerized reservations system is in enormous demand. Moreover, agency locations had been proliferating at the rate of 5 to 10 percent a year, making new owners desperate to hire agents with two years of ticketing experience to meet the Airlines Reporting Corporation appointment requirements. All of these factors are helping to improve salaries.

Increasingly, travel agencies are attempting to improve compensation through more use of incentive programs, whereby agents earn a base salary plus commission. At Rosenbluth Travel, a Philadelphia-based mega-agency with an innovative incentive program, agents were able to increase their compensation by 27 percent.

Benefits Vary

Most agencies view travel as their employee's primary benefit, but policies on travel vary markedly. Generally, agencies offer four to six days of familiarization trips depending on experience plus another eight to fourteen vacation days. According to ASTA's 1989 "Agency Salary and Benefits Survey," most agencies provide at least some type of paid familiarization trip annually but some require the agent to pay for all or part. Most agencies provide free or reduced-rate travel as well as career-related educational benefits.

However, agencies tend to be weak in providing most other benefits. Only one-third of all agencies pay the full cost of employee hospitalization and major medical insurance; 40 percent provide no such insurance at all (a legacy from the time when most agents were mature women whose husbands' jobs provided health coverage). Only 10 percent of all agencies offer a retirement plan; a slight majority of agencies provide employee bonuses; nearly half of all agencies provide five or more days of paid sick leave. Less common benefits are dental insurance, disability insurance, life insurance, and maternity/paternity leave.

Who Becomes an Agent?

In a business where experience is becoming increasingly important, a sizable proportion of the work force consists of newcomers, which largely reflects the astronomical growth of the field since 1978. According to a survey by the Travel Education Center (TEC), a Cambridge, MA-based travel school affiliated with Thomas Cook/Crimson, some 12.9 percent of agency employees have been working less than one year; only 32 percent have been in the business more than five years. Even owners are new; 16 percent have been in the business less than three years.

While we tend to think of "entry-level" workers as people who are just starting out in their careers, the travel agency industry has traditionally been a popular one for people who are changing careers, starting over after raising a family, or retiring from something else. This is convenient, too, because many agencies openly admit that starting salaries would be inadequate for someone who depended solely on the one salary.

Increasingly, though, people who are becoming travel agents are coming from burnout professions like teaching and nursing, which are higher-paying fields. While these people are content to take lower pay initially, they are still forcing new standards and expectations.

"People who are changing careers don't care so much about money," said Zoe Wakefield, an administrator with TEC. "They want an atmosphere that they are comfortable with."

"A lot had well-paying jobs, but are willing to take less because of job satisfaction," added Paula Wagner, president of the Colorado School of Travel, Lakewood, CO.

Sharon Caldwell, for example, was a teacher for seven years and then a nurse before becoming a travel agent. "As a nurse, you deal with patients, families, life and death. It takes a lot of energy on a consistent basis. Travel agency work is relaxing in comparison. As an agent, you're dealing with people and dealing with problems, but these are happy problems. I like travel; I like selling it. I love to travel—and I do.

"I had wanted to be an agent for a long time, but stayed away because of the salary," said Caldwell, who had also tried real estate sales and, though a full-time travel agent now, continues to work as a nurse every other weekend.

Though more men are coming into the field than before, men still account for only about 15 percent of new agents—mainly because of the low pay. "They can't live with it, even in the short term," said Wagner.

The low pay is the major reason, however, why few who are becoming travel agents today intend to stay on the front line forever. They have ambitions of becoming a manager, an owner, or even an outside salesperson. "Part of the American dream is to be a manager or owner," observed Martin McArthur, placement director for the Southeastern Academy, Kissimmee, FL. "Most come in realizing that salaries are low, but they come in with an eye to the future. They see being a travel agent as 'paying their dues,' a steppingstone. A far higher proportion [than in the past] want to go into management."

One reason why more people are coming into travel agency work is that "travel agent" is becoming a more recognized and highly visible profession. Kate, on the TV show "Kate and Allie," was a travel agent, and, in a revival of the "Gidget" sitcom, the grown-up Gidget was a travel agent.

"Young people are thinking about becoming a travel agent," said Doris Davidoff, vice president of Belair Travel, Bowie, MD. "Fifteen years ago, the average kid coming out of high school or college hadn't even heard of a travel agent. It wasn't even listed in the Labor Department's list of careers. People didn't think of it until after they had traveled, and then tended to stay home until their kids were grown. They could take a 'fluff' thing that wasn't threatening to their husband's professional role. But it was exciting, glamorous. For these women, it didn't matter how much money they made."

Joanna Bartolotta, a corporate agent on Long Island, NY, started out as a travel agent just out of high school. "My mother wanted me to be a stewardess, but I decided to be a travel agent when I was in the tenth grade. I just love hearing about different places; I love sending people away—it makes them happy. But it's nerve-racking. It takes a lot out of you; people are constantly changing their mind, and businessmen are rough—they actually want you to build them a plane sometimes."

Meanwhile, the traditional source of new travel agents—mature women returning to work after they have reared their children—is drying up since many fewer women are staying home with their children. They are building careers and staying in them through their childbearing and childrearing years.

Today, the fact that most travel agents are women in their childbearing years raises a new problem for agencies—how to keep their trained professionals once these women have babies.

Consequently, travel agencies are trying to improve the position of travel agent and make it more of a career by offering more specialties, more steps on the career ladder, and better pay and benefits. Many, in order to keep valued employees, are allowing new mothers to work from home via computer or are offering flexible and reduced work schedules. A few, like VTS Travel, Montvale, NJ, have even opened an on-site day-care center.

"We are limited in our growth because of the difficulty in hiring people," noted Maryles Casto, chairman of Casto Travel, Inc., a five-office group headquartered in Palo Alto, CA. At Casto's agency, the work-and-family problem is acute: Out of 140 employees, 80 percent are women and 60 percent of those are in childbearing years. "We have four to five pregnancies a year, and more and more women are not coming back after having their babies," she said.

Casto offers many options to retain and attract employees such as a three-month maternity leave with an option to extend, liberal part-time and flex-time options, and job sharing. Casto is also looking into the possibility of subsidizing the cost of child care and allowing new mothers to work from home via computer.

Getting In

Getting into the travel agency business is tough. One of the ironies of the industry is that entry-level jobs are so scarce when the industry is expanding so dramatically.

In the past, the travel agency industry afforded enormous opportunity at the entry level. The industry's version of an apprenticeship was a clerk working for minimum wage but able to look over a more experienced shoulder and ultimately move into a consultant's spot. Many agents started while they were high school students working part-time and summers.

Today, the situation has completely reversed. Computers have virtually eliminated the need for clerks while vastly increasing the complexity and technical knowledge required to do even the most basic functions. The incredibly fast pace of work means that there is no time to train, and the very low profit margins make training a costly exercise. What is more, many managers fear entrusting their clients to a novice when the tiniest missed detail can cost the agency a client, or worse, a lawsuit.

Jobs for neophytes are scarce, while jobs for agents with only minimal experience (knowing how to operate the airline reservations computer) abound. On the other hand, tens of thousands of people are hungry to get into the travel agency business. Drawn by the glamour and opportunity to travel, many are so desperate to get in that they are willing to work for no pay; they just want the chance to gain the necessary experience for a paying job. Some agencies have taken advantage of this situation, hiring people on a commission basis.

One young woman who now owns her own agency recalled her experience of getting into the travel agency business with bitterness. She enrolled in a travel school operated by a prominent agency but realized that "no one would give me a job when I had no experience." She found a Long Island agency that offered to pay her commission on sales she brought in. She worked Monday through Friday from 9:30 A.M. to 5:30 P.M., Saturday from 10 A.M. to 5 P.M. and Sunday from 12 to 5 P.M. After four months, she had earned $4.52 in commission "on a one-way ticket to Florida for my boyfriend. I was a gofer." She was eventually "promoted" and shown how to write tickets and invoices. Finally, she landed a group account.

"Exploited? I felt then I was getting what I wanted–training and experience," she declared.

Another young woman also volunteered to work for nothing for six months in order to gain the requisite experience. "I felt cheated; there was no time to train me as they said."

Moreover, many agency owners or managers do not recognize free work as valid experience. Still, many of these work-in-exchange-for-training programs can lead to jobs, and some managers even insist on "growing their own" through an established in-house training program.

Many agency managers have had to abandon their own training programs because the work environment simply does not allow the luxury. They are being forced out of desperation to draw upon the graduates of vocational and academic travel training programs despite lingering skepticism that such programs do not adequately prepare people.

"I've never yet met a graduate of any travel school who was ready to be a travel agent right after graduation," said the owner of a North Kansas City, MO, agency, who nonetheless hired two.

Indeed, agencies are becoming much more accustomed to going to the placement offices of schools to hire new graduates.

So, while you should not confuse a diploma with a ticket into an agency job, some kind of schooling is becoming more and more necessary to break into the field. Even the most skeptical agency managers appreciate the value of the schools for screening out those individuals who are interested in travel agency work only for the fun and fams. Graduates of such programs are regarded as more serious, more committed, and more realistic about what the business is all about. This is important because agencies make a great investment when they take on a novice.

Fewer than 20 schools were dedicated to travel agency training a decade ago. The numbers have since swelled to more than 1,200.

Today, with better cooperation between the travel schools and the industry, more and more schools are becoming recruitment centers for the entire industry. (There is more about travel schools in Chapter 17). Both the American Society of Travel Agents (ASTA) Scholarship Foundation (P.O. Box 23992, Washington, D.C. 20026, tel. 703-739-2781) as well as the National Tour Foundation, a subsidiary of the National Tour Association (546 E. Main St., Lexington, KY 40508, tel. 800-682-8886), publish directories of schools.

Significantly, some of the large-agency groups, like Thomas Cook/Crimson (which operates the Travel Education Center, Cambridge, MA) and Carlson Travel Network (Carlson Travel Academies), plus scores of smaller agencies, have established their own schools, primarily to meet their own recruitment needs.

Probably the most well-respected educational institution in the industry is the Institute of Certified Travel Agents (ICTA), which bestows on working professionals a coveted Certified Travel Counselor (CTC) title upon completion of a rigorous program. ICTA has introduced a beginners' program that is geared to agents who have just entered the industry but that can be taken by people who want to get in. (For further information about programs, contact Institute of Certified Travel Agents, 148 Linden St., P.O. Box 82-56, Wellesley, MA 02181, tel. 617-237-0280.)

Before you enroll in any program, review the curriculum closely. Hiring agencies are looking for geography, reservations computer training, courses in agency operations and the travel industry in general, and some sales training. Also check that the school is licensed with the state and accredited by appropriate agencies, that instructors have worked or currently work in the industry, and that there is placement assistance (check the track record). Talk with graduates of the program. You may also want to check the school's reputation with local agencies (particularly with an agency that you feel you want to work at), as well as with the Better Business Bureau. ASTA publishes a brochure entitled "Choosing the Right Travel School."

It is not absolutely necessary to go to a school. Indeed, many managers are firm about taking on new talent and training them their own way. The task is to find these people. The best way to start is to network – contact everyone, starting with the agency you or your company uses, your friends, relatives, neighbors. Walk into a local agency and ask whether some entry-level job is available. If you already have work experience, you may be surprised at how applicable it may be, particularly if it is secretarial, sales, or telemarketing. Think about what you can bring to the agency. While a desire to travel and even vast experience traveling are helpful, what an agency really wants is contacts for new business. If you are coming from another industry, you may be in a position to bring in new commercial business to the agency.

ASTA also offers a home-study course on becoming a travel agent.

Working on Straight Commission

The easiest (and the most prevalent) way to get in without prior travel agency experience is as an outside salesperson, working on straight commission. This minimizes the risk for the agency, but be aware: You are unlikely to earn more than a few thousand dollars in the first year and perhaps only $5,000 in the second.

Outside sales agents do not necessarily always work outside the agency, but their function is to bring in business from outside. "You're your own boss," said Bonnie Kogos, a commissioned sales agent for more than a decade with Zenith Travel in New York City. "You have your own clientele. When you change agencies, you generally keep your own clients."

"It is not glamorous at all. You have to slog through each individual booking. You are only as good as your last ticket. You might handle 30 clients at once, do a conference, a vacation, handle commercial clients. I have 40 people going to Bermuda."

The newer agents, she commented, are "computer whizzes but have never been anywhere. The older ones, over 35 years old with ten years in business, are more Renaissance people. I've been to 82 countries and love to look at hotel rooms. You've got many different breeds of cat in the business," said Kogos, who also publishes her own newsletter for agency clients.

A commissioned agent, like any agent, gets better and better with experience; with more knowledge of destinations, facilities, and airfares; and with more contacts at travel companies. The hardest part is getting in, "like acting," she says. At age 32, she worked for $3 an hour in an agency. After two years, she went off on her own as a commissioned salesperson.

"You have to love the business. If I have a conference, I may work 8 A.M. to 8 P.M. Sometimes I wake in the middle of the night, remembering some detail I had overlooked. There are lots of little details. It pervades life. I don't go on vacation: I go on inspection tours. You are always learning."

A commissioned sales agent should negotiate with the boss first. Items to negotiate include the amount of the commission split (half of the 10-percent commission for a fairly experienced agent who does his or her own ticketing, but the amount can go higher; 25 percent for an inexperienced agent who does not do the paperwork); when it will be paid (at the time of booking, when the client pays, or after the trip); and what the agent pays for (use of computer, telephone, supplies, or nothing). You should get promises of a higher pay rate or a future salaried position in writing. Read the contract presented to you carefully, and see what it says about whose clients your clients are (whether you can take them with you if you leave the agency).

Selecting an Agency

If you use reasonable care in selecting a travel agency, take any job with it, even at minimum wage, just to get a foot in the door. If you are interested and a bit aggressive, you will learn by being exposed to various tasks and can create your own position or slip into a vacancy. Once inside, it is easy to move up or to move over to a better position at another agency.

If you are in a position to choose among agencies to work for, there are several matters to consider. Agencies manifest the styles and character of the owner or manager. The clientele and sales volume of an agency (and therefore your own revenue) are further determined by the location, size, facilities such as computers, advertising and promotion budget, and even numbers of counselors or outside salespeople. You can tell a great deal about an agency, for example, by whether it is a storefront on Main Street or in a mall or is an upper floor in an office building; by how many computer terminals there are; by the brochures that are displayed and how they are displayed; and by the general appearance of the office.

Most agencies have a mixture of leisure and commercial business, though the balance may vary (usually 60:40). Some agencies specialize almost entirely in one or the other, and there are gigantic differences in terms of working environments. The leisure agency is generally friendlier; counselors are accustomed to spending a lot of time with clients because they may have to prepare special itineraries.

In the commercial agency, speed and efficiency are everything; the agent does not deal with the traveler as much as with a secretary or corporate travel department; there is little consultation since the traveler will likely have specific requests. Creativity comes in obtaining the lowest fares and best rates. Also, agents in commercial departments do not have the same opportunity to travel since they are not in a position to influence decisions regarding destination and product. Commercial agencies also tend to be larger and more heavily computerized. On the other hand, commercial agents tend to make higher salaries.

There are advantages and disadvantages to starting out in a small operation rather than in a large organization. The largest agencies probably offer more entry-level positions, better training programs, substantially better mobility, and benefits. But they are also highly specialized; you may be required to do reservations for a commercial account (which some compare to a position on an assembly line) for some time. On the other hand, a small agency may also present entry-level opportunities, and the training, while not as formatted, can be excellent, with an opportunity to take on a wide variety of tasks. The rise to a senior position may be more rapid in a small organization, but since there are very few management tiers, fewer senior positions are available. A small agency, though, may offer a homier atmosphere and more opportunity to be creative in travel planning.

The number of personnel agencies specializing in full-time

and temporary travel agency personnel is growing. Check the trade publications and the *Yellow Pages.*

Telecommuting

Telecommuting–working from home via computer–makes it possible for both salaried and commissioned agents to successfully combine work and family life.

McGettigan Corporate Planning Services, Philadelphia, has allowed some of its valued employees to telecommute. "From an employer's point of view, it is so difficult to find skilled people that this was cost-effective for us," commented Mimi McGettigan, vice president.

Kathryn Davis, a Texas travel agent, gave up a job as an office manager and bookkeeper because she was "tired of staring at the same four walls." Instead, she established a relationship with a local agency and, in effect, works on her own, doing FITs (customized itineraries), groups, and corporate travel. "If I choose to let my family take priority, that's my choice," said Davis, who has been working from her home for five years, linked to a sponsoring agency by computer. "I would never go back to an office setting. I would quit completely first. I like the freedom."

One of the advantages of telecommuting is that agents can coordinate their schedule around their families. "What doesn't get done in the day, I can do after hours," said McGettigan's Tina McLaughlin.

Mega-Agencies

More Specialization, New Career Paths

The emergence of mega-agencies–billion-dollar companies with hundreds of outlets nationally and internationally–like American Express, Carlson Travel, Thomas Cook, and Rosenbluth has added the dimension of Big Business to travel agency careers, opened new paths for entry and advancement, and, in all, helped shape travel agency work into a profession.

Small family-run operations–the so-called Mom and Pop shops–may be an excellent training ground for novices, but they offer limited mobility. At a certain point, the only move for an ambitious agent is to go to a larger agency or to open his or her own.

Larger agencies (which generally prefer to be known as "travel management services companies" and tend to derive more than 70 percent of their business from corporate travel sales) have more specialization of function and many more management opportunities. For example, positions may include: quality control coordinators and customer service representatives, account executives, area managers, commercial sales managers, human resources specialists, training and development professionals, MIS specialists, accountants, product development managers, fare analysts and negotiators, public relations professionals, and marketing managers.

Indeed, Thomas Cook, one of the nation's largest agencies, lists 130 different job titles among its three divisions (up from 110 in 1986) with most of the new positions in product development, vendor relations, automation, and quality control. Among the job titles are the following: document control specialist, data specialist, Disney sales administrator, branch liaison coordinator, cruise specialist, promotions coordinator, inventory control coordinator, training coordinator, and senior hotel desk agent.

Because these companies have hundreds of locations nationwide and even global presence, they offer more opportunities to relocate (an advantage if you want to live in different places, but a disadvantage when the company says you have to relocate to Minneapolis or Phoenix or leave). The mega-agencies also generally offer better salaries and benefits and have superior training and development programs.

Travel agencies generating more than a billion dollars' worth of business include the following:

AAA Travel Agency Services, Orlando, FL, an affiliation of 154 clubs

American Express Travel-Related Services, New York

Carlson Travel Network, Minneapolis

Lifeco Travel Service Corporation, Houston

Rosenbluth Travel, Inc., Philadelphia

Thomas Cook Travel, Inc., Cambridge, MA

Uniglobe Travel International, Vancouver, B.C., a franchise organization

USTravel Systems, Inc., Rockville, MD

Other giants include:

IVI Travel, Northbrook, IL

Scheduled Airlines Traffic Offices, Inc. (SATO), Arlington, VA, owned by 13 airline companies

Wagon-Lits Travel USA, Dayton, OH

An Example: Rosenbluth Travel

One of the oldest travel agencies in the United States, Rosenbluth Travel was founded in 1892 as a steamship ticket office by Marcus Rosenbluth, a man who spoke nine languages and would be entrusted to take a few dollars at a time until his client could accumulate the $50 to send to Europe to bring a relative over to America. The agency, now one of the largest in the country, epitomizes the evolution of the travel agency industry: It is a family shop turned mega and, in many ways, still straddles both worlds.

In just 10 years, Rosenbluth went from regional travel agency with 8 agencies and 250 employees generating $150 million in sales (a substantial amount for the time) to a national company with global links and more than 400 offices and 2,600 "associates" (as its employees are called) generating $1.3 billion annually in sales.

Headed up by the fourth generation of Rosenbluths – Harold F., the president and chief executive officer, and Lee, the executive vice president and chief operating officer – the company has grown and prospered because of its focus on technology, innovation, and people.

The company has been able to preserve the essential qualities of a closely held family company, particularly in its attitude toward its "associates" ("People work *with* me, not *for* me," said Lee Rosenbluth), while wielding the power and influence of a mega-agency. The company has the clout to negotiate high override commissions and the resources to invest millions of dollars in state-of-the-art technology to provide value-added services for clients as well as achieve high productivity.

Rosenbluth has applied considerable innovation to its work force. For example, a "Pay for Quality" incentive program for reservationists produced a 27-percent increase in salaries. The company also places emphasis on quality control and customer service programs, employing specialists in these areas, as well as on training and development, and maintains 12 training centers staffed by a department of 20. It recently set up a special reservations office designed to be staffed by people who have been disabled. One of its California outlets employs a blind associate who uses a special machine that converts information on the computer screen to Braille. The company even opened a special data processing center in Linton, ND, in order to create jobs for struggling farmers.

Rosenbluth has also been innovative in its products and services. It tapped into the emerging market of consumers who shop via personal computer by linking up with Prodigy, a joint venture of IBM and Sears (subscribers seeking to book travel with Rosenbluth are actually hooked up to a Rosenbluth agent who works from home so that she can be with her baby). Other innovations include a Family Vacation Station, a specially designed travel agency dedicated to families with a Kid's Test Flight Room; an executive vacation planning program whereby high-level consultants visit with executives in their own offices to help plan their vacations on a one-on-one basis; an in-house tour program; and a travel department for the deaf.

The company is divided into three major divisions: commercial travel (accounting for about 85 percent of business and handling about 1,500 corporations); leisure travel (including a cruise center, 30 vacation centers, and a department that operates cultural tours); and an incentives and meetings division (which handles programs ranging in size from 10 to over 2,000 people).

Apart from travel consultants and reservationists, some of the other job functions include account executives (who interface with major accounts); area managers (who are responsible for overseeing a cluster of agencies and monitoring productivity and quality control); commercial sales managers (who are responsible for winning new corporate accounts); MIS specialists (there are about 60 programmers); and product development people (who negotiate rates with airlines, hotels, and other suppliers).

Lee Rosenbluth's management philosophies, which emphasize open communication and respect, were shaped largely by having come up through the ranks of the company and also by his having worked outside the company. "Most summers, I worked in our company," he recalled. "I started stamping brochures, then bookkeeping, then as an agent. I worked in every phase because I knew I would eventually be in a position to oversee. So I know what the job is like, and I also know how I wanted to be treated."

But Lee, who also has a law degree, applied this background working for a congressman and a district attorney. "This gave me the perspective not to be an owner, but to be on staff."

"Law school taught me I had a greater capacity than I thought I had. Law professors pushed my capacity, forced me to do more. But I knew, even going through law school, that I would be in the travel industry," he said.

The Travel Agency Industry

The travel agency is a relatively new phenomenon. Its origins go back a little over 100 years to the heyday of railroads and steamship lines, when agencies sold tickets on these carriers. With the emergence of airlines as the main common carrier of the twentieth century, travel agencies have become an extension of the airlines. Although they are, in effect, a department store for all forms of tours and travel, the airlines, which account for 65 to 80 percent of an agency's revenues, for the most part dictate the rules and regulations for agency appointments and operations. The appointing bodies are the Airlines Reporting Corporation (ARC), the domestic airline conference, or the International Airlines Travel Agent Network (IATAN), the international conference, a not-for-profit subsidiary of the International Air Transport Association.

In the early days of travel agencies, the clientele was typically affluent, but more efficient and less expensive jet service brought a new era of mass travel. The trend was further hastened by tour packages that combined the airfare and ground arrangements so that the total cost was cheaper than the regular airfare alone. In the 1960s, the predominant low-cost package was the GIT (group inclusive tour); the 1970s saw the liberalization of charter rules and the mushrooming of this new form of package.

A new generation of so-called "jetsetters" was born. Travel agencies flourished, although they dealt almost exclusively with leisure travel–vacation and pleasure trips that are considered "discretionary" because people can choose to take the trips or not. The airlines used low commissions and difficult rules to effectively keep most agencies out of nondiscretionary business travel. The airlines felt that agents were entitled to commission only on business that was incremental—above what the airlines would have had on their own. Moreover, the carriers knew that the leisure traveler takes much more time and personal attention than the business traveler, whose requirements are dictated by the purpose of the trip. Often, the difference is between minutes and hours.

In the mid-1970s, the airlines made a complete reversal in policy. They realized that their overhead for reservationists and city ticket offices was much more expensive than the amount they paid in travel agents' commissions on actual ticketed sales and began to ease agents' way into the commercial arena. At the same time, new computerized reservations systems were introduced, giving travel agents direct access to the airlines' inventory of seats.

The result was dramatic growth in numbers, sales, and proportion of airline sales by travel agencies. In 1974, only 11,400 agency locations were appointed by the Airline Traffic Conference (now called the Airlines Reporting Corporation), and these generated only 40 percent of domestic airline sales. By 1984, the number of agencies had more than doubled, and the agencies' share of domestic airline sales jumped to 65 percent.

A decade after deregulation went into effect, dollar volume jumped 231 percent, but the number of agency locations also doubled, to 29,584. In 1989, agency sales from all sources totaled $79.4 billion, according to the 1990 *Travel Weekly* Louis Harris Survey.

Currently, agents generate 95 percent of all cruise reservations, 90 percent of tours, 85 percent of international tours, 80 percent of international airline sales, 70 percent of domestic airline reservations, 50 percent of car rentals, 37 percent of rail fares, and 25 percent of domestic hotel bookings, according to the *Travel Industry Yearbook: The Big Picture, 1990.*

Deregulation: Boon and Bane

Greater reliance on the travel agency community by suppliers and the computer systems that gave agents unprecedented access to information partly explain the growth in agency numbers and sales. But deregulation meant that commission rates were no longer standardized and regulated; once they were opened, the profitability of agencies improved considerably and scores of new entrepreneurs rushed into the field. Deregulation also unleashed chaos on the public in the form of changing schedules, fares, and even airlines. Sheer confusion drove countless new customers into agencies for the first time, while outrageously low fares, pushed down by bloody battles for market share by upstart carriers, also generated new airline travelers.

Agencies obtain virtually all their revenue from commissions earned on booking arrangements with airlines, hotels, tour companies, car rental firms, and the like; only a few charge service fees. Commissions average 9.9 percent on airline fares (up from about 8 percent a decade ago); 10 percent on hotel arrangements; and 10 to 22 percent on tours and car rentals. So, a medium-sized agency, doing some $5 million in sales, actually earns about $500,000 in commissions. The $500,000 is the agency's operating revenue for paying employees, utilities, advertising expenses, interest on loans, and so on. According to a survey of financial statements submitted to bank loan officers, agencies clear only 2.9 percent in profit before taxes.

A financial study by *ASTA Agency Management* magazine disclosed that the average one or two-outlet agency generates total commission income of $155,245 and has expenses of $122,416, leaving a net profit (before payment to principals) of only $32,829. Reasonable levels of return occur only above the $2-million (gross-dollar) volume level, when the level of return is $80,211.

Travel agencies in 1987 generated $64.2 billion in total travel sales – about 20 percent of the total U.S. travel expenditures domestically and abroad. Of this amount, agents generated $37 billion in airline sales, $10.3 billion on cruises, $7.1 billion on hotels and other accommodations, $5.2 billion in car rentals, $1.9 billion in rail travel, and $1.9 billion in miscellaneous services such as sightseeing, according to the 1988 *Travel Weekly* Louis Harris Survey.

A decade ago, an agency that generated $3 million would have been considered large; most agencies generated under $1 million in total volume and were able to keep only about 8 percent of it to cover all expenses and profits. The average agency might have consisted of two or three people – a husband and wife and an extra agent – a so-called Mom and Pop operation. Today, according to a Louis Harris study, the average agency does about $2.5 million a year; a large agency, on the order of $25 million and up; and mega-agencies and chains, such as Carlson Travel Network and American Express, from $500 million to $1 billion in business.

Because agencies are now free to negotiate commissions based on volume, bigness – and consequently consolidation – is becoming an advantage. The biggest agencies not only have the clout to negotiate favorable rates, but they also benefit from certain economies of scale – the ability to purchase sophisticated computers and software, to advertise, to pay higher salaries to attract top people, and to afford training and development programs.

Though the industry is still very diverse, with 65 percent of all agencies still generating under $2 million in revenue, these generate only 32 percent of all sales. The largest agencies, those generating $5 million or more in revenues, though only 9 percent of the total, generate 33 percent of the sales.

Some travel agencies attempt to provide the full spectrum of services, from corporate to leisure. Others operate more like "boutiques"; they are small and specialized, with an emphasis on service. Some specialize in the "carriage trade" – the affluent travelers who prefer customized itineraries. Others specialize in some special interest, such as adventure travel. About 1,000 travel agencies specialize in servicing government accounts – a $15-billion business – or in handling the military (SATOTravel, a $900-million travel agency network, is owned by 13 airlines). And then, there are thousands of "cruise-only" agencies that do nothing but sell cruises.

An Example: The Travel Spot

Being a travel agent, said Richard Dixon, the owner-manager of The Travel Spot, Cranford, NJ, is the "most difficult job in the world. Customers are often irrational. You have to sift through what they think they want and figure what they really want, then choose among 9,000 potential travel products for the right one.

"In 1965, when I entered the business after leaving Pan Am, this was a regulated business [fares had to be approved by a government agency and were the same for everyone]. Yesterday, we spent the day cutting discount coupons from the newspaper in order to give our customers the best deal.

"It's enormously frustrating. But it's the greatest business in the world. Something is always new."

Dixon, a former fine arts major who found his way into travel, epitomizes the new wave travel agent who clips coupons, keeps on top of the best deals, and uses innovative marketing programs and good business practices.

For example, seeing a weakening in the economy of Cranford, a town of 30,000 people, Dixon joined forces with other local merchants to create a "Home Town Advantage" promotion to stave off competition from surrounding suburban shopping malls and boost traffic into the local stores. Participating merchants cross-promoted: a photo store provided a $25 gift certificate to its customers toward the next vacation booked at The Travel Spot; the local bookstore sponsored a murder mystery weekend at The Sagamore on Lake George, NY, booked by the agency; a local restaurant donated a dinner that the travel agency used as a prize in conjunction with its promotion with the bookstore. A townwide treasure hunt was also planned.

The agency has also been successful in turning individual travelers into groups—thus multiplying sales—and, at the same time, building brand loyalty through its own travel club. Club members pay into an interest-bearing escrow account, with the funds earmarked for some special amenity or activity on the tour. The agency offers six or seven special tours a year for club members.

"We discovered a long time ago that unless people are made to feel special, they will shop price," said Dixon.

Dixon himself helps promote the agency's and his own credibility as a travel expert through a weekly column he writes for the local paper.

Dixon also knows the importance of keeping tight controls on cash flow and scrutinizes corporate accounts (which represent 30 percent of the agency's volume). "Unless they can convert to a seven-day billing [paying as frequently as the agency has to pay the airlines] or a credit card, we say we can't afford to handle them. I have told clients we think they would be happier in a different environment."

The Travel Spot, which does over $3 million in business (70 percent of it in leisure travel), employs 11 agents, all of whom are specialists in some facet of travel. One agent has a great following among senior citizens; Dixon specializes in the United Kingdom and cruises. (The Travel Spot has a sister agency, Camelot, which handles cruises exclusively and employs 9 people.)

"When I hire," commented Dixon, "I only hire from tour and travel programs because I find these people understand the language and have an interest in travel. As an employer, I will refine the interest."

Starting salaries at The Travel Spot are $22,000 for someone with an education. "The more travel and service-related background you have, the better. Sure, someone who wants to be a travel agent should love to travel, love people. But you also need a sense of service, and be detail oriented."

And being a travel agent, Dixon noted, does give you the opportunity to travel: "Travel is a life-changing experience. You don't come back the same, or your heart is dead."

Opening Your Own Travel Agency

In spite of the emergence of mega-agencies, the travel agency industry is still overwhelmingly small business and entrepreneurial. It is still a relatively inexpensive business to start–suppliers even provide your inventory, in the form of brochures. All you do need is an office accessible to the public (which does not prevent you from opening an agency in your home), a telephone, and a manager with two years of ticketing experience (who may be the owner). An agency must post a bond or letter of credit of $20,000 and be open a certain number of hours. (Some airlines also impose a rule that no more than 20 percent of your business can be done with yourself in order to prevent corporations from setting up their own travel agency to save commissions). It is increasingly necessary to have an airline computerized reservations system which probably will add about $1,000 per month to operating expenses. Still, you can open an agency with only about $75,000 to $100,000 in operating capital.

While there is no federal licensing, some states may require a license. The Airlines Reporting Corporation (ARC) and to a lesser degree the International Airlines Travel Agent Network (IATAN) set out the rules and regulations for appointments and operations.

Donna Conklin, formerly assistant director of ARC, now has a service to assist people in obtaining ARC appointments (Conklin & Associates, 4216 Evergreen Lane, Ste. 115, Annandale, VA 22003, tel. 703-941-5486). "Virtually everyone gets approved," she noted. The fee, including application fee, is about $425 and takes about 30 to 35 days (compared with 90 days if you do it yourself).

The more daunting obstacles to opening your own agency are likely to be the lease on office space (typically three years) and an automation contract (typically five years, which can amount to $60,000). You will be liable for both if you have to close.

Travel agencies used to be opened typically by doctors' wives and divorcees or were used as tax write-offs or for the purpose of obtaining free travel for the owners. That is, they were used for a tax loss and not for profit; consequently, nearly half were operated at a loss.

However, the steady increases in commission levels have made the travel agency business, if not lucrative, at least profitable. In 1990, domestic commission rates (before override) averaged 9.8 percent, and international commission rates averaged 12.8 percent, with agents netting $4.9 billion in all. Still, after expenses, travel agencies typically clear 1 to 2.5 percent, a dismal profit margin compared with most other retail industries. Nonetheless, the industry now attracts serious professionals—often people retiring from other businesses.

Travel agencies had been opening at the rate of 9 to 10 percent a year (about 3,000 new outlets) to the point where there seemed to be travel agencies literally on every corner. In recent years, the rate has slowed down; in 1990, the number of retail locations grew by only 2 percent to 32,077. However, there has been an explosion in STP (satellite ticket printer) locations—actually a device located in the office of a large corporate client—which grew by 49 percent in 1990 to 5,730 locations.

To open an agency, you have to choose a location, which means evaluating potential customers, the competition, and the overhead costs (rent, utilities).

Doug Thompson, in his book *How to Open Your Own Travel Agency* (Dendrobium Books, 76 Gough St., San Francisco, CA, 94102), recommends telephoning agencies within a five-mile radius of your proposed location as though you were a potential customer to find out about their hours, specialties, policies on ticket delivery, staff, special services, and brochure offerings. Then you should go through the process of booking a trip in person to see how the competition operates. Thompson now sells two different start-up programs for new agencies as well. ASTA also offers a manual on how to start a travel agency.

The ease of opening an agency dupes many people, particularly those who have been successful in other businesses, into believing that the business is also easy. Operating a successful travel agency is deceptively difficult; there are nuances to the business that have tripped up some of the mightiest companies, including ABC Network, which thought it could make a go of it and then failed.

Consequently, instead of starting from scratch, many newcomers buy an existing agency or purchase a franchise. There are advantages and disadvantages to buying an existing agency. You may, in fact, be buying an agency with a poor reputation or poor business methods. Look for one where the owner is retiring after a successful career, and retain his or her services on a consultant basis.

Franchises and Consortiums

Travel agency franchises sell for $10,000 to $32,500 and are not of the same value as real estate or fast-food franchises. Unlike the hamburger, which can be standardized from restaurant to restaurant, or the home you buy once in five or ten years or a lifetime, travel is a service purchased frequently. Success depends on personal relationships between the agent and the customer.

When you franchise, you get assistance with site selection, training, help in hiring a manager with the necessary experience for the agency to become appointed, and promises of advertising. Usually, there is also a program for obtaining override (bonus) commissions from preferred suppliers. But the franchiser may also take a royalty of sales plus annual fees.

Since the travel industry has not had an especially good track record with franchising, you should scrutinize the company carefully, do background checks, and interview franchisees. Check to see whether there are legal actions against the franchise company.

Among the more successful franchise operations are the following:

American Express, New York, NY

Carlson Travel Network Associates, Van Nuys, CA

Empress Travel, New York, NY

International Tours, Tulsa, OK

Uniglobe, Richmond, British Columbia, Canada

Travel Agents International, Seminole, FL

Check the *Franchise Annual* published by Info Franchise News, Inc., Lewiston, NY.

In the travel agency business, many of the services performed by franchise organizations are available through cooperatives and consortiums, which enable the agency to preserve its independence but have the purchasing power and clout of a group. Indeed, membership in some sort of network or association has become increasingly essential, both to earn higher override commissions from suppliers and to provide clients (particularly commercial accounts) with the wide-reaching services they require. In addition to the value they offer a new agency, management of these multi-agency groups has become a career path in itself.

Among them are:

Action 6, Lowell, MA

Gem, Inc., Massapequa, NY

Giants, New York

Hickory, Saddle Brook, NJ

TIME (Travel Industry Marketing Enterprises), Massapequa, NY

Travelsavers, Manhasset, NY

Travel Trust International, Washington, D.C.

Woodside, Boston

Rent-A-Desk

A new concept and an alternative to opening your own agency is "rent-a-desk." This concept affords the best of both owning your own agency and working for someone else in the form of independence and an opportunity to retain 100 percent of the commissions on travel bookings, but with lower overhead and reduced risk (and stress). Instead, agents pay a monthly rental and, in exchange, have access to computer reservations systems and the use of an appointed outlet.

One of the first to be successful at the concept is The Travel Society, Denver, founded in 1987 by two travel industry veterans, one from the travel agency side and the other from the airlines.

Bill O'Connor, the cofounder, quickly noted that the concept is more akin to a "cooperative" than to "rent-a-desk." In effect, the individual "associates," who pay a fixed fee ($1,600 a month), are set up as if they were branch offices. They keep 100 percent of the commission on the travel they book plus a majority of overrides and, in exchange, are provided with delivery service, accounting, and automation. The agency negotiates overrides with preferred suppliers; commissions are sent to the agency and then distributed on a pro rata basis.

"It's really more like a microfranchise, or an executive suite, or a cooperative," said O'Connor. As such, the arrangement frees up the associate to concentrate on being a travel arranger rather than a financier or an accountant. Agents are provided income statements, balance sheets, commissions tracking (so they know which suppliers are paying what), accounts payable and receivable, vendor analysis, and corporate reports.

So far, the company operates two offices in Denver, with a total of 27 associates, who have generated a total of $15 million in sales, or about $650,000 each. If the associates were working as employees, they would likely earn about $20,000 a year; as associates, they net $40,000 on average.

The program works best when an agent comes with his or her own following rather than when someone just enters the field, O'Connor advised. Other outlets are planned in new markets. (For more information, contact The Travel Society, Ste. 100, 600 South Cherry St., Denver, CO 80222, tel. 303-321-0900).

A variation on the theme is an enterprise that sets agents up in home-based businesses (cottage agencies) linked by computer to an appointed agency. Pacifica Plaza Travel, Culver City, CA, is one of these businesses.

Future Trends

The travel agency industry is evolving in response to changing market conditions. The past few years have been a period of transition and shakeout, of consolidation and retrenchment. The industry is still very new to discount pricing, and, frequently, agencies do not know the true cost of handling an account when they make a bid that includes a rebate to a client. Negotiating rates and marketing services are still new concepts.

Airlines are actively introducing technology that gives commercial and leisure customers direct access to their schedules and fares on personal computers. They are also moving to a "ticketless ticket," which could make it easier still for passengers to book air tickets directly with airlines.

Travel agents, meanwhile, are moving into several new areas. They are working with banks to set up retail travel agencies; beginning to sell their services through personal computers; installing satellite printers outside the agencies; establishing travel clubs, promotional programs, and frequent traveler clubs, and generally becoming much more marketing and sales oriented. Many are establishing travel schools not only as a source of new staff but also for the substantial profits the schools generate.

The radical changes unfolding in the industry are producing more jobs, more specialization, and more professionalism. The industry is becoming much more marketing and sales oriented as well as much more computer oriented. New methods of retailing (or merchandising) travel have been introduced, and agents are beginning to take advantage of them. Negotiations skills, forecasting, and preplanning are becoming an increasing part of travel agency operations and will result in new kinds of jobs. The emergence of massive travel agency organizations, many with global links, will result in new tiers of management, new specialties, and greater opportunities for graduates of four-year and business administration programs.

"You get satisfaction in making someone's dreams come true, of doing things for people they can't do as well for themselves," concluded Joseph Hallissey, president of Hallissey Travel, a founder of Conlin-Hallissey Travel Schools and a former chairman and chief executive officer of the American Society of Travel Agents. Added Hallissey, who entered the travel business in 1968 after being a social worker for 18 years, "We are dream makers, still."

Contacts and Sources

Leading trade associations that can provide information about the industry and contacts include:

American Society of Travel Agents (ASTA), P.O. Box 23992, Washington, D.C. 20026, tel. 703-739-2782.

Association of Retail Travel Agents (ARTA), 1745 Jefferson Davis Highway, Ste. 300, Arlington, VA 22202, tel. 703-553-7777.

Airlines Reporting Corporation (ARC), 1709 New York Ave., NW, Washington, D.C. 20006, tel. 202-626-4076.

International Airlines Travel Agent Network (IATAN), 300 Garden City Plaza, Ste. 418, Garden City, NY 11530, tel. 516-747-4716.

Institute of Certified Travel Agents, 148 Linden St., P.O. Box 82-56, Wellesley, MA 92181, tel. 617-237-0280.

Society of Travel Agents in Government, 6935 Wisconsin Ave., NW (#200), Washington, D.C. 20815, tel. 301-654-8595.

Leading travel industry publications include:

Travel Agent Magazine

Travel Weekly

Tour & Travel News

Travel Management Daily

Travellife

ASTA Agency Management

3

Corporate Travel Management

A Career in Its Own Right

Corporate travel management, a career path and a steppingstone for commercial travel agents, is emerging as a career in its own right.

"Corporate travel management is the growth industry for the decade," declared Mary Kay Dauria, director, Worldwide Travel Services, American International Group (AIG), New York. "The field is just coming into its own."

Currently, the responsibility of overseeing corporate travel is usually left to the company's purchasing or personnel department or is put under the controller's office or, sometimes, under the purview of a secretary (who often emerges as the corporate travel manager). Only a little more than half of the Fortune 500 companies have travel managers at all.

Though in the past the corporate travel manager's position in the corporation had little clout, the spiraling increase in travel expenses and the recognition that travel is the third greatest controllable expense (after personnel and data processing) have catapulted the job to a higher status.

"Corporations recognize the need for the position when they

start realizing how big the travel expenditure is and that they have an ability to impact on that expenditure," said Ed Rathke, corporate travel manager for Aetna Insurance Company, Hartford, CT, and a former president of the National Business Travel Association (NBTA), the Alexandria, VA-based trade association for corporate travel managers. "The larger the company, the more the emphasis, and the higher the position."

No longer just a service for the employees, corporate travel management is becoming appreciated as a means for a company to achieve its business goals, help other departments reduce their costs, and, increasingly, serve as a profit center. Moreover, following the Persian Gulf War, corporate travel managers were recognized as critical advisers on safety and security concerns.

Staffing

Members of a company's corporate travel department are generally employed by the company itself and receive comparable salaries and the same benefits as other employees. They are responsible for arranging travel for the company's employees, arranging meetings and conventions, and managing travel budgets that can amount to millions of dollars.

Companies may employ a single individual to be responsible for setting up a travel budget, establishing policies for employees to follow (such as who can travel first-class), and acting as the liaison with an outside travel agency that actually handles the arrangements. Or, an entire staff may be organized to function much like a commercial travel agency. Sometimes, an outside travel agency establishes an "inplant" on the company's premises, which operates like a branch office of the travel agency to handle the company's travel arrangements exclusively but is staffed by the company, the agency, or a combination of both. This arrangement enables the company to recover some of the travel expense.

Corporate agents do not have the reduced-rate travel privileges of agency personnel, but their salaries and employee benefits are the higher, better ones of a big business. On the other hand, the corporate travel department (because it is typically perceived as a service and not as a profit center) is one of the first to be pruned during business downturns. Moreover, mobility can be limited (but is improving considerably): Within the department, there are generally few senior positions and only one corporate travel manager. Agents tend to move up to a higher position by transferring to the corporate travel department of another company.

Broad Responsibilities

The responsibilities of corporate travel management go well beyond booking airlines and hotels for executives. When they are part of the personnel department, the responsibilities may also include personnel relocation and coordination of training programs. They may involve meeting and convention planning. Many corporate travel departments also administrate corporate aircraft, car pools, and possibly group recreational trips or vacations for employees. The manager may also negotiate barter deals and discounts with travel suppliers.

A strong business background is desirable for a corporate travel manager (who may also be called a travel administrator or a transportation specialist). The manager has to oversee staff and forecast budgets; handle accounting and reconciliation; choose preferred vendors; negotiate contracts for lower rates on airlines, hotels, and car rentals; establish travel policy; select a travel agency through a bidding process; and help implement complex management information systems (MIS).

"You have to follow and understand travel industry jargon, read the trade press, keep up with industry trends and forecasts which change daily," advised Dauria. For example, you have to be alert to an impending airline strike or new service or a change in oil prices that could affect fares, as well as who is buying aircraft and who is paying bills on time.

You also have to be the neutral arbitrator standing between the company and the travel agency and other vendors. "Sometimes I am accused of being on the payroll of the travel agency, but you can't automatically assume that the agency is wrong," said Dauria, whose company generates $100 million in travel. AIG is one of the largest international insurance companies, with 130 offices (125 in the United States) and more than 500 locations of travel.

Dauria is working on a pilot project to globalize and consolidate travel as was done in the United States. The 125 different U.S. locations that worked with 100 different travel agencies now work with one. Dauria is working next to bring in the foreign locations.

But corporate travel management is very much a service business. "You have to be someone who gets self-gratification and not live for pats on the back," observed Dauria. "You don't hear from people except when there is a mistake." You need to be a self-starter, someone who is hardworking but likes change. "You can work for months on something, and then something changes." You need excellent communications skills, a "calm spirit," and diplomacy.

While companies used to promote people from other departments into travel management positions, this is becoming less and less possible as corporate travel management is increasingly becoming a specialized profession.

"Corporate travel tests your business acumen. It is a fast-moving, changing specialty area of business. It is fun because the people are fun," said Dauria, who started out in urban planning and moved into corporate travel management more than 12 years ago. "People in the industry have open minds; they are well traveled. They help each other, even if they don't know somebody. It is a tight network."

Advantages and Disadvantages

The disadvantage for someone in Dauria's position is that 80 percent of the time is spent on the road. "It is *not* fun. It is *not* a vacation. When I am on the road, I am working from 8 A.M. to 8 P.M. It is a misunderstood industry—and you have to be able to explain it" and continually fight the perception that you are out sightseeing when traveling.

On the positive side, there is tremendous growth opportunity ahead because so many companies have yet to designate a corporate travel manager and because other avenues for mobility are opening up. "You have access to every department and access to the highest offices. There is high visibility, great contacts," Dauria noted. Other career paths are into consulting, into large corporate travel agencies, or into vendor companies like airlines. Also, there are more and more training programs, particularly through NBTA.

Salaries

Salaries for in-house reservationists range from $15,000 to $40,000; managers, directors, and vice presidents can make between $20,000 and $100,000. Dauria took a $10,000 cut in salary when she moved to corporate travel from an airline, but she tripled her salary in a six-year period.

Corporate travel management has been an excellent field for women. According to a survey by NBTA, 56 percent of corporate travel managers are women. Also, while 57 percent have a four-year college degree, 31 percent have only a high school diploma. Salary medians, according to the survey, are as follows:

	Low	*High*	*Average*
West	$32,500	$ 82,500	$52,000
Midwest	21,000	110,000	47,500
South	27,000	57,500	41,000
Northeast	21,000	82,500	47,000

An Example: Aetna Insurance Company

Aetna Insurance Company separates its corporate travel function into three areas: executive travel (which handles the top 50 executives in the country, scheduling corporate aircraft and ground transportation); conference services (which handles the company's vast meeting and convention planning and special functions and administers the Aetna Institute, an apartment complex for the company's trainees in what amounts to a 300-room hotel); and corporate travel (which arranges travel for employees at headquarters as well as hundreds of field offices throughout the country).

The corporate travel department is a $40-million operation including $30 million in airline sales (booking 4,000 tickets a month). The department, which utilizes Thomas Cook as its agency, has a staff of 40 Cook employees plus 9 Aetna management people at the headquarters and a regional office in Dallas.

Aetna hires its reservationists directly from commercial travel agencies. A minimum of two years of experience is required, but seven years of experience is more typical. A starting reservationist (with Sabre experience) earns $19,000 in Hartford (more in New York City). A reservationist can make up to $27,000 in Hartford (more in New York City).

In the past, those who tended to move into corporate travel management at Aetna were agents (usually women) who had been working for ten years or so and were no longer entranced by the travel benefits but were lured by the better salaries, security, and retirement benefits afforded in a corporate environment. This distinction has blurred somewhat since the mega-agencies and large, regional travel agencies that specialize in corporate travel have come much closer in salaries and benefits.

Contacts and Sources

Trade associations for corporate travel managers that can provide information include:

National Business Travel Association (NBTA), 1650 King St., Alexandria, VA 22314, tel. 703-684-0836; offers a Certified Corporate Travel Executive program as well as education programs.

Association of Corporate Travel Executives (ACTE), P.O. Box 5394, Parsippany, NJ 07054, tel. 800-ACTE-NOW (201-379-6444); has instituted an executive recruitment service through The Management Network, Inc., Millburn, NJ.

Leading trade journals for corporate travel include:

Business Travel News

Corporate Travel

Travel Weekly

Travel Agent

4

Tour Operations

Dream Makers or Merchants

Whale-watching in Baja, California; ballooning across the chateaux country of France; riding a wagon train through the Bad Lands of South Dakota; climbing the Himalayas; or camping in a Mongolian yurt—these are no longer wild fantasies. Nor are the Pyramids of Egypt, the Great Wall of China, the Incan city of Machu Picchu, the North Pole, or even outer space beyond the reach of ordinary people. The dream makers who turn these fantasies into realities are tour operators—a small, highly specialized segment of the $350-billion travel and tourism industry.

Typically, tour operators are people who have been smitten by the travel bug themselves. Possessed by an insatiable desire to see and experience new places, new cultures, and new ideas, they bring their entrepreneurial talents, creativity, "gamesmanship," and love of travel together in the business of designing, producing, and marketing trips for other people.

Tour operators put together all the elements of a trip—transportation, accommodations, meals, sightseeing, and the like. They work with other segments of the industry—hotel companies, airlines, car rental firms, bus companies, cruiselines, local ground operators, and government tourist offices. They negotiate rates and block space, coordinating all the intricate details of an itinerary so that every moment of time can be accounted for. Then they "package" the product (the tour) in a brochure for sale through retail travel agents to the public. Tour operators (who create as well as market the package) or wholesalers (who do not operate the program but rather distribute it) then market the product, generating awareness and brand-name identification among retail agents and the public.

Foreign and Domestic Tours

Much more common in Europe, tours have never gained truly wide acceptance in the United States. According to the U.S. Travel Data Center, packaged tours account for about 22 percent of all person-trips of five nights or more duration, and foreign tour packages account for 20 percent of all U.S. foreign travel.

The industry is still evolving. Tour companies developed in an era of the Grand Tour of Europe, and there has always been a core of deluxe tour companies. But the packaged tour business really took off in the jet age. Operators devised the GIT (group inclusive tour) as a device to obtain a low fare, and the mass travel business was born. Sometimes, the land package was only an excuse to qualify for the low fare—a "throwaway" and the accommodations provided might have been at some isolated inn for ten nights. When the airlines introduced low fares that did not require a tour package, the price-oriented operators had to come up with packages that people really wanted to use.

"The idea of a package tour evokes a mental picture of a group of geriatric dodderers in rimless glasses and cast-iron permanents getting on and off a tour bus," quipped one tour operator. Another popular image arose when a trip to Europe was considered a once-in-a-lifetime event and travelers sought to cram as much into a single trip as possible. Tour-goers were treated to what seemed to be seven countries in eight days, giving rise to the expression, "If it's Tuesday, it must be Belgium."

But tour products have changed considerably since then. "Tour operators don't do 'packages' anymore," asserted Raymond M. Cortell, who grew up in his father's tour company and who now heads R.M. Cortell & Associates, New York. "Seventy-five percent of the products are independent and only 25 percent are escorted. The American mentality is antagonistic to groups."

Most people who take escorted tour packages want the security and convenience of having everything done for them—transportation, accommodations, meal arrangements. Other people look to a different sort of package, one that offers economy. Still others take tours because they provide access to places and sights not easily visited by individuals (China and the Soviet Union are examples). New-style programs cater to a traveler's sophistication and desire for independence and adventure.

The market for the tours is growing along with the expansion of the product offerings. There are tours for every budget, taste, interest, age group, and lifestyle. Examples are a journey by covered wagon (Wagons Ho, Phoenix); a mystery tour by bus where the destination is a surprise (Bixler Tours, Hiram, OH); a "Flight Through Fantasia" in the American Southwest (Special Expeditions, New York); ballooning in France (Bombard Society); an archaeological expedition (Crow Canyon Archaeological Center, Cortez, CO; Dinamation International, San Juan Capistrano, CA); bicycling (Backroads Bicycle Touring, San Leandro, CA); an agricultural tour (Farm Tours, Etc., Tulare, CA); travel for women only (Mariah Wilderness Expeditions, El Cerrito, CA); travel for the disabled (Flying Wheels, Owatonna, MN); health and fitness enthusiasts, (Global Fitness Adventures, Aspen CO); and tours for the young (Contiki Holidays, Anaheim, CA) and the old (American Express's program for the American Association of Retired People).

There are religious tours (Western World Tours, Santa Barbara, CA); professional tours; ethnic tours; reunions for veterans; and tours for musicians (Performing Arts Abroad, Richland, MI). There are also tours for artists, runners, students (Voices of the Future, New York), gardeners, nudists, and people who collect doll houses, study caves, or want to go dog-sledding. There are companies that specialize in the more exotic, adventurous, and cultural programs (Special Expeditions, New York; Society Expeditions, Seattle; Abercrombie & Kent, Oak Brook, IL; Mountain Travel & Sobek, El Cerrito, CA, two famous adventure companies that merged).

The new trend among tour companies is to focus on ecotourism (so-called green travel). These tours are oriented around and in turn are concerned about protecting the environment (Biological Journeys, McKinleyvile, CA; Geostar Travel, Rohnert Park, CA).

Indeed, noted guidebook author Arthur Frommer has targeted a "second revolution in travel" (the first, mass travel to Europe, launched with his book *Europe On $5 a Day*). The new revolution is oriented around "cerebral" and experiential travel—travel for ideas, learning, people. This kind of travel "shakes you up, introduces you to lifestyles, philosophical viewpoints." In his book *The New World of Travel,* he lists 1,200 companies offering programs to places like personal-growth centers, utopian villages, and centers for alternative teaching (one company with this focus is Shelter International, Boulder, CO).

Literally thousands of companies operate packaged tours, but only about 350 operate on a nationwide basis and sell their product chiefly through travel agents. Fewer than 50 of the companies handle as many as 20,000 passengers a year and only about 10 to 15 handle more than 100,000 passengers a year. This is in marked contrast to Europe, where massive travel organizations move hundreds of thousands of tourists a year; some handle one or two million packaged trips a year.

In summary, tour companies differ markedly in their style and structure. They may specialize in certain destinations (Europe, the Caribbean, Asia); activities (river rafting, visiting museums); markets (singles, youth, women, retirees). They may be geared to the deluxe, middle, economy, or budget market.

A Time of Radical Changes

An intensely competitive industry, tour operators work on very low markups (about 20 to 25 percent, compared with clothes-retailers' 100 percent markup). After expenses, pretax profit averages 3 percent. This is a business where volume really pays off, yet ironically, the rising costs of advertising, printing, and postage are factors keeping operators within small, specialized niches.

The changeability of airfares, volume-based pricing, market segmentation and rising costs of marketing and selling tour products, and the volatility of key suppliers like airlines are all forcing radical changes among tour operators. One aspect of this is a shift away from small, entrepreneurial, family-owned companies to Big Businesses with specialized functions. Furthermore, a communications revolution is changing the makeup of the professionals inside the industry.

"This the Electronics Age," declared Robert Whitley, president of the U.S. Tour Operators Association (USTOA), a membership association of about 40 of the largest tour companies. "The industry is hiring more and more technical people – computer specialists, telephone salespeople, marketers."

"We used to create a tour and then worry about operating it," reflected Cortell. "It was magical, creative then. Now we first have to consider whether the tour is operable from the computer end, or whether the cost of writing the software would exceed the profit potential.

"The criteria are changing for everything. Years ago, we would put out a 'dream' tour. Now it is all boiled down to airfares and body counts. We're not selling dreams anymore. We create a product we can operate the best – one where we can handle a booking in four minutes or less."

In Cortell's view, the focus has shifted from operating the tour to distribution and delivery – that is, marketing and sales: "The challenge today is the cost of getting the message out to the people, and still make a profit."

Not everyone has lost the "magic," however; one company was formed to do space travel and was even building its own rocketship. There are countless other examples of small companies bringing to life the creative imaginings of their founders: One trip recreates the voyages of Jules Verne; another explores Antarctica; yet another involves sailing up the Grand Canal through China.

Risky Business

Tour operations is one of the riskiest businesses in the travel industry. Operators deal with the most perishable commodity possible. Their product is space in time, like a seat on an airline flight or a room in a hotel on a particular night. Storing the product on the shelf for a markdown sale after the departure is not possible. They deal with foreign currencies that are subject to wide fluctuations. They are vulnerable to strikes, political upheavals, natural disasters, economic downturns, and simple changes in the tastes of the traveling public.

"The business is more nerve-racking than people realize,"

Whitley said. "It is a constant condition of management by crisis. You have to make quick decisions. It is difficult to plan ahead, yet you have to plan ahead. You need to be able to change plans at a moment's notice.

"You could be a Hawaii operator, for example," said Whitley. "Things are going great and you staff up and advertise. Then United Airlines [the biggest carrier to Hawaii] goes on strike for three months. Or you specialize in Russia and plan for the 1980 Olympics. You go through the negotiations, print the brochures, advertise. Then the U.S. government boycotts. You put together your program to Europe or to the Middle East, and the Persian Gulf War erupts and no one is traveling abroad at all. You have to cope with the economy of this country and the rest of the world. You have to anticipate what will happen to currency.

"You have to have patience and be able to handle details."

Getting In

On one hand, tour operations is one of the most creative areas in the travel industry and affords some of the best opportunities to fulfill dreams of traveling to exotic locales. On the other, however, job opportunities are limited and mobility is much more restricted than in other areas largely because most of the companies tend to be small, entrepreneurial, or family-run.

Tauck Tours, a leading domestic tour company based in Westport, CT, for example, "is geared for us to take over," said Peter Tauck, the third generation in the company. "We have five kids in the family, and all of us believe in nepotism." Still, Tauck employs about 45 people at headquarters plus another 55 to 100 tour escorts.

A company that sends some 20,000 people abroad may have only six to ten people in any position of real power. The vast majority of jobs are in reservations.

Nonetheless, tour operations is one field that utilizes virtually every type of professional. Doctors are involved in coordinating professional tours or assisting with programs for the handicapped; former journalists handle public relations and marketing functions; artists and musicians create and lead tours to the major art and music events of the world; former educators organize trips for teachers and students.

Salaries tend to be low (decent at top management positions). A low salary is somewhat compensated for, however, by the opportunity to take the trips a company offers.

"This business is designed for someone who starts very young, even part-time, when at school," said Jeffrey Joseph, an industry veteran who started in travel more than 20 years ago at the age of 18 working as a ticket agent for an Israeli domestic airline, ultimately wound up in New York where he heard of a new tour company opening, and landed the top spot despite the fact that, as he admitted, "I had no credentials at all."

He related, "We don't look for degrees, we look for personality, good communications skills, friendliness, helpfulness, and a desire to please. The whole industry is highly mobile. It's a matter of being in the right place at the right time, being motivated, intelligent, and capable. You have to be flexible and willing to move. Success doesn't depend so much on your education as your perseverance and ability to capitalize on opportunities. Anyone that shows promise always finds positions at mid-level."

Evolution of a Tour

A basic schedule for a ship or some major event or attraction may serve as the "embryo" of a tour package, with the rest of the itinerary organized around it. (A trip to Machu Picchu, for example, involves not only plugging in extra days in various cities in order to acclimate tour-goers before they go up to such a high altitude but also taking into account limited departures of small airplanes that tend to be canceled due to weather).

Next, the schedule may go to the tour development manager, who fills in the spaces, accounting for virtually every moment of time. Negotiators then block space and negotiate for rates from suppliers (airlines, hotels, ground transportation and sightseeing companies, restaurants) based on an expectation of how many passengers the program will carry.

Then, the material goes to the production department, which creates a brochure. This is the actual product that goes out to retailers for sale to the public, as well as to marketing for further promotion.

Once the tour is available for sale, it comes under the aegis of the operations and reservations departments. Reservationists take orders from travel agents and from the general public. The operations department gathers necessary documents and mails them to passengers, keeps track of tours as they are sold out or overbooked, and sends out passenger lists (manifests) to hotels. Tour escorts are assigned.

The visa department gathers the documents needed by foreign governments in order for the passengers to be admitted.

Tour operators may also have sales and marketing specialists who are responsible for promoting the program to travel agents and the public and public relations, personnel, and accounting professionals.

Salaries

Salaries are tremendously divergent (even among comparable companies) and do not always reflect the level of responsibility. Salaries generally depend on the size of the company (number of passengers carried), geographical location, number of people managed, and prior experience. International operations and in-house operations of airlines generally pay better than domestic travel companies (even those motorcoach companies that expanded into international operations).

Starting salary for a reservationist with one year of experience is about $18,000 to $20,000; after five years with a company, a reservationist can make from $22,000 to $25,000. Other examples of positions and salaries are as follows:

Hotel Negotiator, $20,000 to $40,000

Air Negotiator, $30,000 to $45,000

Air Desk Director, $30,000

Flight Operations Department Manager, Southeast, $30,000

Manager of Marketing Development, International Operator, $35,000

Operations Manager, $30,000 to $52,000

Regional Sales Manager, $45,000

Salaries for top management positions are quite satisfactory. Examples include:

Vice President, Operations, $55,000

Vice President, Sales and Marketing, $78,000 to 80,000

President, $80,000 to $100,000

For the near-term at least, there will be greater opportunities in operations (including MIS, reservations, customer service, and quality control) than in sales and marketing. "There are many jobs in tour operations," commented Lars-Eric Lindblad, a pioneer in the field. "But what has been lacking is trained people – the idea of going to a university to learn tour operations is new."

Contacts and Sources

Organizations that can provide information include:

U.S. Tour Operators Association (USTOA), Ste. 4B, 211 E. 51st St., New York, NY 10022, tel. 212-944-5727; represents some of the most prestigious and best established tour companies (mainly international) in the industry; has stringent membership requirements including bonding, and publishes a membership listing.

National Tour Association (NTA), 546 E. Main St., Lexington, KY 40508, tel. 606-253-1036; has directory of 600 tour operator members.

American Society of Travel Agents (ASTA), 1101 King St., Alexandria, VA 22314; publishes list of tour operators participating in bonding program.

Publications include:

World Travel Directory

Specialty Travel Index, 305 San Anselmo Ave., Ste. 217, San Anselmo, CA 94960.

Official Tour Directory, Thomas Publications, 5 Penn Plaza, NY 10117-0074.

The Educated Traveler Newsletter, P.O. Box 220822, Chantilly, VA 22022.

Other travel industry publications include:

Tour & Travel News

Travel Weekly

Travel Agent

Also check consumer travel publications and Sunday travel sections in newspapers.

Domestic Tour Operations

Just as there are international tours for every taste and lifestyle, there is an extraordinary range of options for domestic trips – everything from a journey by covered wagon (Colorado Wagon Train, Crawford, CO) to a mystery tour by bus where the destination is a surprise (Bixler Tours, Hiram, OH). Though similar to international tour companies, domestic companies have different origins and have evolved differently. They tend to have an atmosphere that is more conservative – even provincial – one that is more oriented to serving a local community rather than a national market.

Deregulation of the motorcoach industry has opened the way to innovation and made it possible for operators to creatively fashion programs that appeal to contemporary lifestyles and needs.

Prior to deregulation, rules restricted the use of other forms of transportation (such as airlines) in conjunction with motorcoach. For example, if you had a cross-country trip by bus, you were required to bring the people back the same way. There were incredible restrictions of operating authorities, which meant that a bus could only go through a state for which it had obtained costly licenses. To become licensed, an applicant had to prove a need for a service. That is, incumbents, like the two giants Greyhound and Trailways (now merged into Greyhound), did not have to prove that a new service would somehow be detrimental. Moreover, a motorcoach company could obtain rights to a service and then not exercise them, blocking a newcomer. Also, the motorcoach tour operator (called a broker) could not be the motorcoach operator, with the exception of Greyhound and Trailways, which had "grandfather rights." That is, both services had operated prior to the Interstate Commerce Commission Act of 1939.

All of this changed with deregulation; entry into motorcoach operations, charters, and tours was vastly eased. The result was that literally hundreds of new companies opened almost overnight and the numbers of passengers traveling on motorcoach tours and charters increased dramatically. The National Tour Association (NTA, the largest domestic travel organization with 4,000 members including 600 tour operators, 2,800 suppliers, and 650 destination marketing organizations) estimates that the industry carried 56.3 million passengers and grossed $5.6 billion.

While the industry had its origins in escorted motorcoach travel, now programs encompass many modes of transportation. Tours range in duration from one day to several weeks, and prices range from $35 for a day-trip to nearly $10,000. The most popular trips are five to seven days, and cost $400 to $500.

Domestic tour operations may be smaller in scale and more narrowly focused than international tour operations but currently offers greater growth and more career opportunities. In many respects, domestic tour operations affords greater creativity; so many more markets are available for domestic tour products than for international products, and the industry has really only just begun to tap them. Indeed, domestic tour operations has in a sense been reborn, and newcomers to the field have a chance to be in on the ground floor.

Tour participants still tend to be senior citizens, but the average age of all tour-goers is beginning to come down as new tour products are introduced to appeal to a younger, more active market. Indeed, the emerging specialties include programs oriented around ecotourism and cultural tourism (art, music, museums, cultural events), family travel (particularly "grandtravel" joining grandparents and grandkids on a tour), and such innovations as "hub and spoke" itineraries. While a typical domestic package might be a six-day fall foliage trip through New England, new products include a three-day rafting outing geared to singles (introduced by Bixler Tours, the Hiram, Ohio, company that developed the mystery tour).

The elements of domestic tour operations are essentially the same as in tour operations generally. They are product development (creating new products), sales and marketing, reservations and operations, and distribution.

Significantly, according to a membership survey by the National Tour Foundation (NTF), a subsidiary of the NTA, most tour operators' marketing strategy is oriented to product development (developing new products for current customers) and market development (finding new customers for current products). Few focus on market penetration (selling existing products to current customers) or diversification (creating new products targeted at new markets), but these represent growth areas for the future.

The industry is made up of a few large firms with a substantial number of employees and hundreds of smaller enterprises with fewer than 10. Most tour companies are relatively small: More than two-thirds have annual gross sales of less than $1.7 million; nearly one-fourth are mid-sized with sales from $1.8 to $7.5 million; only 8 percent have sales of $7.5 million or more, according to the NTF membership survey. The vast majority (of NTA members at least) have been in business for 10 to 16 years.

The average company usually employs 4 people plus 2 part-timers, operates 81 tour departures, and handles 2,500 customers a year. The largest companies employ more than 200, operate 10,000 departures, and handle 100,000 customers a year. The vast majority draw their customers from within their local area; but nearly one-fourth of all customers come from far away, making it necessary for operators to have links with travel agents.

In most of the tour companies, the owner is mainly responsible for tour development. Then the program is given over to a tour-planning department to find hotel rooms, negotiate rates, and figure out what attractions or sightseeing to include.

The field is becoming more professional (less "Mom and Pop"), along with most segments of the travel industry. In the domestic tour business, too, there are some consolidations into larger corporations (but not to the same degree as in other segments), greater sophistication in business operations, and more automation. Automation is playing a growing role, making management more efficient by enabling managers to keep track of reservations, how tours are selling, load factors, and the like.

Domestic tour operations is also becoming much more sales and marketing oriented. Field salespeople are being hired to call upon travel agents and groups (senior citizens clubs, church groups, and schools).

High Mobility, Low Pay

Though there tends to be little turnover of staff (less than 1 percent), considerable mobility exists within companies, probably more so than in international tour companies, mainly because domestic tour companies are not yet large enough to hire specialists; they hire generalists instead. It is common for tour escorts to rise within the company to the highest levels.

According to the NTF survey, no consistent effort is made to recruit managers and employees with previous experience and provide them with competitive wages and incentives. This field is still one where people can get in with relatively little experience; however, salaries reflect it. Consequently, people can stay in a company, taking on enormous responsibility, and still earn modest salaries. Consider the following examples:

- A woman with 12 years of experience with a company, rising up from a clerk typist to operations manager, was earning $30,000.
- The director of operations for a company, who rose up from a tour escort over a seven-year period, was making $30,000.
- Another person, with 11 years with the same company, rising from air tour coordinator to manager of tour development, was making $25,000.
- Another person, who was with a company for six years, rising from tour escort to supervisor of tour and development, was earning $23,000.
- The vice president and general manager of a company, with 24 years at the company, was making $47,000.

Domestic tour operations is one of the lowest-paying fields in the industry. Indeed, the NTF's first-ever salary survey disclosed:

President–only 52 percent earn over $40,000, 17 percent earn $30,000 to $39,000, and 20 percent earn under $20,000.

Vice President–42 percent earn over $40,000.

General Manager–24 percent earn over $40,000, and 38 percent earn between $20,000 and $29,000.

Operations Manager–41 percent earn between $20,000 and $29,999, and another 32 percent earn between $30,000 and $39,999.

Sales and Marketing Manager–only 8 percent earn over $40,000, 30 percent earn $30,000 to $39,999, and 39 percent earn $20,000 to $29,999.

Reservations Manager—only 4 percent earn over $20,000, 33 percent earn $15,000 to $19,999, and 62 percent earn under $20,000.

Tour Planner—only 7 percent earn over $30,000, 27 percent earn $20,000 to $29,999, and 53 percent earn under $20,000.

The rewards, however, come from having considerable responsibility, the diversity of tasks, the product, and the people you deal with. What compels people to stay? As one tour professional exclaimed, "In the tour business, you work with all components of tourism—hotels, restaurants, events, attractions, destination marketing organizations. You never get bored!"

Contacts and Sources

The National Tour Association (NTA) has a listing of members and further details about the domestic tour operations industry. NTA provides some placement assistance via notices in its "Tuesday" newsletter (for a $50 fee).

National Tour Association (NTA), 546 E. Main St., Lexington, KY 40508, tel. 606-253-1036.

The National Tour Foundation (NTF) assists students with internship placements in the tour business. NTF manages the Certified Tour Professional (CTP) program, the premier certification for tour professionals. It offers professional development seminars at its convention.

Major trade publications include:

Courier (NTA's magazine)

Tour Trade

Tours!

Tours & Travel News

Travel Weekly

Travel Agent

Inbound and Reception Services, Ground Handlers, and Sightseeing Companies

Americans generally think in terms of outbound travel and rarely realize that there are people at the other end to service the travelers with transportation, sightseeing, and other facilities. Those that handle incoming visitors, coordinating their stay and escorting them about, are called "inbound," "reception services" or "ground handlers." Most U.S. travel agencies are solely involved with sending visitors out from their areas to other states or countries, whereas most foreign travel agencies handle both outbound and inbound services. In this country, reception services are usually carried out by specialists, though many travel agencies are moving into the field.

Handling reception requires some specialized skills and services–multilingual guides, for example, and contacts with travel agents abroad–for handling foreign groups. But groups also come from other parts of this country. The key ingredients are a thorough knowledge of your locality and contacts with local attractions and facilities.

A Coral Gables, FL, agent, for example, handled a group of Norwegian zoo owners who were visiting to learn about facilities for captive animals in southern Florida. Besides arranging visits to such facilities, the agent also had to coordinate matters concerning passports, visas, lost luggage, and sickness among the tour members.

The reception service works in concert with the tour packager or the travel agent sending the group. Frequently, the travelers are completely unaware that they are being handled by an agent for the tour company with which they booked.

Many large companies, particularly motorcoach operators, specialize in reception services (sometimes known as Visit USA operators). Among them are American Express and Greyhound. Many small companies, including travel agencies, however, are getting into this area.

Convention and visitors bureaus are excellent sources for names of companies operating in your area. The New York Convention and Visitors Bureau (2 Columbus Circle, New York, NY 10019), for example, publishes a directory, geared for travel agents, which includes a listing of reception companies.

In addition to full-service sightseeing and transportation companies, there are specialized reception services. For example, New York Fashion Works specializes in a "shopping extravaganza" in New York's garment district and department and specialty stores; Overseas International Tours hosts groups from abroad; Accent-on-Theatre Parties obtains blocks of tickets to theater, dance, music, and special events; Art-in-Action arranges for art programs as well as shopping; Behind-the-Scenes looks into New York life-styles, antiques, fashion, finance, food, and interior design; Doorway to Design "opens doors to spectacular design" and arranges visits to "trade" interior design and fashion showrooms; and Harlem Spirituals is one of several companies specializing in tours of that celebrated district.

Cary Frederick, a Hoosier from Indiana who made his home in New York, knew what it was like to be an out-of-towner in the Big Apple—the fears, confusion, expense, wonderment, and delight. So, he set up his own personalized guide service, appropriately named "Rent-A-New-Yorker," to help visitors to the city, individually or in small groups. He draws upon his skills as a trained librarian to research and plan itineraries and to prearrange hotel accommodations, restaurants, theater and events tickets, and sightseeing. He even stands on line at the TKTS booth to obtain Broadway theater tickets at half price for his clients.

"Everyone talks about personal service," he said. "I am like a friend in town."

As companies like Frederick's expand, due to repeat business and referrals, they generally take on associates or add staff.

The American Society of Travel Agents (ASTA) has been actively working to help its member travel agencies to cultivate reception services, and several hundreds have already entered the field, with several hundreds more moving in the same direction. This usually involves adding staff.

ASTA member Rex Fritschi, president of Rex Travel, Chicago, launched a reception service a decade ago, providing sightseeing programs in Chicago. His company, Chicago Welcomes, handles groups mainly from overseas, including England, France, Germany, and Switzerland.

"It's a completely different ball of wax from the travel agency," said Fritschi, "different selling, marketing approach, and different handling. The wants, needs, expectations of foreign travelers are different."

It takes several years to become established in receptive services, to develop the contacts abroad, to gain the name recognition. Help in penetrating markets is available from the U.S. Travel and Tourism Administration, a section of the Department of Commerce in Washington, D.C., and, often, from state and regional travel offices. Also, ASTA has a listing of receptive services as well as an international membership division. International airlines can also be valuable allies.

Skills that would be excellent assets for working in reception services are knowledge of foreign languages (although not necessarily a prerequisite), experience of living abroad, contacts with travel companies abroad, and knowledge of a locality or special interest. Good planning and organizational skills, high creativity, and maturity and patience are also very important.

Reception services also offer a means of entry into the travel business without your having to give up your current job. Many reception companies need part-timers to help as escorts or guides (some areas, like New York City, require guides to be licensed) or associates to plan and coordinate trips. These companies afford much of the excitement and sense of traveling without your ever leaving town because the clients are from faraway places.

A job as a professional guide can be an excellent entrée into the travel industry and can be a challenging, creative, and financially rewarding position. Guides can freelance for travel companies, developing relationships with tour operators, travel agents, reception companies, and hotels. Guiding provides an opportunity to maximize your knowledge of foreign languages, art, history, architecture, clothes, music, theater, entertainment, and virtually any special interest. Some areas may require licensing; New York City's Department of Consumer Affairs, for example, administers a test that qualifies an applicant to become a professional guide. There are several entities in New York that place guides.

Reception services is a highly entrepreneurial field. If you are considering opening your own reception service, consider what your locality has and what it does not have. Talk with the local convention and visitors bureau or chamber of commerce people.

There is tremendous opportunity particularly because of the

continued growth in travel into the United States, fueled in part by exchange rates that have made the United States such a bargain, but also because of the appeal of the United States as a destination. "Foreigners have 'done' Disney World and New York and want to see what more of the U.S. has to offer," said Fritschi. "There is great, great potential."

It is possible that your own professional area can be a starting point. For example, one company (Cityscapes) specializes in finding the right locales for meetings, film shoots, receptions, and the like.

There are so many reception services and ground handlers that one of the greatest needs for individual companies is marketing. American Sightseeing International (ASI) was formed to meet this need. It is an association of sightseeing and tour companies in more than 100 major tourist markets (40 U.S. cities, 60 countries). Gray Line is another.

Sightseeing is probably one of the more limited occupations in the travel industry. In sightseeing companies, most people in positions of prominence have come up through the ranks of a bus company. Rather than travel industry professionals, they tend to be bus industry specialists.

The appeal of the sightseeing business is that it is intensely people-oriented. Escorts, ticket sellers, and bus drivers are all in constant contact with the public.

Deregulation has forced everyone to be more creative, innovative in terms of product and marketing, because there is so much more competition.

"This is a growth area – any city can have a sightseeing company," said Richard Valerio, ASI president. "There are new hotels, convention centers opening all over the place. Call the convention and visitors bureau to see what is happening."

Ground transportation companies do not only handle sightseeing. They may also handle transfers from airport to hotel or to sites for special events. They are used to a great extent in conjunction with conventions and meetings (even "spouse" sightseeing and shopping programs while meetings are going on).

One of the ASI members is Shortline Tours, which is unusually large for a bus company. Shortline had three buses when it started more than 20 years ago to provide transportation to rural areas. Later, the company bought up a sightseeing operation. Now, Shortline has 220 buses and 350 employees. The operations are so computerized that even sales locations on the road are tied to the main office in Manhattan. Bus maintenance – even when to change tires – is also logged in a computer inventory. The company has four levels of sales – marketing, sales, sales support, and an art department to produce brochures.

Why go into the ground transportation/sightseeing business? "The excitement of being part of a worldwide community," declared Valerio, "of hosting visitors, conveying civic pride, being creative."

Contacts and Sources

Apart from local convention and visitors bureaus, other organizations that provide information include:

U.S. Travel and Tourism Administration, 14th and Constitution Ave., NW, Washington, D.C. 20230, tel. 202-377-0136.

American Society of Travel Agents (ASTA), 1101 King St., Alexandria, VA 22314, tel. 703-739-2782.

Professional Guides Association of America, 241 S. Eads St., Arlington, VA 22202-2532.

Travel Industry Association of America, 1133 21st St. NW, Two Lafayette Centre, Washington, D.C. 20036, tel. 202-293-1433.

Travel for the Disabled

An infinite variety of tour companies specialize in some interest, activity, or demographic group and fall into the category of "special-interest operators." In recent years, however, the travel industry has become mindful of a huge group of people who had a deep desire to travel but due to some disability were unable to take advantage of conventional programs.

According to some experts, there are about 43 million Americans with disabilities, with a potential of generating about $60 billion in travel sales. A whole new industry has sprung up catering to these travelers. It is potentially so large and so specialized that handicapped travel is actually considered a separate field of tour operations.

Edna Davis, a former travel agent, was brought into the field quite by accident when her son, the captain of his school football team, was tackled down and did not get up.

"In the year that he spent at the hospital, people would hear I was in the travel business and ask me for help arranging travel for them. I realized no one knew anyone to help them. I handled groups, then tours, now reception services, also." Even Disneyland has called her for assistance.

The disabled, Davis stated, "are not content to fit into the mold. They seek freedom of movement. They won't be content sitting still. Disability does not mean inability."

Other companies have made this same realization. Flying Wheels Travel (P.O. Box 382, Owatonna, MN 55060), for example, tailors tours for the physically disabled. Evergreen Travel Service (19505L 44th Ave. W., Lynnwood, WA 98036) "does whatever anybody else would do who is able-bodied, but we do it slower."

This field of travel offers special opportunity for people trained in physical therapy, nursing, medicine, and psychology, as well as for people who are themselves handicapped. Travel agencies, for example, are becoming very involved in serving disabled travelers, both on a group and an individual basis, and may be very amenable to hiring someone with familiarity with serving the disabled traveler. Indeed, a registered nurse, Pam Erickson, set up a business (Professional Respite Care, Denver, CO) to provide nurses as medical travel companions for the disabled and seniors.

According to Davis, getting into the disabled travel market requires a knowledge about particular details as well as meticulous efficiency in anticipating every need and making arrangements for these travelers. "Introduce yourself to a wheelchair," she advised. "See how it works. There is no one easy source of information. No two disabled people are alike. All are individuals. Each must be counseled individually—their needs, desires. Always discuss with a carrier and check and recheck. Leave nothing to chance. Don't be timid; ask direct questions. They know they are disabled—they live with it. Their problems need to be discussed openly."

Two laws, the Air Carriers Access Act of 1986 and The Americans with Disabilities Act of 1990, will force widespread improvements in access for the disabled and spur many travel-oriented companies to cater to this market. The 1990 law specifically prohibits discrimination in transportation and public accommodations, including hotels and restaurants.

Hyatt Hotels Corporation, for example, launched a major program to increase accessibility at 107 of the chain's hotels and resorts, as well as a nationwide recruitment program for persons with disabilities. The company hired Barrier Free Environments, Inc., Raleigh, NC, an architectural and product design firm specializing in building design for persons with disabilities, to help develop the guidelines.

Moreover, under the Air Carriers Access Act, travel agencies, as agents for the airlines, are actually required to be able to service handicapped people who wish to travel by air. This opens the way for qualified people to approach an agency and create their own position.

Contacts and Sources

Sources of information and leads for potential employers include:

Society for the Advancement of Travel for the Handicapped (SATH), 347 Fifth Ave., Ste. 610, New York, NY 10016, tel. 212-447-7284; publishes a list of tour companies specializing in disabled travel as well as various guides.

Travel Information Center, Moss Rehabilitation Hospital, 12th St. & Tabor Rd., Philadelphia, PA 19141, tel. 215-329-5715; dispenses information by phone or mail.

Tour Managers

Many people expect that they can start a career in tour operations as a tour manager (also called a tour escort or tour director). In many companies, this job is relatively easy to obtain; in others, some very sophisticated background and skills are needed. For example, leaders of China tours may need to speak Mandarin and have strong academic backgrounds as sinologists (specialists who are highly knowledgeable about Chinese culture).

Most tour operators contract tour managers on a freelance basis since the work is so highly seasonal. Tauck Tours, a premier escorted motorcoach tour company, is unusual because it hires its own tour directors (paying salary and benefits) and tries to keep as many as possible working year-round.

Randy Durband, Tauck's manager of tour directors, is responsible for hiring. As many as 150 tour directors are hired in peak season; about 80 are employed year-round. Durband's position is a key spot because at Tauck all positions in middle or upper management are filled from the escort staff. This is because, as Peter Tauck, director of reservations, explained, "We organize the tour here and sell it to travel agents, so the only way one would see the product is to be a tour escort. Then you see the hotels, how they function. You are more able to handle the day-to-day decision making. It is hard to teach the product by showing someone the brochure. You have to experience it." Even Peter, the third generation at Tauck Tours, has been a tour escort.

Though tour escorting is often a steppingstone, it is emerging as a career in itself, albeit one that is hard to keep up after marriage and children.

"Things have changed," reflected Dick Sundby, a tour escort for 12 years, who served as Tauck's tour director supervisor for a while before returning to being a tour escort (leading the trips to the Canadian Rockies). "People are beginning to look at tour directing as a career. Many are writers and musicians. They want to work for five or six months and have their own thing to do in the off-season.

Still, "It's a strange lifestyle for a married person or parent," noted Durband. "It's like being a professional athlete – does anyone question whether Bo Jackson should be on the road? But it gives you very little opportunity for parenting. Most who do this who are married just do it in the summer."

No specific skills are required, but there are many things you have to be. "Like the Boy Scouts, you have to be honest, cheerful, brave, courteous, reverent," said Sundby. "You have to have the understanding and patience to deal with clients. You have to be able to go the extra mile to take care of people on an individual basis – that is equally important to knowing dates and places. It takes a special person to do a complete tour during the day and then handle individual requirements in the evening. You have to be a leader and be a friend."

Tour escorts need to be good communicators and diplomats.

They must be detail-oriented, well-organized, and highly responsible because they frequently have to manage through emergencies as well as handle considerable sums of money. Tour escorts also must have a deep curiosity, desire to keep learning, and an inner desire to do a better job than the time before.

Tauck has an intense training program in which escorts (who range in age from 21 to 60) learn how to deal with potential problems and emergencies. A rookie is put together with a more experienced driver and escort. Also, Tauck maintains special telephone lines should escorts get into difficulty along the way. The guides do a complete narration. "Clients expect a guide to know everything," Sundby said.

Tour escorts at Tauck typically make $250 to $450 a week before tips (but tips can amount to two-thirds of the escort's income). Tauck also provides group health insurance benefits to tour escorts, which is unusual.

Some tour escorts are married, but this arrangement generally does not work out well for long. Married couples will sometimes work the same itinerary but for different groups (but they still do not get to see each other more than once a week).

The work is emotionally and physically demanding. It involves working 15 to 25 weeks straight, 7 days a week, with no days off and only a limited amount of free time. There is little chance to sit down when you have to help lift out luggage and run around keeping everyone happy.

Despite this rigorous schedule, Tauck has a fairly low attrition rate. People either leave after one season or stay a decade. "It suits your personality and lifestyle or it doesn't," said Durband.

It can be a lonely job. But, "you develop camaraderie with the hotel people," remarked Sundby. "You develop friendships in the towns you visit, and it is like going home each time."

Normally, a tour escort will run one itinerary exclusively for one year; the next year, two itineraries; the next, three. With seniority comes more choice of itineraries, but selections are made by performance.

Out of 500 résumés, Tauck may hire 20 or 25 escorts. So many résumés come in unsolicited that Tauck does not have to do any active recruiting. "Persistence is the key," Sundby noted. "I tried to get into Tauck four or five times before I got in."

Because so many résumés come in, "it's difficult to tell a good candidate," Sundby advised, "so try to make personal contact." Friends who work in hotels or who are escorts can provide leads. It is also important to demonstrate some kind of familiarity with the product (the tour) and the destination.

Some companies may require a master's degree in botany or some other specialty. "But for most tours, good general knowledge suffices," said Sundby. "I became an expert in wildflowers and trees just by doing the same tour over and over and researching the questions the passengers asked."

The International Association of Tour Managers (IATM) has 2,000 members worldwide. Only 100 of these are in the United States mainly because most domestic tour companies employ local guides rather than escorts (who accompany a trip throughout its itinerary).

Most tour escorts are freelance, working for such companies as American Express, Trafalgar, and the like. They earn a minimum of $50,000 a year.

Dom Pasarelli, who is the main contact for IATM in the United States, noted that the association, which often acts as a referral service, has stringent membership requirements including five years of experience working as a tour manager. This kind of "chicken and an egg" situation can be overcome by working like an apprentice parallel with someone experienced and starting with a small tour company or a travel agency that operates groups. Membership also requires that the tour manager spend 180 days on the road and that escorting be the primary source of income. The vast majority of tour managers in the United States work part-time; only about 1,000 are professionals.

It is a highly specialized field – and one that is fairly elite. The IATM membership roster includes people who have doctorates, speak various foreign languages, and specialize in architecture, art, culinary arts, and the like. Also among the IATM members are three barons, two counts, and a prince.

"We're all crazy, eccentric," commented Pasarelli, who holds a doctorate in foreign cultures and has been a tour manager since 1962. "There is tremendous responsibility; you have the lives of 48 people in your hands. You have an awful lot of power; like a ship captain, you can put someone off the tour. I've had to ship some home, including one in a body bag. And people end up in hospital or lose a passport."

Though some passengers may initially regard their tour escort as a kind of lackey to help with the luggage, this image changes. "You live with them for many days; they get up when they are told, eat where and when they are told; listen and learn. You function as an interpreter, a Big Sister, and their 'bridge over the cultural gap.' It's fun, and you get paid for it," summarized Pasarelli.

But, he warned, tour managers can also be held liable and some have been sued.

Contacts and Sources

International Association of Tour Managers (IATM), 1646 Chapel St., New Haven, CT 06511, tel. 203-777-5994; has an annual membership fee of about $100.

Training programs include:

International Tour Management Institute, 625 Market St., Ste. 1015, San Francisco, CA 94105, tel. 415-957-9489; is the first and the biggest school (also in Boston and Los Angeles) and the one from which most tour operators recruit.

Other programs that have cropped up include:

American Tour Management Institute, New York

International Guide Academy, Denver

Tour Director Institute, San Diego

Lucas Travel School, Virginia Beach, VA

Educational Center, New Haven, CT

Starting Your Own Tour Company

Most tour companies start in a small niche and grow slowly. A small company can be set up with about $50,000. A company that aims to reach a national market needs about $2 million to start primarily because of the expense of printing and distributing the volume of brochures necessary for a national market, as well as advertising and promoting the product.

The tour operations field is very difficult to break into since, chances are, there are bigger, stronger, better-financed, better-known competitors. Moreover, there have been failures even among big, household-name companies, such as Rand-McNally, when they ventured into the market, mainly because they underestimate what tour operations is all about, tend to throw money into the trappings and fail to give enough attention to winning the loyalty of travel agents. Furthermore, companies from outside the travel industry are accustomed to much higher profit margins and are not willing to hang in when acceptance takes longer than anticipated (usually two to three years).

More worrisome is the recent failure of well-established and well-respected tour companies with a great following among travel agents and consumers, such as Lindblad Travel (whose name was synonymous with adventure travel) and Four Winds Travel. Their demise demonstrates the difficult financial waters that tour operators must navigate. They simply couldn't survive the multiple assaults of a declining economy that cut demand for travel, spiraling costs, and fear of terrorism, which caused Americans to all but cease traveling abroad altogether.

Much of the problem can be traced to the peculiarities of the business. For example, tour operators' biggest competitors these days are the airlines that they depend upon for space and good rates. Many major airlines have their own in-house tour operations, such as American's FlyAAWay Vacations and TWA's Getaway.

Many people who launch tour companies do so because they have some special interest (or passion) and want to build a business around it. Tom Hale, for example, "jumped in head over heels" when he set up his own tour company, Backroads Bicycle Touring, San Leandro, CA, in 1979. He was in environmental planning "and just decided I didn't want to do it anymore." He took a 5,000-mile bike ride through the West and then started Backroads. "I had an interest in doing something different and an interest in bicycling and just decided to do it."

Operating a tour company proved to be more expensive and harder to get off the ground than Hale thought it would be. To sell the tours nationally, he had to advertise. The company has grown steadily, however, with the rate faster now than at the beginning. Currently, the company handles more than 2,000 customers a year and has a staff of 15 including 10 tour leaders. The remaining staff are in reservations, marketing, bookkeeping, and equipment.

Hale himself plans the itineraries but confessed, "I didn't

know anything about the travel field. I didn't even know what a tour operator was. The thought of a motorcoach tour of Europe sickens me."

Backroads operates one- to ten-day bicycle tours, year-round. Offering bikers "pampered camping," the tours are deluxe and feature first-class hotels, country inns, and mountain resorts.

"I really like what I do," Hale asserted, but he only recommends starting up a tour operation to a small number of people. "There are obstacles at every corner. It takes someone with a fair amount of long-term outlook to get over the short-term frustrations. You have to plug away. There are financial obstacles. You don't make any money for a long period of time – until you get to a size customer base to support the operation. Like any business, you've got to pay your dues."

While Hale launched a successful tour company based on his special interest, other people may do so by virtue of a special way of selling.

"If it was just Jeffrey Joseph opening another tour operation, I'd say it was a thankless task, very difficult to do," said Joseph when he was about to open his company Spa-Finders, which specializes in selling packaged spa vacations through a catalog. "There are so many companies, and so many well-financed ones already established. This is not an easy field to get into. Yet there are areas of travel that have hardly been touched – special markets, special ways of selling. That's where I feel I can come in – I won't have thousands of competitors.

"I said to myself, 'I can run a big company, and if I am working that hard, I should be seeing more of the profits in my own hands.' The problem always was, what to do?"

Joseph was confident of his own success. "It's not the product that will be different; there are products for everybody already. It is the way of selling. Essentially, the method of marketing tours has been unchanged – companies either sell directly to groups or through travel agents." His strategy was to reach consumers directly.

Five Key Considerations

To start up your own tour company, there are five key areas to consider, according to Raymond M. Cortell, whose early tour operations experience came from his father's tour company Europacar (which mushroomed into the Cortell Group and was family owned and operated until it was swallowed up by a high technology company) and who has launched several new ventures. The five areas are (1) product, (2) customer target, (3) promotion, (4) distinction, and (5) pricing.

1. Product: Consider the destinations chosen; suppliers selected; type of travel, such as cruises, educational tours, or fly/drive trips; and class of product, such as deluxe or budget.
2. Customer target: Tailor the product to a demographic characteristic such as income or geographic location (a trip to Hong Kong can be a weekend shopping spree to a West Coast traveler but a two-week exotic Orient adventure to someone from Boston). Consider the "psychographic" characteristics of potential customers (are they, for example, retired, yuppie, or single).
3. Promotion: Plan not only the theme and execution but also the dollar amount in relation to size and frequency of the program. Plan the method, such as advertising, direct mail, or personal sales calls.
4. Distribution: Get the product out to consumers. Even consider items like the physical aspects of the brochure (4 by 9-inch versus 8 ½ by 11-inch, for example) and the kinds of distribution channels to be used, such as travel agents, clubs, or consumer-direct marketing.
5. Pricing: Position the product in relation to both the psychographic characteristics as well as the competition. The idea is to maximize profit without crossing the "price breakpoint," at which you price yourself out of the market. Pricing is critical to marketing strategy because it is one of the key decision factors consumers use to choose a tour product. The difference in price must be substantial enough to capture the target market's attention and motivate a shift in sales, while still leaving enough margin to make a profit. You must be able to sustain the price over a period of time.

Setting up the tour program—plotting out the itinerary, negotiating for space and rates—is only one aspect of establishing a tour company. How you will handle reservations should not be underestimated. You have to consider the kind of telephone system, a computer system (if any), and who will take the reservations. This last factor is so strong that many companies are moving their reservations centers to Denver, Atlanta or Las Vegas, where there is availability of cost-effective staff.

You can also get tripped up with distribution. Just getting a brochure into a travel agent's hands does not ensure that the agent will sell your tour, particularly when the agency is hooked up with "preferred vendors" who can afford to pay a higher override. More importantly, with so many companies failing, agents are skittish about linking up with an unknown, unproven supplier. And the cost of advertising directly to the consumer in order to drive customers to the agent can be prohibitive.

Tour operators are experimenting with alternate forms of distribution, such as computer-based shop-at-home services like CompuServe and Prodigy (a joint venture of IBM and Sears). Cortell himself is developing a company (TravelFax) that is aimed at reducing operators' cost of distributing brochures to agents by using fax linked to a computer database.

Newcomers can surmount many of the obstacles by focusing in on specific niches–special interests–where the main purpose of the trip is not the destination but a particular activity or interest. Specialty markets are more defined, easy to reach (through clubs and specialty publications), and more committed to travel.

"The specialty traveler is willing to pay more for the special features of a tailored itinerary," said Ann H. Waigand, who publishes *The Educated Traveler Newsletter.*

5

Incentive Travel

The Ultimate Motivator

The corporate version of tour operations, incentive travel – the use of a trip as a prize or premium connected with some action performed by the winner – is among the most creative fields in the travel industry. It is also among the most demanding in the amount of detail and responsibility, interesting in that it combines expertise in marketing, advertising, and promotion as well as travel, and fascinating in terms of the people with whom it brings you in contact.

Incentive travel also is one of the fastest-growing segments within travel, offering some of the best opportunities for jobs. Yet incentive travel is one of the least known and understood segments – probably because most of the major incentive companies do not consider themselves part of the travel industry at all. Rather, incentive travel is usually considered part of the larger, motivation field; travel is only a means toward an end, a small element in a much larger motivational program.

"I don't sell toasters. I don't sell travel," said an account executive for Carlson Marketing (formerly E.F. MacDonald), one of the giants in the field. "I sell ideas. We sit down with the vice president of sales and the marketing people. They tell us what their problem is–increase their share of market, move some item before the new inventory comes. Then we sit down with our people and design the program."

Jobs in the incentive travel field can be found among incentive "houses," which handle all facets of motivational programs including travel; specialty incentive travel companies; destination management companies, which put together the travel program for an incentive company; travel agencies; and suppliers like airlines, hotels, and destination tourist offices. Jobs can even be found among major companies and associations that regularly mount incentive travel programs.

Travel is just one of the incentives and premiums compelling millions of people each year to exert themselves to hit some target, exceed some quota, meet some goal, or fulfill some specified requirement in order to win. Cash, television sets, video cassette recorders, automobiles, radios, computers, and cameras are only a few of the others in a long list of items.

But ever since the 1950s, when travel first began to be regularly used as an incentive, it has proved to be the "ultimate" motivator. More people will work harder and exert more effort to win an incentive trip than they will to win any of the cash or merchandise items. The reason is that travel plays on more of the psychological forces that go into motivation, such as status, peer recognition, dream fulfillment, and the desire/need to get away. Moreover, unlike a color television, which anyone can purchase (and probably already has) at an established price and have for years afterward, an incentive travel program is an experience that cannot be bought at any price, cannot be stored on the shelf, but must be renewed each time.

The Special Difference

The incentive trip is different from the typical packaged tour. Indeed, though many travel agents are expanding into incentive travel as an extension of their corporate, groups, or conventions and meetings business, the trips are intrinsically different in their make-up and must be specially created.

"Incentive travel is a party, a celebration," declared John Kiley, president of EGR International, a New York-based meetings and incentives company, and a former president of the Society of Incentive Travel Executives (SITE). "It is about 'making it' in the business world. It is an extraordinary event. It shouldn't be predictable. It should be full of surprises. And the source should appear to be the sponsor company and not the travel coordinator."

For example, a $459,000 incentive travel program in Hawaii that Kiley's company arranged for Avon (where spouses tend to be husbands) was capped by a luau at Sea Life Park. Just as the 500 people were gathering for the show, three men in hang gliders, specially painted with the company's logo, leaped off the cliffs and performed an aerial ballet.

Traveling Like Royalty

The other distinguishing aspect to incentive trips is that you are not dealing with travelers at all, but winners, each a VIP. The trip is always first class and sometimes ultradeluxe–with a chauffeured Mercedes to drive couples around Switzerland for a day, for example. Generally, the incentive trip is structured so that the winner will not have to reach into his or her pocket at all, not for a tip, not for a taxi. Some programs even provide postcards and stamps.

Shaklee Corporation of San Francisco has one of the largest in-house incentive travel departments in the country and has won awards for its creative programs. One program offered a top prize of a six-day trip to Montreux, Switzerland, which was won by 310 people. Since Shaklee believes strongly that participants should not have to pay for anything, the company even provided some spending money. The winners also found little packages awaiting them in their hotel rooms, complete with gift cards thanking them for their hard work. Shaklee rented an entire train for an excursion to Zermatt, had it decorated, and arranged for a band to give the riders a send-off. There was continental breakfast and entertainment aboard, and, on arrival at Zermatt, they were met by Saint Bernards with casks of Shaklee liquid protein around their necks.

For traditional incentive companies, travel is only an incidental in an overall marketing campaign that can last a year. The program starts and ends with marketing. It kicks off with that first encounter with the vice president of marketing when the incentive travel specialist says, "You've got a problem, and I can solve it, and it won't cost you a dime." It ends with the sales results being tallied and the kickoff of the following year's campaign.

A Winning Situation

The beauty of incentives is that it is a "win-win-win" situation: The sponsoring company pays for the awards out of incremental revenues (money it would not have had were it not for the incentive campaign); the winners get a priceless trip, fantasy-come-true, for free, plus peer recognition; and the incentives company clears about 12 to 15 percent of the total bill.

For example, suppose that a company wants to increase its sales volume by 20 percent. The incentive planner would structure a program by first figuring the gross profit that the additional income would produce and then applying a percentage of this amount (12 percent is typical) as the budget for the incentive travel program. The budget for the program involves much more than the trip. It also includes the cost of promoting the contest, monitoring contestants' progress toward meeting the goal, and planning and operating the trip.

Incentives can be used to solve any number of marketing or operational problems, such as the following:

- Stimulate the sales force.
- Introduce new products or models.
- Boost sales volume.
- Extend the distribution area.
- Move slow items.
- Open new accounts.
- Sell special consumer promotions.
- Revive inactive accounts.
- Stimulate sales in a slow season.
- Push new uses or combinations of items.
- Offset competitive promotions.
- Aid in sales training.
- Gain higher visibility at the retail level.
- Back up special promotions to the retail trade.

- Gain sales help from nonselling employees.
- Cut employee turnover.
- Recruit.
- Extend a peak season.
- Clear inventory.
- Help collect past-due accounts.
- Obtain competitive market information.
- Improve working habits.
- Reduce absenteeism.

How It Works

Example: A modest-sized small-appliance manufacturer, GEE, has 100,000 ice-cream makers that must be sold by December in order to make room for new inventory. Solution: Rather than spending $100,000 on an ad campaign to inspire consumers to buy the product, the company decides to offer an incentive travel program to its 200 distributors. The retail price of the ice-cream maker is $30, and GEE makes $2 on each item. The payback to GEE, then, is $200,000 if all 100,000 units sell. The contest is designed so that each of the 200 outlets has to sell 500 units. If this target is hit, then the manager of the outlet wins the trip. The incentive travel planner has a budget of $110,000: $1,000 to spend on each winning couple and $10,000 to spend on the promotional campaign. The $1,000 per couple includes the incentive company's commission of $125. The planner expects 100 to win the prize but will allow a buy-in (whereby people who do not meet the quota are allowed to pay the difference, thus enabling the operator to fill the blocked space) for the unsold units, at $2 a unit. GEE sells off the units, makes $90,000 profit, and, in the bargain, boosts the support of its distributors.

In addition to solving specific marketing problems and building good will among the sales force, distributors, retailers, and the like, incentives also provide measurable results that an advertising campaign does not. Travel has advantages over other awards because it is a more powerful motivator, builds good will, and (unlike a toaster or a TV) provides a vehicle for bringing top producers together with corporate top brass. A trip can also be used for a sales meeting, educational program, or product introduction.

Selecting the destination is a critical aspect of the program since the destination itself has to be the primary motivator. The destination must have a certain status and excitement, but it must also meet practical criteria. Most companies do not want their key producers to be away for very long; thus traveling time is a consideration. Also, the destination must be within the budget and have the necessary space. It must also be relatively safe and secure since incentive programs are usually decided upon two or more years in advance. The destination name must be very promotable, even if the participants do not know precisely where it is. Top incentives destinations are London, Paris, Hawaii, and Las Vegas, but incentives companies have also created programs to more far-flung points such as Hong Kong, China, and the Soviet Union.

Incentives are a vital source of tourism for many destinations, and many tourist bureaus frequently become actively involved in helping incentive planners and decision makers to recognize the appeal of their locality and to make inspection tours. Australia, though a long distance away, is working hard to entice incentive movements, as is the Montreux, Switzerland, tourist board.

A Growth Industry

Incentive travel has burgeoned in recent years yet is still only a fraction of what is could potentially become. "Productivity is the name of the game today, and productivity and incentives fit together," declared one veteran incentives executive predicting continued growth in the industry. "We have historically been involved in white-collar travel, and white collar is the growing portion of the workforce. At banks, fast-food restaurants, and the like, we can help develop good work habits, apart from just boosting sales."

National Cash Register Company (NCR), Dayton, OH, was the first to use incentive travel when, in 1906, the company awarded 70 salespeople who qualified for its 100-Point Club diamond-studded pins and a free trip to company headquarters. In 1911, winners received a trip to New York.

The first regular use of incentive travel began in the 1950s, with the advent of mass travel and the airplane. In one year, some 45 companies awarded top producers trips totaling $50 million. By 1990, businesses were spending $2.6 billion on incentive travel awards.

In the early years, incentive travel was limited to a few incentive houses that specialized in handling massive groups and were prepared to take the risk of chartering whole aircraft. With deregulation of the airline industry, incentives were no longer confined to charter movements and whole planeloads; instead, operators could purchase small blocks of seats on regularly scheduled aircraft. This brought down the size of incentive groups from the hundreds to perhaps 50 or fewer people–a number easily handled by a travel agent or meetings planner–and minimized the risk. Indeed, the burgeoning growth in the incentives industry is due to the huge numbers of small incentives groups. Now, 48 percent of all incentive trips are arranged by travel agents rather than by incentive companies, according to *Incentive Magazine*.

Apart from travel agents, the number of incentive travel companies is small–perhaps only 100. Only five companies are considered major, full-service incentives houses:

Maritz, St. Louis County, MO

Carlson Marketing (formerly E.F. MacDonald), Minneapolis

S&H Motivation, Hillside, IL

Business Incentives, Minneapolis

Top Value, Dayton, OH

Besides the incentive travel companies, travel agencies, and meetings and conventions planners that arrange these trips, incentive specialists are in heavy demand at companies that are the biggest users (like Shaklee, Merrill Lynch, Fedder's, General Electric). Tourist offices, like the British Tourist Authority, French Government Tourist Office, and Irish Tourist Board, also employ incentive specialists, both to promote these kinds of trips to their destination and to help planners coordinate their programs. Many travel suppliers, such as airlines, hotel chains, resorts, car rental companies, and cruiselines, also employ incentive specialists.

The "theoretical flow" of the incentives program process starts with the account executive in the field (Los Angeles, New York, Chicago, for example) who talks to a potential client about its "challenge" (usually regarding the sales of a specific line). Based on the problem, the account executive brings in the marketing department, which takes this input, couples it with what they know about the industry and what has worked in the past, and makes a proposal that represents the "solution" to the problem. "Everybody has a different problem; every program is different," said an incentives executive. The presentation may involve anything from a flip chart to a "dog and pony show" of live actors to give the potential client the feel of how the agency would kick off its program. The solution usually involves "motivation/incentive" in the form of merchandise, travel, and/or recognition items.

Twenty years ago, the awards were 30 percent travel and 70 percent merchandise. "Travel was reserved for the very top producers—the sizzle and the steak, the icing on the cake," he said. "It was highly promotable, highly visible, but reserved for the elite group."

Now, travel accounts for 70 percent of the awards, which challenges incentive companies to come up with new destinations and a broader range of travel categories. "We're stretched," the executive continued. "Many clients take two trips a year. We have to give more emphasis to theme parties, new and exciting things to do, such as renting a limo to go across Europe, renting private homes and condos for the top winners."

Once the concept is sold, the motivation program is designed. Design takes into account contest promotion, rules and administration, and awards. It is vital for the program to have measurable results so that the company can demonstrate a return on investment to the client.

Considerably more detail is involved in coordinating an incentive trip than a regular trip. "Some are intimidated by the size of the movements—500 to 1,000 people are not unusual," noted the executive. One meeting involved an overnight trip to Atlanta for 2,400 people, which was "scary to do just from the point of lost luggage."

Getting In

Incentives companies are organized much like advertising agencies. They have account managers, who generally are business and marketing specialists and who sell the incentives programs to companies and act as the liaison between the incentive companies and the clients; a creative department, consisting of writers, artists, and audiovisual and graphic arts specialists; and a travel department, consisting of people who scout new destinations and facilities, trip planners, and coordinators.

The entry-level position is typically the account coordinator, who is involved with coordinating the incentive trip. This position provides a locus for learning the whole incentives process from conception to operation and servicing. On a major promotion, the coordinator may even participate in the trip. The account coordinator manages transportation, works with the pretrip department on mailings, and funnels information to client and account executive.

The marketing department tends to have many people with M.B.A.'s as well as people who grew up in the industry, worked for a client, or came from an advertising agency where they dealt with the marketing concept. One account executive, for example, came out of an incentive department of a bank. Account executives and motivation salespeople may be stationed in sales offices located around the country.

The kinds of jobs at a major incentives house include data processing, administration, customer service, purchasing, graphic arts, marketing, print buying, accounting, transportation coordination, and mail room work. "The types of jobs are everything you can imagine," said the incentives executive.

Why go into incentive travel? "I'm not only involved in our business, but all the others – Chevrolet, Avon, Merrill Lynch – and how they go to market," he said. "We know the motivation business, the travel business, and our clients' businesses."

For someone who has reached the level of an account executive, the business also "gives me freedom," said one who held the position at Carlson Marketing. "You're your own boss, with your own accounts. This isn't monotonous."

The field can be lucrative as well. "The salary grows with your bottom line," he continued. The structure is generally a base salary plus commission. "It can pay well, but it takes a bit of luck in addition to skill and creativity. You have to be there at the right time, when the client is ready for a new idea. I sell ideas."

Salaries tend to be better than in the travel industry as a whole, particularly among the account managers. In general, salespeople and account executives earn more than operations people. Operations managers earn from $30,000 to $40,000; sales executives can earn as much as $50,000.

An account executive for Boston-based Tri Companies and a former advertising executive commented, "I enjoy seeing the project succeed. It excites me when the goal is reached." The ability to manipulate people is also intriguing.

Who should go into incentives? The answer is someone who loves challenge and problem solving, someone who is excited by being on the edge of a crisis. "There is always the panic moment," one executive said. "We all like that challenge of feeling we can't resolve the problem, and then we do."

"Someone who is achievement-oriented," answered Robert Guerriero, president of The Journeymasters, Salem, MA. "This isn't a job; it is a way of life. This business is not for everyone. There are constant emergencies, constant challenges, constant excitements, and constant rewards. Everyone is divorced whose spouse is not also in this business because they can't understand the demands. We sell achievement. We sell joy."

"This is a high-pressured business," said James Kimball of Kimball Travel Consultants, Salt Lake City. "You have to make decisions on the spot. You need good business sense."

Other important criteria include good communications skills, creativity, imagination, self-confidence, and being a good listener.

Because the emphasis in incentives is on marketing, the industry draws more heavily on business executives than on travel professionals. Advertising professionals are also in demand. At Maritz, even the so-called travel director, an entry-level job, generally requires a college degree and business experience. Travel directors also tend to be "bright, attractive, generally youthful, and comfortable with more mature individuals," one executive observed, since they are the client-contact people who actually go out with the incentive groups and are on site, coordinating sightseeing trips and troubleshooting.

Whereas many come to incentive travel from other travel fields, Maritz prefers to go out and recruit top-level people for the travel directors positions. "They are our first line of contact. The service they give, their attitude, can determine whether that company comes back to the company another year," an executive said.

The largest companies, like Carlson Marketing, Maritz, and S&H, probably have the greatest number of entry-level positions and the best training programs, but the competition for these jobs is also stiff. The 50 to 100 smaller companies may offer a better opportunity to get in and take part in a greater scope of the business; rising through the ranks may be faster, though how far you can go more limited than in a large company. Still, small companies can be steppingstones to the larger firms.

The field is growing as more companies begin to understand what incentive travel can do and how it can be applied.

Moreover, there is greater use of travel awards in consumer promotions as well. Indeed, this is where the whole concept of incentives and premiums began, when, in 1851, B.T. Babbit, a soap manufacturer, printed coupons on the backs of the soap wrappers that consumers could exchange for lithographs. Later, companies buried dishes within the soap boxes to induce people to buy their product. One travel agency, The Happy Traveler, Somerville, NJ, cashed in big on repeating this same concept of exchanging soap wrappers for travel in a huge promotion for Procter & Gamble.

In addition to jobs at incentives companies and travel agencies and as conventions and meetings planners with incentives divisions, there are incentive travel specialists at hotels, cruiselines, airlines, and tourist offices. This field is one where you can literally create your own job because the opportunities to apply incentives are unlimited.

Incentive Houses

An Example: Maritz

At Maritz, one of the largest incentive houses, 2,000 of the 5,000 employees are in the travel area alone. Of these 2,000, there are 1,500 who are the incentives professionals within the motivation and travel companies.

Among the incentives professionals are program administration personnel who develop administrative procedures, issue standings reports, send Award Credit checks to participants, and handle all other details of the program; computer programmers and operators who are responsible for sales reports for clients and assist with the program administration; and direct mail specialists who process and mail all communications material and customer service personnel. Incentive travel sales amounts to $300 million out of $600 million in total travel sales.

Occupying a 100-acre complex, Maritz operates five separate divisions of which travel is one. Maritz is a full-scale motivation, communications, research, and training company. Frequently, the different companies work together. Maritz creates incentives with both travel and merchandise awards, coordinates business meetings, and handles all the audiovisuals needed for the program.

All the motivation/incentive programs are sold by the account managers. These people tend to be mature, be in their thirties, and have eight to fifteen years of experience in the business world, though not necessarily in incentives. They need a business or marketing background to best understand how products load a market, how a company is organized, and how to determine what a client's need is all about.

Creative people, who develop programs and do the promotional campaign, come from among travel directors. Maritz maintains sales offices around the country, but nearly all the creative work is done out of its St. Louis headquarters.

Maritz handles only the vary largest corporations, but the incentive trips may range in size from as few as 25 to 50 winners to as many as 5,000 to 10,000. Trips are intricate to plan and coordinate; one trip, for example, involved a succession of bicycle treks through South Africa over a six-month period. Specialists work as a team on a program.

The company has a policy of promotion from within, and, according to the executive, there is a great deal of movement inside. "We want our people to enjoy upward mobility," which can mean within divisions and to other divisions.

Another Example: The Journeymasters

There are perhaps 100 smaller incentive companies, which consider themselves the "boutiques"of the industry. The Journeymasters, Inc., Salem, MA, is probably one of the most creative incentives houses around. The company's client list is small, but all blue chip–General Electric, Tupperware, General Felt Industries, Toshiba, Mita, Sherwin-Williams. Yet the staff numbers fewer than two dozen.

"We're massively elite," commented Robert Guerriero, president. "We do things the big guys can't do. We don't do anything less than 100; a typical group for us is about 200."

He described his operations department, with about five people, as "the factory—they create the details of the trip, prepare the costing, work with the hotels and airlines." Two others make up the advertising and sales department. "We do all our own copy, including the letter shop, printing, typesetting, and pasteup and creative portions." Freelancers are also employed.

One of the most exciting incentive programs he operated, he recalled, was billed as the "Rally to the Renaissance" and involved a road rally by Mercedes through Italy for Knoll Furniture, a top-of-the-line furniture manufacturer.

Guerriero maintained that it is not necessary to actually know the client's business; but the incentives specialist must know how to familiarize the client with the value of incentives as a marketing tool. "We'll never know their business as well as they do. But what we can do is show how they can operate a $100,000 contest and it won't cost them a thing."

The Journeymasters believes that a travel incentive needs to have "poetry" and that the company offers "poets of imagination."

Contacts and Sources

The Society of Incentive Travel Executives (SITE) is the main trade organization. SITE conducts excellent training programs and seminars. It also publishes job openings in its newsletter and offers a free, confidential employment service. A membership directory is available free to members and for a fee to nonmembers.

Society of Incentive Travel Executives (SITE), 271 Madison Ave., Ste. 904, New York, NY 10016-1001, tel. 212-889-9340.

Some excellent trade publications that provide leads and contacts include:

Incentive

Corporate & Incentive Travel

Corporate Meetings & Incentives

Meetings & Conventions

Successful Meetings

6

Meeting and Convention Planning

Meeting Planning

"Show business" is how one meeting consultant described his field. Putting on conventions, meetings, or trade shows offers the technical and logistical challenges as well as the thrill, excitement, and creative fulfillment of a theatrical production. Many conventions even incorporate Broadway-quality entertainment into the program.

Meeting planners work for individual companies, associations and trade groups, government, and educational and religious organizations and in independent consultancies, incentives houses, travel agencies, hotels, conference centers, and convention bureaus. The field is mushrooming in people as well as influence; about 8,000 people in the United States belong to Meeting Planners International (MPI) out of a total membership of 10,300 in 31 countries. This trade association had only 150 members when it was founded in 1972.

Collectively, the MPI membership puts on more than 233,000 meetings – new product introductions, sales meetings, board meetings, annual conferences, conventions, educational seminars, workshops – that are attended by 42 million attendees who generate $13 billion in spending a year. In all, the meetings industry generated $54.6 billion in 1990. The average MPI member is responsible for an annual budget of $2 million, plans 16 meetings, and accounts for an average of 1,200 room nights a year. More than a dozen MPI members plan meetings attended by 90,000 delegates at a time, and a few handle meetings of more than 100,000 attendees.

Not long ago, the task of planning meetings and conferences typically fell to a person holding some other job, like the Director of Sales or Vice President of Marketing. Even now, corporate meeting planners may also be responsible for education and training, while meeting planners attached to associations are frequently also responsible for membership services.

But as the cost, intricacies, and options available in arranging meetings have escalated, the function has emerged as a profession in its own right. Whereas meeting planners of a decade ago might have learned through "trials by fire," now it is more necessary to have some formalized training. Even within the field, there is growing specialization of function. MPI, which has a training program, also has its own certification process.

Meeting planners are the producers, directors, writers, and ticket takers of every event. They have to plan for every detail, every eventuality, so that everything flows smoothly. Then they have to solve problems and deal with the inevitable crises that crop up, such as airline strikes, power failures, and lost freight.

"This is an artistic business, as well as a scientific one," said Phil Lee, president of California Leisure Consultants, Inc., a San Diego-based meetings consultancy.

"You work six days a week, 18-hour days, and get paid lower than the legal minimum wage," asserted Ann Raimondi, president of The Raimondi Group, New York. "You have to be tireless because you need a lot of physical stamina and common sense, which gets you through a lot of unknowns."

MPI has sorted out 25 main functions of a meeting planner. They are as follows: establishing objectives of the meeting; selecting the site, hotels, and facilities; blocking space; negotiating rates; setting budgets; making reservations for airlines and hotels; arranging air and ground transportation; planning the program; choosing speakers and entertainers; planning food and beverage functions ("You have to know what people are eating these days, and not to overfeed them at lunch because they fall asleep, and not to serve chocolate at the coffee break," advised Raimondi); arranging for all facilities, such as audiovisual equipment; providing necessary security; setting up meeting registration; providing support services; coordinating with the convention center or hall; planning with convention services manager; arranging a preconvention meeting; taking care of shipping; setting up function room; preparing exhibits; scheduling promotion and publicity; orchestrating guest and family programs; providing meeting materials; taking care of gratuities; and supplying a postmeeting evaluation. Apart from these functions, a meeting planner also has to do budgeting, know how to use computers, be able to manage people, and, above all, be diplomatic.

In the past, meeting planners functioned much like travel agents—merely taking orders of how many people would need transportation and accommodations at a specific site. But increasingly, instead of just handling the logistics, planners are more crucially involved in negotiations that save the organization enormous sums of money. The planners also play more of a role in the corporate image/public relations aspects of meetings and are becoming more involved in setting goals and objectives of meetings and in giving advice and counsel on how to make meetings more productive and cost effective. Planners have a key responsibility for site selection, a decision that might be made as much as eight years in advance. They must be aware of world affairs and economic trends in order to make judicious decisions.

In many meeting planning offices or departments, a single individual sees a meeting through from beginning to end; in others, functions are divided up among specialists such as those who negotiate with facilities and those who actually operate the meeting and arrange travel. Often, the travel arrangements are separated out entirely and handled by an outside travel agency.

Meeting planning is negotiating, planning, and management. It is very much a people business, involves creativity, and affords considerable (even too much) opportunity to travel. It has an element of glamour, and there is enormous challenge. It is also a business of problem solving and crisis management.

A meeting planner has to have excellent organizational skills and, more importantly, the ability to manage a project. "Loving people is basic, but everybody does," said Phil Lee. "You need the experience of handling a project that might have started on a cocktail napkin, progressed to a meeting, and come back into your lap. You have to procure services, harness them, and make sure everything performs where hours and minutes and seconds are critical, and then move on and start all over again. You only need to know half of all the information in the *Encyclopedia Britannica.*

"It is not quite the entertainment industry," said Lee. "You can't wear lavish clothes. But it has the excitement of the entertainment business. Each meeting is a production. There is excitement that emanates from the stage. There is an audience. You get a little depressed when the show ends. It is just like show business, but you have to be more responsible."

A Calling

Meeting planning is not for everyone. "You have to have the calling," said a meetings professional. "This is a group communications process. People who are successful are those who understand the components–like putting on a party in a house." You have to be sensitive to what people are going to want and need in terms of the environment you create for the meeting, convention, or conference and the creature comforts you provide. "No matter how good the program, it is not going to work if the environment is not conducive and the expectations of attendees have not been met."

A person who becomes a meeting planner, cautioned Raimondi, must be someone "who enjoys doing a job for which you get no thanks. You can't expect your ego to be fed all the time. You are the unseen and unsung hero. After all, you don't make money for the company; you save it."

Good communications skills and excellent organizational skills are critical. Meeting planners also have to be extremely adept at handling people, at being diplomatic. A sense of humor also helps.

A meeting planner may travel one out of every four weeks of the year, choosing sites, making preconvention inspections, and, finally, attending the major meetings or conferences he or she has arranged.

The frequent travel and the fact that meeting planners are wooed by hotels, airlines, and destinations all the time create an aura of glamour that is hard to dispel. "People perceive the job as fun and games–being wined and dined," one planner remarked. "But it is hard work. All the hours of work that go into putting on a meeting, the worry about every little detail that becomes second nature, and the miles and miles of travel wear thin."

Apart from the energy, excitement, creativity, and responsibility that are part and parcel of the job, the growth of the field means that advancement opportunities are excellent.

"It is a fascinating industry," said Raimondi. "I knew I wanted to stay in it. It is hard to get in, but then you can make your own opportunities."

Getting In

The profession is relatively new, and many of those in the field came in "through the back door," basically from jobs with limited planning responsibilities that expanded into full-time jobs. Even now, many planners do meeting planning in conjunction with jobs in communications, public relations, marketing, human resources, and administration.

The new breed of meeting planners who have targeted this career generally have a four-year college degree with an emphasis on business, good written and verbal communication skills, and good people skills. They are detail-oriented and organized, are able to work well under pressure and make quick decisions, have a working knowledge of the travel industry, and are able to take frequent business trips.

People typically come into meeting planning through the hotel side, where they gain experience in dealing with meetings and meeting planners, negotiations, and the fundamentals of handling the logistics. Apprenticeships come in the form of positions such as "assistant meetings manager" or "meetings coordinator."

Large corporations or associations that hold many meetings probably offer the best opportunities for entry, but getting in is tough. Legions of people are drawn to the field by the opportunity to travel, deal with people, and have the kind of responsibility that a meeting planner has. Large corporations and associations offer more routes into meeting planning, such as through secretarial work or some other clerical capacity. Entry-level positions are low paying: In major cities, starting salaries are in the high teens to the mid-twenties. The field can pay fairly well at the highest levels, however.

"Meeting planning has finally come into its own as a profession," stated Raimondi, who was the corporate meeting planner for the Touche Ross accounting firm until she set up her own consulting company. "Hoteliers are now used to dealing with professional people expert in negotiating." Deregulation of airfares, making that segment also subject to negotiation, is also a factor in the greater acceptance of the profession.

Pointing to how tough getting into the field has become, Raimondi advised that it is frequently easier to get into an organization or company department as a secretary or in some other clerical position. An organization like the American Institute of CPAs, for example, has 12 planners at various levels and is willing to hire entry-level people who are able to move up through the hierarchy.

There is more specialization of function. Meeting planners are diversifying into experts on audiovisuals, food and beverages, entertainment and meetings content, incentives meetings, and logistics and negotiations.

Job listings, Raimondi said, are "hidden in the *Wall Street Journal* and *New York Times* under such headings as 'meeting planning,' 'special-event coordinator,' 'public relations,' and 'hotel-convention services' " (which means the employer wants someone with no experience because they want to train you their way at low pay).

Salaries

"It scares me that so many people want to get into the business," Raimondi added. "It will bring down starting salaries. People want to come in because they want to travel and they like people. But after one or two years, you become disillusioned with travel. It loses its appeal. You do it so much (50 to 80 percent of the time), it becomes a chore and kills your social life."

Starting salaries (which still means having some basic experience) are in the $20,000 range; planners with one to two years of experience earn in the $30,000 range. With three to five years of experience, they can earn $40,000 to $75,000. A director, with a staff, can make $60,000 to $75,000. Salaries can go well into six figures but usually only for someone like a Vice President of Marketing who oversees meeting management.

The average salary in the United States for meeting planners in 1990 was $37,478 (for females, the average was $34,824, and for males, $52,101) according to a survey of MPI members by *The Meeting Manager* magazine. Planners with fewer than three years of experience average $27,290; with three to five years of experience, $32,146; six to nine years, $39,232; ten to fourteen years, $41,964; and more than fourteen years, $52,653. Those who work in the corporate market earn $1,192 more annually than the average; planners in the health care industry also are paid on the high side. Those working for associations, in government, education, and religious organizations and as independent planners earn lower-than-average salaries.

Getting Ahead

Meeting planners can rise to the head of their department in a corporation or association, becoming a Corporate Vice President in charge of meetings and conventions, for example, but rarely higher. Those who harbor higher aspirations generally wind up setting up their own meeting and convention planning consultancies, as Raimondi did.

There are about 700 to 800 consultancies. The largest of them might have seven people, and many are solo operations. They tend not to be as lucrative as other kinds of consultancies because the work is very labor intensive.

Middle-level corporate meeting planners are being hired by travel agencies to head up new conventions and meetings divisions.

Thus, despite some limitations on mobility, meeting planning is emerging as a career. Some planners even become very involved with the management of major corporations and associations.

Meeting Planners International conducts a number of educational programs, including one-week institutes geared to entry-level, intermediate, and advanced professionals. MPI also publishes various resource books and maintains a resource center, which can provide "career packages" consisting of information gathered on how to get into the field (price is about $30).

MPI works with the Convention Liaison Council, which provides a program toward a Certified Meeting Professional (CMP) title. Several local chapters offer a job bank for members, and MPI is compiling an on-line employment bulletin board (for members only).

American Society of Association Executives has an executive referral program (tel. 202-626-2723) for a fee. Other meetings industry job banks include the Society of Corporate Meeting Planners (tel. 408-649-6544), Professional Conference Managers Association (tel. 205-823-7262), and National Coalition of Black Meeting Planners (tel. 202-628-3952).

Meetings industry recruitment and employment specialists include Lerner Associates (tel. 516-767-7074, 301-549-7455); Rod Abraham & Associates, who specialize in placing freelancers on-site (tel. 215-923-4913); and Travel Executive Search (tel. 516-829-8829). Trade journals provide other recruitment possibilities.

Convention Center Management

If working as a meeting planner is like "show business," then working for one of the hundreds of convention centers throughout the country is like "opening a Broadway show every day"—especially if the convention center is just across from New York City's Great White Way.

Of the 1,000 jobs at the Jacob K. Javits Convention Center of New York, 700 are part-time or daily (principally workers who move equipment in and out) and 300 are full-time. Of the full-time workers, half are "blue-collar" (mainly union), such as electricians, plumbers, and guards. Only about 125 are actually the core management staff, consisting of marketing, public relations, personnel, administration, finance, and operations people.

Rachel Dahbany, director of administration and personnel, drew a parallel between convention center management and real estate management, the area she worked in before going to the convention center: "This is a great big corporation that manages a building but also does marketing and public relations." But there is an important difference: The convention center, unlike most office buildings, never closes. After the day's activities conclude or a trade show closes, teams come in to break down one show and set up for another on one floor, while on another, a grand banquet may still be going on.

Convention center management involves extremely complex logistics. The New York City center is as big as the Empire State Building would be if standing on its side, and, in any one day, some 70,000 people can be going and coming. "There is nothing more exciting," Dahbany said. "Tens of thousands of people scurrying about every day. There is madness at night. This building is alive."

Among the positions that are fairly unique to convention center management are the Director of Transportation, who is responsible for getting the convention-goers from their hotels to and from the center, trafficking trucks in and out of the building, working with the city to make sure that streetlights are working and enough police are on hand when necessary, and dealing with the city's Taxi and Limousine Commission to make sure that there are adequate services for the center; a Director of Public Safety, who is in charge of the safety of the people and the equipment; a Director of Fire Safety; and an Events Coordinator, who is something like a meeting planner but is at a much higher level. A center the size of the Javits Center has six or seven Events Coordinators working under a Director of Event Services.

Entry-level jobs for the "white-collar" positions in management might be as a receptionist, a mail room worker, a messenger, or a secretary. New centers tend to hire only experienced people in key positions–generally from hotel-convention sales, meeting planning, show management, and convention and visitors bureaus–because there is not enough time to train them.

In essence, the convention center provides the space and facilities; individual show managers provide their own creative people, interior designers, audiovisual technicians, and the like.

Most convention centers operate much like a private enterprise but are generally owned by state or local government. The New York City center is owned by both state and city government. Political contacts can come into play in getting jobs.

The 1980s was a period of extraordinary growth. It seemed as though every town was building a convention center and every city was building a newer, bigger one. Convention center management offers interesting and unique opportunities for those seeking jobs in the 1990s. Contact local convention and visitors bureaus for further information.

Conference Center Management

Apart from convention centers (generally stand-alone structures that do not provide accommodations on-site), there are hundreds of conference centers. These complexes combine accommodations (up to 300 rooms) and food and beverage facilities with meetings facilities, according to the International Association of Conference Centers.

Conference center management essentially couples hotel and resort management with convention center management, usually with separate categories of professionals.

An executive conference center has a median staff size of 15 in the conference service department; a corporate conference center has a median staff size of 7, while a resort conference center has a median of 6.

Professionals who work in conference centers have "high-impact" positions involving face-to-face contact with attendees. Front-desk personnel and those who pick up the attendees at airports and bus or rail terminals, as well as conference service coordinators (who are involved with anything having to do with the conference itself, from booking the meeting, to servicing it, to following up with a postmeeting evaluation), are all on the front line. The sales department, assistant manager, and general manager are also all highly visible.

A career path can be drawn from the front desk to the assistant coordinator to the conference coordinator and up. How fast you rise depends greatly on the size of the center.

In the past, many people entered conference center management from education (former teachers, for example, who became involved in coordinating educational programs), from hotels, and from meeting planning departments at corporations. But this field, as virtually every other in travel, is becoming more professional.

The International Association of Conference Centers is working with a university to create a curriculum for a conference center management program. It also provides continuing education for those who have already come into the field from other areas. The association holds a "Career Mart" and keeps résumés on file for six months so that its 141 members (centers and suppliers) can call when new staff are needed.

Contacts and Sources

Apart from local convention and visitors bureaus, other organizations that can provide information include:

Meeting Planners International (MPI), 1950 Stemmons Freeway, Ste. 5018, Dallas, TX 75207-3109, tel. 214-746-5222.

Society of Corporate Meeting Planners, 2600 Garden Rd., Ste. 208, Monterey, CA 93940, tel. 408-649-6544.

International Association of Conference Centers, 900 South Highway Dr., Fenton, MO 63026, tel. 314-349-5576.

Trade publications include:

The Meeting Manager

Successful Meetings

Meetings & Conventions

Meeting News

Business Travel News

Hotel & Resort Industry

Corporate Travel

Association Trends

Travel Suppliers

7

The Hospitality Industry

Hospitality Industry Overview

It was only a 300-room hotel in a metropolitan area with hundreds of hotels. Nonetheless, the opening of the Charles Hotel at Harvard Square in Cambridge was cause for (then) Massachusetts Governor Michael S. Dukakis and Speaker of the House Tip O'Neill to come to officially cut the ribbon and for the movers and shakers from Boston's political, financial, and real estate elite to turn out in their finery.

Hotels are more than a bed and a hot meal. They are frequently a linchpin for commerce. They can literally put a destination on the map as a commercial center or a distinctive place where visitors should come. Invariably, hotels are a key element in a community's economic base because they generate jobs and draw in visitor spending to the area, bringing in new money and support for many other businesses. The grocer who supplies the hotel's restaurants, the laundry that cleans the sheets and tablecloths, and the souvenir shops, restaurants, local attractions, and sightseeing companies frequented by tourists and business travelers all benefit. Indeed, through the ripple effect, it is estimated that what each visitor spends multiplies four times through the local economy.

In many parts of the world, a hotel has been the foundation for a tourism industry that turned a depressed area into a vital one, such as Kyong-ju in South Korea and Khajuraho in India. Closer to home, in Lake George, NY, the reopening of The Sagamore, a grand resort built in the Gilded Age, was a major event for the community; the largest single employer in the area, The Sagamore was the first hotel to remain open year-round.

Employing some 1.6 million people in some 44,000 properties in the United States and paying out some $17.4 billion in salaries and wages, the lodging industry offers the greatest opportunity for jobs of any single segment in the travel industry in terms of numbers, future growth, and advancement. Indeed, the lodging industry, which totaled $57 billion in sales in 1989 (a year when 2.8 million new rooms went on the market), is expected to generate some 400,000 new jobs during the 1990s; in 1989 alone, 53,000 new jobs were created. The number of desk clerks, 113,000 in 1988, is expected to grow to 142,000, or by 26 percent, by the year 2000.

The growth in new properties has slowed since the boom of the 1970s and 1980s (an estimated 6,000 properties opened between 1985 and 1990), when building was propelled by real estate tax shelters. Hotel owners did not have to make money on rooms; they could get their money back through tax write-offs and then hope to see a profit when they sold the property at an appreciated value. "With construction costs currently amounting to $350,000 to $500,000 a room, that would mean a room rate of $420 a night in order to make money," said John Beier, regional vice president of Loews Hotels, New York. "There will be a shakeout period."

So far, the shakeout has consisted of buy-outs rather than bankruptcies. For example, the mega-company Holiday Corporation—at its height a $5-billion company with 1,700 properties and 200,000 employees worldwide—was acquired and broken up into Holiday Inn Worldwide, owned by Bass PLC, a British conglomerate, and The Promus Companies, Inc., which operates Embassy Suites and Homewood all-suites, Hampton Inns, and Harrahs Casinos/Hotels. Holiday Inn Worldwide now consists of Crowne Plaza, Holiday Inn, and Holiday Inn Express, which employ 1,700 people in the United States and 52,000 worldwide; another 150,000 employees work in franchised hotels. Promus, meanwhile, still one of the largest hotel companies in the world, recently formed an international division to expand the company's operations in Europe and Asia-Pacific.

The lodging industry will expand for all the same reasons that the travel industry will expand – the maturing of society into demographic categories that tend to travel, more dual-income families, and greater value placed on travel. Other factors also come into play – the mobility of society (the fact that children tend to move away from parents, prompting much long-distance leisure travel) and the specialization and globalization of commerce (which spur growth in business travel).

Continued growth in the hospitality field will accelerate the already rapid career advancement characteristic of the lodging industry. The lodging industry has a long-standing tradition of taking people with minimal experience into specific entry-level positions, training them, and moving them up through a hierarchy. It is not uncommon for someone to rise to a general manager's position within five to ten years. Among the success stories are the chairman of Hyatt Hotels, Pat Foley, who started out as a front-office supervisor in Seattle about 30 years ago, and Hyatt's president, Darryl Hartley-Leonard, who started out as a desk clerk at about the same time.

However, many people in the industry fear that a threatened shortage of skilled workers in the 1990s may prevent companies from realizing the full potential of growth in demand.

"The decrease in the size of families is a double-edged sword," declared one hotel executive. "Smaller families will probably mean a significant increase in per capita discretionary income which can be spent on travel and leisure. However, a decrease in the available workforce suggests a shortage that will affect all service industries.

"We will have to be more flexible in establishing split-time and flex-time for our employees and exert a recruiting effort beyond anything we have seen before because if we can't service the market, we will lose it."

Consequently, companies are stepping up efforts to hire from nontraditional sources, including retired, disabled, and economically and educationally disadvantaged groups. Hyatt Hotels Corporation, for example, launched a nationwide recruitment program of people with disabilities (and is instituting guidelines for "barrier-free" hotels). "Providing job opportunities for persons with disabilities is not only morally right, it also makes good business sense," stated Darryl Hartley-Leonard.

More hotels are also making the work-and-family problem easier for working parents. Twin Towers Hotel and Convention Center, Orlando, FL, opened a satellite public school within the hotel so that parents could have their children nearby. And, to further spur people to pursue careers in hospitality, the American Hotel and Motel Association (AH&MA) is working to step up efforts by hospitality educators to recruit high school students into their programs.

The Oldest Profession

Long an esteemed profession in Europe, hospitality as a service industry is just coming into its own in the United States. Indeed, the AH&MA, representing about half of all lodging properties in the United States, at one point joined with the National Restaurant Association to mount an "Image Task Force" to create an industry-wide "Image/Employee Recruitment" campaign.

Innkeeping is probably the oldest "tourist" entity still surviving intact. The tradition of innkeeping that served pilgrims and merchants thousands of years ago is still fundamental to the lodging industry. The essence of bed and board is preserved in bed-and-breakfast establishments (seeing a new revival), inns, motels, and the new class of so-called economy hotel.

However, hotels today take many different forms and offer many different services and facilities beyond bed and board. Many hotels are more like minicities, offering a full complement of services and a range of professionals to match. Hotels are restaurants, catering services, meeting and convention facilities, and sites for weddings, family functions, and other special events. They are sports facilities, retail malls, and tour operators. Many stage live entertainment; some are gambling establishments.

Far more than bed and board, the hotel business involves real estate, finance, food and beverage, tour packaging, meeting and convention planning, education and development, engineering, energy management, purchasing, architecture, interior design, maintenance, information management, franchising, entertainment, recreation, telecommunications, and computer systems. It also involves sales and marketing, administration, and public relations.

People are most familiar with the chain properties because they are the most visible. Most of the chains do not own all their properties (70 percent of commercial properties are independently owned) but manage them for private or even government owners or franchise the name. Still, it is the chains that usually set the tone and establish the trends and standards for the industry.

Industry Dynamics

The distinctive dynamics of the hotel industry derive from the high capital requirements, the time between planning and opening a hotel, and the fact that a hotel is "brick and mortar" and cannot simply be moved if the destination or location falls from favor. Location is nearly everything in the hotel business.

The location will largely determine whether a hotel is geared to business or pleasure travelers and which time periods are busiest. Every hotel has the problem of leveling out peaks and valleys of occupancy—a task of the marketing department. A conference center such as Arrowwood of Rye Brook, NY, a full-service hotel specializing in conferences and meetings, solves the problem by introducing summer vacation packages. A city-center hotel like Vista International in New York City, which caters to midweek business travelers, creates resort-type packages for the weekend. A resort like The Sagamore, which traditionally relied on summer travel, now cultivates incentive travel and meetings, spa programs, and family-activity packages to boost fall and winter travel.

Competition is intense in the hotel industry—and not just from other hotel properties. Only 44 percent of all trips involve commercial lodging, according to the U.S. Travel Data Center; the majority of travelers stay with friends and relatives, or at campgrounds, or in recreational vehicles and vacation homes.

Though demand has continued to increase for commercial lodgings, so has competition. Hotel companies have thus been forced to wage more aggressive marketing campaigns and to expand their sales and marketing forces.

Segmentation, or product differentiation, has also continued, as hotels have sought to expand their market share by offering new products from high-end accommodations to all-suite hotels to a variety of new inns and motels. New specialized companies are springing up, and older established chains are diversifying more than ever before.

In short, proliferation, competition, market segmentation, diversification, and increased utilization are the key issues facing the lodging industry.

What the Hotel Business Offers

"This is such a dynamic, high-energy business," commented L. Antoinette (Toni) Chance, former vice president of personnel for Omni/Dunfey Hotels and now an industry consultant.

"Opportunities in the hotel industry are unlimited," she said. "There is no more exciting industry, or more opportunities available in any other industry in the country, including high tech. The variety of positions one can have, the flexibility, the freedom to test your wings in other areas with few restrictions, the high status of certain positions.

"I would be bored working for a widget manufacturer. The hotel industry offers a dynamic quality unlike any other. I can't see myself in any other business. I've seen people leave for a 9 to 5, weekends-off job, but wind up coming back later. They miss the energy and excitement. Once you get into the hotel business, you're in it for life."

"Hotels are theater," stated Beier. "In fact, a lot come to hotels with a theater background. You can live a lifestyle that you couldn't otherwise afford."

The lodging industry offers considerable glamour; the chance to mix and mingle with the powerful, successful, and rich; an opportunity for enormous responsibility at an early stage; and tremendous advancement prospects. Few industries offer as much chance to live and work virtually anywhere in the world. In fact, a career in the lodging industry almost necessitates frequent relocation. Each type of property and each location present their own challenge and distinct atmosphere.

"If you graduate from a hotel school or learn from the ground up," an industry executive observed, "the skills are equally as valuable in Seattle as Miami Beach or Bangkok. If you want to pull up stakes and move, you can. It's not like working in aerospace or in automobile manufacturing, where the key companies are concentrated in only a few places. Hotel skills are in demand everywhere, and if you like to travel and see new places, you can."

The lodging industry also offers a chance to do many different jobs in the course of a career; you are not pigeonholed in any one area. Indeed, wide experience is encouraged for anyone aspiring to a general manager's position.

The business is very much about people–there is constant interaction with guests and coworkers–and it is very literally a service business. "It's a service business–not servitude," stated Beier. "But Americans generally don't understand service."

The hotel industry remains very traditional and very hierarchical, much in keeping with its European heritage. A definite value is placed on "paying dues."

"Being a bellman or a front-desk receptionist is okay, but there is the nagging feeling that 'I should be doing more,'" said Beier. "But you have to systematically learn the business. No one doubts what a chef has to go through, the training in all the positions, but too many people in other positions in hospitality think, 'If I'm not the general manager within the year, I failed.'"

Though patience is a virtue, there is relatively fast progression toward accountability and the higher-paying positions. "You can be accountable for millions of dollars by your mid-thirties," said the human resources vice president of a major chain. "There is power and responsibility at a relatively early age." Even with relatively little supervisory experience, within only two years, you can find yourself overseeing 40 people.

However, the fast track (known for rapid burnout rates) with frequent hops up the career ladder is no longer favored. "Companies want more stability," noted Dawn Penfold, formerly with ITT Sheraton and now an industry recruiter with Lerner Associates, New York. "They want a sales staff to stay a minimum of three years. They don't want people who jump around."

What It Takes

The lodging industry demands dedication, sacrifice, and sheer hard work. Hotels do not shut down at 5 P.M. or even midnight; they are open 24 hours a day, weekends, and holidays. The work hours are very long: A group sales coordinator, for example, might have to be at the hotel at 3 A.M. on a Sunday to greet a group and stay until 8 P.M. to resolve a problem. Given the number of hours that mid- and senior-management positions require, the hourly rate is not very substantial. Moreover, there is no such thing as a totally protected holiday.

As a service business, the hospitality industry demands far more of employees than merely "liking people" and enjoying contact with them. "We're looking for people who have warm, outgoing personalities, who see a dignity in serving others and are not resentful of providing service," said a human resources executive.

Personnel people look for a take-charge person who wants accountability and autonomy early on yet can be a team player and is service- and people-oriented, flexible, adaptable, adventurous, hard-working, and self-disciplined. Since the work is physically demanding, they also look for energy and stamina.

"Everyone puts such emphasis on technical expertise," commented Jim France, former general manager of the Charles Hotel, Cambridge, MA, in describing what he looks for when hiring.

"Technical expertise is the last thing you need. You can have the most brilliant hotel man, but if he can't handle people–the staff or the guest–then he should be an auto mechanic."

"A hotel may have lovely appointments, but it is essentially brick and mortar. The only thing that makes one hotel better than another is the staff. I would fire an employee who is rude to a guest faster than one who makes a mistake. We can teach a person not to make a mistake, but rudeness to the customer destroys the business."

People looking for a career (not just a job) in the hotel business should be willing and able to physically move about frequently and be interested in doing so. (France's own career proves the point: In 20 years in the business, he moved 13 times.) However, the need to uproot family, leave friends, and relocate frequently in order to rise up the career ladder can strain relationships.

The hotel environment can be extremely disciplined, if not autocratic. Front-desk clerks, bellpersons, and waiters, for example, are drilled in techniques; their movements are choreographed, their remarks rehearsed. The Charles Hotel in Cambridge even has an operating manual 84 pages long, describing every detail about what to say to guests, how to present restaurant checks to patrons, and what the menu will be like. At the same time, as one general manager noted, a hotel must operate democratically, involving individuals in the operation.

"We don't want automatons," added Chance. "We want to see 'scenarios' but we don't inhibit personal style."

What to Go in For

Work environments and advancement potential and even job categories differ greatly in the hotel field depending upon whether the property is a city-center hotel, a highway motel, a vacation resort, a conference center, or a country inn; whether it is full-service or economy class; and whether it is a chain or an independent property.

There are eight major categories of function. Depending upon the size of the property, functions can be separate jobs or combined into one.

Front-Office Staff. Responsible for direct personal contact with the guests, reservations, special needs, check-in, and check-out. Positions include front-office manager, assistant manager, room clerk, reservation clerk, cashier, information clerk, and telephone operator.

Service Staff. Responsible for greeting guests, handling baggage, and assisting with travel plans. Positions include superintendent of service, concierge, lobby porter, bell captain, bellperson, and doorperson.

Accounting. Responsible for tracking financial information. Positions include controller, assistant controller, credit manager, purchasing agent, food/beverage controller, income auditor, food/beverage auditor, general cashier, cashier, accounts payable supervisor, accounts receivable supervisor, payroll supervisor, night auditor, ADP systems supervisor, and secretary. The controller can play a key role as a financial advisor along with the general manager and professional staff; the assistant controller serves as office manager.

Food Service. Positions include food/beverage director, catering manager, maître d'hôtel, captain, waiter/waitress, busperson, bartender, wine server, food checker, and dietician.

Example: a food/beverage manager for a hotel that generates $10 million in annual volume is responsible for keeping costs down by controlling inventory and obtaining better prices (as well as for serving as the liaison between the company and outside contractors and unions, determining how to upgrade restaurant operations, achieving "harmony" of the staff, planning work schedules, overseeing accounts payable and receivable) and is ultimately responsible for profit and loss.

Food Preparation. Positions include executive chef, first assistant, second cook, fry cook, roast cook, garde-manger, vegetable cook, pastry chef, butcher, pastry supervisor, and steward.

Housekeeping. Positions include executive housekeeper, floor supervisor, room attendant, serving specialist, and houseperson.

Sales and Marketing. Responsible for promotions; special arrangements for events such as meetings, banquets, and weddings; sales to the travel trade (travel agents, tour operators, car rental companies, and airlines); rate setting; and decision making regarding products and services. Positions include marketing director, sales director, sales representative, group sales coordinator, banquet manager, and food service staff coordinator.

Maintenance and Operations. This area has been greatly elevated in status since the energy crisis of 1973, which saw energy and maintenance costs of hotels skyrocket. Positions include chief engineer, air conditioning engineer, plumber, carpenter, electrician, and laundry and kitchen equipment service representatives. The director of engineering does not necessarily have to have a degree in engineering; rather, this position requires experience in building maintenance and equipment. The director of engineering usually supervises five or six people and maintains a $50-million building.

Special Opportunities

The lodging industry is expected to continue to expand at the rate of 1.0 to 1.5 percent a year, with 11,000 to 16,500 new jobs created each year. Demand for particular specialties flows in cycles, however. At present, the food-and-beverage area is very active, particularly with regard to positions for food-and-beverage directors, restaurant managers, and executive chefs; a few years ago, sales and marketing slots were prime possibilities.

"Demand runs in spurts because turnover runs in spurts," said Sue Gordon, vice president of human resources for Radisson Hotels and a member of AH&MA's Human Resources Council. "The executive housekeeper position comes and goes; also controller, director of sales, and food and beverage director. All positions are opportune areas for people wanting to make careers in lodging."

One of the less known positions is that of the stewarding manager, who is responsible for all the ware washers, pot washers, and silver burnishers. The stewarding manager is responsible for distributing all the china, silver, and utensils, and keeping track of all that would be used for a banquet for 2,000 people, for example, is quite a responsibility. This position is usually a steppingstone to higher positions in food and beverage.

Growing sophistication, specialization, and greater service orientation among the hotel industry's properties are also producing new positions and shifting emphasis. For example, there is substantial growth in concierge positions as part of an industrywide push in the guest services area. Convention services has come into its own as more and more properties are appreciating the potential of the groups and meetings business; director of catering has thus become a key position, with a new emphasis on promoting banquet sales (much like room sales). The popularity of health spas, golf courses, tennis courts, and other sports and entertainment facilities at properties makes the lodging industry an important employer of these kinds of professionals as well.

Computers have become an essential tool in hotel operations. They are used in reservations, accounting, energy management, and sales. Consequently, most hotel companies have MIS departments, and MIS analysts are in demand.

Shifts in emphasis and changes in services and management techniques directly affect the position of general manager. General managers are much like city mayors in that they have the ultimate responsibility for perhaps thousands of guests and employees. They are also chief executives of large, complex businesses and must be responsible for financial management and for providing leadership.

Not everyone working in the hotel industry aspires to be general manager, and, with the expansion in the numbers of properties, there is actually a shortage of talent. Becoming a general manager is a very attainable career goal.

But, warned one hotel executive, "People don't have a realistic view of the demands. They see 'Hotel' on television, see the glamour side of wining and dining celebrities. But that is only a very, very small part of it. Being a general manager is a demanding, highly responsible job, 24 hours a day, 7 days a week. There are a lot of nitty-gritty, dirty types of things that need to be done to meet guests' needs."

Finally, chains and hotel networks have positions in regional, national, and international offices, although these positions are relatively scarce. A major international chain with hundreds of properties worldwide might have about 200 such positions, which include marketing, sales, public relations, personnel, business development, and franchising.

Salaries

While entry-level jobs are relatively low paying, mid- and upper-management positions pay well, as represented by the salary figures for various hospitality industry positions shown in Table 7.1.

Getting In

Entering the hotel industry is difficult. While this segment of the travel industry has the greatest number of entry-level positions, applicants outnumber openings by about 20 to 1. If you have set your sights on working in the lodging business, take any available position. Even if you start as a secretary in a sales office, it is fairly easy to move up or over to another job. Because commercial lodgings operate around the clock, it is usually possible to work in at least a part-time job to get a taste of what the work is like, gain valuable experience, and be in a good position to land a full-time job.

Many hotel companies recruit directly into management training programs from major colleges with four-year degree programs in hotel management (including Johnson & Wales, Cornell University, Michigan State, and Florida International) as well as

Table 7.1
1991 U.S. Hospitality Industry Salary Outlook

	Low ($000s)	*Median ($000s)*	*High ($000s)*
Hotels–Corporate			
Chief Financial Officer	99	100	125
Corporate Controller	40	45	55
VP-Operations	55	73	110
VP-Sales/Marketing	68	77	95
Director-Yield Management	40	50	60
Corporate Food/Beverage Director	50	55	63
Corporate Chef	59	60	72
Director-Development	53	61	74
Director-Construction	45	75	90
Director-Human Resources	40	52	65
Director-Purchasing	23	35	53
Regional Manager	37	43	55
General Manager	43	55	73
Hotels–Operations			
General Manager	42	53	62
Assistant Manager	28	34	45
Controller	32	38	45
Manager-Human Resources	25	36	44
Rooms Division Manager	30	33	45
Front-Office Manager	21	24	34
Food/Beverage Director	32	41	47
Asst. Food/Beverage Director	23	24	28
Restaurant Manager	26	28	33
Maître d'Hôtel	26	31	35
Beverage Manager	26	29	32
Banquet Manager	22	23	26
Director of Catering	27	30	35

Table 7.1 (Continued)

	Low ($000s)	*Median ($000s)*	*High ($000s)*
Hotels—Operations (cont'd)			
Catering Sales Manager	23	25	32
Executive Chef	35	38	45
Chef	29	30	35
Sous-Chef	26	29	33
Pastry Chef	26	30	36
Banquet Chef	22	24	28
Director–Sales/Marketing	28	35	50
Director of Sales	27	36	48
Director of Marketing	33	45	65
Sales Manager	26	28	33
Conference Manager	20	27	28
Executive Housekeeper	23	33	38
Assistant Housekeeper	18	26	29
Chief Engineer	29	35	41
Motels/Resorts			
Guest Services Manager	28	37	48
Motel Manager	22	25	26

Source: Roth Young Personnel Services, New York.
Hotel salary guideline: low = 100–400 rooms; median = 400–700 rooms; high = 700–1,000 rooms.

other disciplines (including business, engineering, marketing, and accounting).

The American Hotel & Motel Association, representing about 10,000 properties nationwide, has established a junior organization called "The Future Hoteliers of America" for those enrolled in vocational, hotel school, or college programs in order to involve people in the industry early on.

"The number one thing I look for is whether the school has an internship program and the student has worked each year in the industry in various capacities," said the vice president of human resources for one hotel company. "A dishwasher gets equally good experience as a front-desk person. I look for a grasp of the realities of our industry. And the reality is, there is a tremendous amount of hard work."

Every hotel has entry-level positions, for example, in sales and reservations or as a front-office clerk, cashier, convention services manager, or floor manager in a convention services department. While headquarters offices receive many résumés, most personnel directors advise new entrants to contact the hotel where they want to work directly.

The next level after the entry level is a team leader supervisory position, perhaps in housekeeping. From there, you can become an assistant manager in housekeeping or rooms or a front-office supervisor. There may be similar positions in food and beverage.

When a new hotel opens, management generally tries to hire as many local people as possible. While experience is helpful, it is not always necessary; it is more important to demonstrate willingness to work and ability to learn. A major hotel company may interview 6,000 to 8,000 candidates to hire for 400 positions.

A newly opened hotel may offer more opportunity for novices than an existing hotel, as well as a better chance of growing into more responsible positions as the whole operation matures. The Charles Hotel, Cambridge, MA, for example, filled most of its 341 positions locally from among inexperienced people. "What I look for," said France, the hotel's first general manager, "is personality, attitude–the [person] who smiles and is friendly, is guest-oriented." France's method is to have candidates go through several screening processes–personnel, the department head, the division head, and, finally, the general manager.

Chain Properties, Sophisticated Training

Chain properties generally offer the best opportunities for new entrants. They have the most sophisticated training and development programs as well as the best chance for advancement within a single organization. Companies such as Omni, Hyatt, Marriott, Westin, Sheraton, Hilton International, and Radisson have excellent programs.

Marriott Hotels, which exploded in growth during the 1980s, growing from 100 properties to 600 worldwide, does most of its hiring for properties locally. The personnel office usually opens and begins advertising for positions three months ahead of the scheduled hotel opening.

"We have a profile of a 'Marriott' person, whether they come to us as a housekeeper or front-desk person," one executive said. "We look for people who are energetic, like people, problem solvers, people who are interested in an opportunity to grow to their fullest extent, who work to their maximum ability." On average, the hotel hires one employee per room; a 400-room hotel would have 400 openings.

When the staff is put together, rather than sending neophytes to "school," Marriott forms a task force of the "best of the best" from around the world, including PBX operators, waiters/waitresses, housekeepers, and doorpersons. Someone might be taken from Torrance, CA, and sent to Hong Kong to help train and work side by side with the new staff for a two-month period to teach them "the Marriott way."

For the vast majority of employees who start in entry-level jobs, the jobs are precisely that—steppingstones to higher positions. Fully 40 percent of Marriott's management started out as housekeepers, waiters/waitresses, or doorpersons. Moreover, people can move from any position in Marriott to any other. The company, which earned $3.8 billion from hotel and food and beverage receipts in 1990, plus another $3.7 billion from contract services, employs 200,000 people worldwide, including 3,500 at headquarters.

A major growth area for the company will be the development of senior resort/living communities, employing an average of 150 people each. The company anticipates building 150 of these communities during the decade.

Small Properties, Big Opportunities

Small operations should not be overlooked, however. While there are fewer entry-level positions, the ones that are available could entail greater responsibility and put you in position to accept a higher position at a larger property. At Balsam House, an inn in upstate New York, a busboy became a chef and a front-desk person assumed the position of a marketing and promotions specialist without the usual years and tiers of experience.

Small, independent properties may also be a better starting place because they cannot afford the same recruitment programs and high salaries to draw graduates of hotel management schools. But, while there may be an opportunity to rise to mid-management or gain diversified experience, there is a limit to how high you can rise in small properties since positions at the top tend not to turn over frequently, if at all. In contrast, positions in upper management turn over every few years at a major chain.

Another consideration is the mix of properties in a chain or hotel group. A company like Omni/Dunfey, which has virtually every size property, can give people opportunities very early on to take on responsibility as a general manager or a food and beverage director. In other companies, where there are only large hotels, the general managers tend to be older and it takes longer to attain the seniority required.

Other points to look for include where the hotel is located, which will largely determine the clientele, and the product mix, or how fast the company (if it is a chain) is expanding; the reputation of the hotel and its professionalism; the track record in retaining people; its financial record; the philosophy of upper management; its human resource policies, particularly those concerning promotion from within; and its training and development programs, salary and benefits, and degree of specialization/generalization of function and tiers of hierarchy.

Stay in School

Even executives who rose up through the ranks or entered from other fields agree that some schooling is necessary to advance. While increasing professionalism and sophistication in the industry are part of the reason, sheer competition for new jobs is the most compelling one. A degree in hotel management can give you the edge in getting a job and put you on a faster track.

"A degree helps you move up quicker but won't give you a higher position starting out," said Beier. "We're not in brain surgery. We're in the job of selling a room, cleaning a bed. It's a simple thing."

In an effort to increase professionalism in the industry, the

AH&MA created the Educational Institute. The institute produces resource materials for the industry and schools and administers its own in-class and homestudy programs. The courses, coupled with work experience, lead to a degree as Certified Hotel Administrator (CHA), Certified Rooms Division Executive, Certified Engineering Operations Executive, Certified Food and Beverage Executive, Certified Human Resources Executive, Certified Hospitality Housekeeping Executive, or Certified Hospitality Supervisor.

Course selections include human relations, communications, food production principles, marketing, energy management, law, accounting, resort management, sales promotion, convention management and service, and food and beverage controls. Tuition is $175 for each course, with discounts for a multiple-course sequence. The program is geared to people who want to enter the hospitality industry and move up from the entry level and to working professionals who seek to advance to higher management.

Because the hospitality industry is probably the biggest single segment in travel and tourism and because of the anticipated growth, hotel schools and academic programs are opening widely. The best known four-year programs of hotel and restaurant management are at Cornell University, Michigan State, Pennsylvania State University, University of Denver, and University of Houston.

The Council on Hotel, Restaurant, and Institutional Education (CHRIE), a nonprofit organization, publishes *A Guide to College Programs in Hospitality and Tourism* (Wiley). This guide provides a list of colleges and universities across the United States that offer hospitality curriculums, as well as a list of a variety of scholarship resources and key industry organizations. The AH&MA also provides information that answers questions about career opportunities ("When Planning a Career . . . Check into Hotels and Motels").

Having a degree in hospitality is very helpful in obtaining a job in the industry since many chains and independents recruit on campuses. Graduates usually enter at a higher level because of the experience as well as specialized knowledge gained in the program. However, you will still most likely do only the traditional entry-level jobs (dishwasher, reservationist, front-desk clerk) during your schooling.

Contacts and Sources

Sources of information and leads for potential employers include:

Educational Institute of AH&MA, 1407 S. Harrison Rd., P.O. Box 1240, East Lansing, MI 48826, tel. 517-353-5500.

Council on Hotel, Restaurant, and Institutional Education (CHRIE), Henderson Human Development Bldg., Rm. S208, Pennsylvania State University, University Park, PA 16802, tel. 814-863-0586.

American Hotel & Motel Association (AH&MA), 1201 New York Ave., NW, Washington, D.C. 20005-3917, tel. 202-289-3100; for information on career opportunities, send a self-addressed business-sized envelope with postage for two ounces.

Industry references such as the *Hotel & Travel Index* list properties, addresses, and general managers. Major trade publications such as *Hotel & Motel Management* and *Lodgings* magazine point to where new hotels are opening and which are expanding and opening new services and divisions. You can also check local newspapers, convention and visitors bureaus, and chambers of commerce. Keep on the look out for newly built properties and try to contact the general manager or director of personnel.

A battery of employment, placement, recruitment, and search firms specialize in the lodging industry. Among them are:

Roth Young Personnel Services, New York (and other cities)

International Hospitality Advisors, Inc., New York

Judith Stanton Assoc., New York

Hospitality Associates, New York

Lerner Assoc., Sykesville, MD (and New York)

Travel Executive Search, Great Neck, NY

Also check local chapters of the American Hotel & Motel Association.

Getting Ahead

The lodging industry has some of the best systems for tracking, tapping, and training employees for advancement. Omni/Dunfey Hotels, for example, maintains a "people-power" computerized inventory of 1,000 management-level employees (out of 9,000 employees systemwide). The computer keeps track of where these people are in their careers, where they want to advance to, and what training they need in order to achieve their objectives. Most of the large, sophisticated companies maintain a similar computerized inventory of people targeted for management positions.

Radisson Hotels has a "This Way Up" program to identify people in the company with the talent, skills, and potential to rise in management. Selected individuals have two counseling sessions a year with their general manager and personnel director, who might recommend in-house training programs, courses at a local college, the AH&MA Educational Institute program, or an assertiveness training seminar. A skills inventory card is maintained by Radisson's Human Resources Office, which matches individual profiles with available jobs. Other major hotel companies maintain similar inventories. Most hotel chains hire for properties that they either own or manage, but not for franchised properties.

The ability and willingness to relocate are important factors in how far and how fast you rise in a hotel organization. While in the past a management person might have been "blacklisted" for refusing an appointment, most major chains have become more sensitive to this issue.

"When I started in the hotel industry some 20-odd years ago," related Gordon, "when the company said you were going to Oshkosh, you only answered, 'What time do you want me there?' Now people are considering offers and turning them down because of their families. We as a company have been supportive, liberal. We haven't been dictatorial. We try to work with them. We don't blacklist."

"This industry is one of the last to come to grips with the fact that people prize their personal life," said Chance. "It is only recently that management people feel comfortable in refusing a move."

Career Pathing

The traditional path to the general manager's seat was through the rooms division—from front desk, to housekeeping, to resident manager or executive assistant manager of rooms, and, finally, to general manager. The route is now wide open.

"Career paths are changing," said Sue Gordon of Radisson. "Doors are more open. At Radisson, we are encouraging people to 'cross lines.' Technical knowledge can be picked up if you have the basic skills and aptitudes. We are identifying skills and talent needed for the general manager's spot, so someone can come from accounting, rooms, food and beverage, sales. It is good to have experience in other areas. We are no longer pigeonholing people." The necessary skills involve being able to lead others, allocate tasks, control finances, and coordinate all work functions.

She also pointed to a trend among hotel companies to "streamline" positions and "flatten out" layers of management. The positions of executive assistant manager of the rooms division and executive assistant manager of food and beverage, for example, might be combined so that a director of operations would handle both areas. "This is out of necessity," said Gordon. "Hotel owners are suffering because of the economy and change in tax laws. There is a lot of pain out there that can only be remedied through better ways of operating."

By eliminating layers of management, more decision making will be pushed further down in the organization, resulting in empowerment. "Empowerment means more satisfaction for the workforce. There are more opportunities to attract and retain people when more decisions are made at lower levels."

It also means that people will have wider authority and more opportunity to learn different skills within the same hotel: "The more cross-trained you can be, the better for the company," said the director of personnel for Hyatt. "You progress by moving from hotel to hotel, company to company."

More opportunities are open for women. Although women were always highly represented in sales, personnel, and housekeeping departments, few achieved the general manager's spot, much less chef or department head. But this has changed. Women now occupy positions as general managers, food and beverage directors, and chefs; some have become executive chefs and even corporate vice presidents of operations.

The industry prefers to tap people with hotel experience for management positions. Nonetheless, it is possible for people to transfer their experience from other industries, particularly in sales, personnel, public relations, and marketing capacities.

Rising to the Top

Jim France's rise to general manager of the Charles Hotel typifies the traditional career path, lifestyle, and dedication that a hotel career exacts. Born in Scotland, "where if you came from a middle class family on the wrong side of the tracks, you had no way to change," France was the son of a hotelier "and knew that I wanted to be one my whole life."

While attending the renowned Lausanne Hotel School in Switzerland, he took jobs in hotels as dishwasher, waiter, cook, accountant, front-desk person, and steward. After graduating, he gained experience in convention services, sales, and food and beverage. He was a food and beverage director for eight years before moving into management.

France, who has since become a specialist in opening new hotels for companies, moved 13 times in 20 years (6 times in 10 years of marriage) and, in the course of his career, worked with some of the major chains. He moved to Boston to open the Charles Hotel for a private hotel company (Interstate) that planned on expanding aggressively.

His wife, Dale, said philosophically, "It is the fate of a hotel careerist – constant moves with every promotion. If you are adventurous, it's okay. You take away a little of every place. But it is difficult when you have children."

France agreed. "The spouse has to be adventurous, willing to give up family ties and friends and be adaptable."

Foreign assignments are particularly difficult because you have to get to know the culture, learn how to communicate in a different language, and know how to function on a day-to-day basis. Mrs. France learned Norwegian during her husband's posting there.

He recommended that new entrants to the field apply for any job at a new hotel and go through community employment agencies, but he counseled those serious about a career to go to a hotel school. "You get a better grounding. It doesn't mean you will get a job and advance quicker. A streetwise person who comes up through the ranks who is good with people can rise faster. The whole industry is people."

Being Keeper of the Inn

Kathi Ransom, who graduated with an M.P.S. in hotel administration from the Cornell Hotel School in 1983, left a job as a training supervisor at Westin International where she had interned, to become innkeeper of the Lake Placid Manor, a charming 38-room Adirondacks inn in upstate New York. The daughter of an innkeeper, she saw this as an opportunity to get back to her roots.

Innkeeping is probably the most ancient form of the lodging industry, and it retains a very distinctive character. An innkeeper has to be considerably more than a general manager. "There are days I have to make the beds, cook, and do the accounting," Ransom related. "There are a lot of hours."

Working in a small organization rather than a large one has advantages. "As an innkeeper of a smaller property," said Ransom, "you are involved in all aspects of the operation; in a larger organization, you are more concentrated.

"You do get to meet a lot of interesting people, and it is very satisfying when you put on an interesting dinner. There is a lot of ego involved, but it is fairly internalized—you know when you've done a good job.

"Innkeeping is creative. It is very much a reflection of your personality. But there are a lot of hours, it is very demanding, and you probably don't make as much as in another profession. You learn to bite your tongue a lot and not to take everything personally. You have to love the work."

Ransom, who had had some thoughts about eventually owning her own inn, later left Lake Placid Manor to go back to Westin.

Operating a Bed-and-Breakfast

Barbara Notarius opened her six-bedroom Victorian mansion as a bed-and-breakfast place after she had a baby because she wanted to work from home. She left her job as a psychologist, opened her B&B, and also launched a bed-and-breakfast reservations service.

Common in Europe, this concept of private individuals opening their homes to guests and providing them with lodging and a morning meal is relatively new in the United States. A variation of innkeeping, bed-and-breakfasts offer cozy, comfortable accommodations in a homey environment.

Sometimes, bed-and-breakfast rates are lower than motel rates; sometimes, they are higher, depending on the particular bed-and-breakfast. Often, the homes are the main attraction; often, the hosts are.

Many people operate bed-and-breakfasts to supplement their income and cover the costs of a large house. Others operate their bed-and-breakfasts like small inns to provide the sole income for a family.

Time-Sharing and Other Innovations

Time-sharing is one of the many innovations going on in the lodging industry. Like so many other innovations, it has had its share of controversy.

Rising out of the ashes of the 1974–1975 real estate recession, time-sharing has grown from less than $10 million in sales in 1972 to about $2.0 billion in 1989. Some two million owners have a share in more than 2,000 time-share resorts worldwide. Nonetheless, time-sharing has always had a somewhat tarnished reputation.

In 1981, when time-sharing expanded into a $1.5-billion business and was forecast to reach $2.5 billion in sales by 1982, about 350 companies were involved in time-sharing. But, after the first flush, time-sharing languished; many of the leading companies failed. The weak economy was partly the problem; but such extraordinary growth levels were also hard to maintain, and many who thought time-sharing would be a way to make a quick fortune found it the road to financial ruin. In some areas, questionable business practices tainted the industry.

The concept, now championed by star-studded companies like Disney, Marriott, Hilton, and Sheraton, is being reborn. A zesty combination of real estate, travel, and resort operations, time-sharing (also known as interval ownership) allows consumers to purchase the use of a vacation place for a specified period of time, for example, one week in December for 25 years.

There are two basic styles. In the first, the individual actually purchases the property for either a designated period of time or in perpetuity, owns the deed, and may resell it or will it. In the second, the individual purchases only the right to use the apartment or condominium for a period of years (typically 20 or more) but does not have ownership interest in the real estate. Current costs range from $1,500 to $25,000 per unit plus annual maintenance fees.

At first glance, you might wonder why anyone would want to commit to spending the same week or two of every year in the exact same spot. Time-sharing has proved appealing for a number of reasons, and there is more flexibility than you might think.

First, vacationers are seeking protection from inflation that may put the cost of owning a vacation home or even taking a traditional resort vacation out of the family budget; time-sharing is viewed as a way to control the escalating cost. Second, time-sharing suits people who are concerned about the shortage of desirable accommodations in the most popular resort areas, like the ski resorts of Colorado and sun resorts of Florida and Hawaii. Third, interval owners are not confined to using their own time-share property year after year; trading clubs such as Interval International, South Miami, FL, and Resort Condominium International (RCI), Indianapolis, which have burgeoned into massive travel companies, enable owners to trade their right to use their property with another member, and there are members all over the world.

Partly because of its newness and partly because of its innovative structure, time-sharing has drawn people from virtually every professional background. "They come from all over," noted a spokeswoman for the American Resort & Residential Development Association, a trade association representing time-share developers. "It is a multifaceted career, needing broad experience from different fields. Almost everything you learned or know would not be wasted."

Specific skills in finance, resort management, public relations, advertising, and marketing are needed due to the broad range of activities associated with time-sharing. There are companies that specialize in planning (accounting, architecture, economic research and feasibility, engineering, environmental and financial analysis, land planning, landscape architecture, law, marina planning, design and layout, market research and feasibility, site selection); development and construction; marketing and sales; financial services; publishing; and tours and travel services.

Moreover, time-sharing is not confined to resort properties. It is being used by city-center commercial hotels as well. Yachts and campsites are also being offered for interval ownership.

Exchange companies like Interval International and RCI are essentially computerized inventory and reservations systems that enable member time-share owners to trade their rights to use their properties with other members. These two companies are also emerging into massive retail and wholesale travel companies in their own right; both companies have introduced in-house tour packaging divisions. Interval International, for example, has Worldex, a travel company generating more than $200 million in sales; RCI operates Endless Vacations Travel.

Condo Networks

Similar to the concept of time-sharing is the concept whereby owners in condominium communities use the properties for only two weeks of the year (in order to qualify for hefty tax benefits) and give them up for rental by resort management for the other 50 weeks. Companies such as Condo Network, Mission, KS, and Creative Leisure/Condominium Vacations, Petaluma, CA, package programs and provide reservations service. Condominium Travel Associates, Stamford, CT, an entrepreneurial endeavor, provides a national network for member travel agents to book condominiums.

Senior Resort/Living Communities

Looking ahead to the "Graying of America," Marriott Hotels and Hyatt International are taking the condo concept a step further by developing quasi-resort/living communities for seniors. Marriott has formed a Senior Living Services division as a new side of hospitality management to build life-care communities, which essentially are full-service resorts designed with health care facilities.

There are two basic product lines. Independent full-service communities will offer residents (who pay an entrance fee plus monthly rental) a full spectrum of care ranging from independent living to assisted living to skilled and intermediate nursing care. Prototype communities, developed nationally under the name of

Stratford Court, typically accommodate 300 to 350 people and employ 120 full- and part-time employees. Custom-designed communities are also being built in conjunction with affinity groups such as military organizations and universities.

The second type are catered living communities, developed for seniors who already need some type of assistance with daily lifestyle activities. These communities are being developed nationally under the name of Brighton Gardens. In all, Marriott plans to build 150 of both types of communities during the decade and will employ hotel and restaurant, as well as health care, professionals.

Summing Up

The hospitality industry offers perhaps the best opportunity for jobs of any single segment of the travel/transportation/tourism industry. It not only offers sheer numbers of jobs, 1.2 million with 250,000 more expected by the end of the decade, but also is a growth industry offering extraordinary opportunity to rise rapidly through the ranks, often starting out with little or no education or experience.

Hotels are like minicities; chains are like states. Both afford vast opportunity for a full spectrum of professionals, ranging from those who are unique to the lodging industry, like front-desk clerks, to those who are more specialized, like architects, interior designers, and energy managers, to those who are common to most businesses, like public relations experts, sales and marketing managers, and administrators.

The lodging industry is first and foremost a people business, affording considerable contact with other people but also demanding a commitment to service. The hospitality field provides a chance to perform a variety of different jobs during the course of a career yet not be locked into any one area or specialization. It also provides an opportunity to take on enormous amounts of responsibility and to attain a position of power and status (with fairly good compensation in management positions). Working in the hospitality industry offers diversity, challenge, and a good deal of glamour and excitement, but it also requires an enormous amount of hard work, commitment, and personal sacrifice.

Contacts and Sources

American Hotel & Motel Association (AH&MA), 1201 New York Ave., NW, Washington, D.C. 20005-3917, tel. 202-289-3100.

American Resort & Residential Development Association, 1220 L St., NW, 5th Floor, Washington, D.C. 20005, tel. 202-371-6700.

8

The Ski Industry

Ski Industry Overview

Like riding a lift to the crest of a mountain, most senior executives in the ski industry started at the very bottom and rose to the top of their profession. This up-through-the-ranks rise has continued despite the evolution of ski areas into Big Business destination resorts.

Much more than the lift, ticket booth, cafeteria, and ski school/equipment rental facility that characterized ski areas of a generation ago, ski resorts have evolved into complex, multimillion dollar entities with such diversified enterprises as real estate development, hospitality and restaurant management, tour operations and reservations centers, nurseries, and day camps. They are now somewhat of a cross between a city, a resort, and a theme park.

There are 21 million skiers (those who have skied within the past two years)—less than 10 percent of the population. The ski industry generates nearly $2 billion in revenues on about 55 million skier visits and pays out $400 million in salaries. The 27 members of Colorado Ski Country, USA, alone attracted nearly 10 million skier visits in 1991 and employed 7,500 people year-round (12,000 in peak-season).

There are about 590 ski areas; only about 100 of them are true destination resorts (places where people come from outside the immediate area and overnight). Due to the high costs of operating ski areas and the increasing pressure to offer a full complement of ski and nonski activities to attract the sophisticated, affluent clientele, small areas have tended not to do well. The trend has been toward large, multipurpose ski companies–big businesses–and foreign ownership (particularly by the Japanese). Many are tied to real estate development and management. Moreover, because skiers are discerning (they go where the snow is the most consistently the best), ski companies have had to invest enormous sums on snow-making and grooming and on faster, state-of-the-art lifts, which adds an extra technological dimension to this industry.

Easing off a Plateau

Despite an outpouring of hundreds of millions of dollars, the ski industry has had a fairly stable base of skiers for the past 10 years, a cause of major concern for an industry banking on growth. There is an industrywide effort to "grow" new skiers through learn-to-ski promotions and special events; family packages and children's programs; new nonski activities and facilities like spas and athletic centers; and programs targeting women, seniors, and handicapped skiers. Efforts are also being directed toward developing entirely new markets including incentive travel and toward enticing the international market (Europeans, Asians, South Americans).

The industry has also made a greater effort to reach new skiers through the travel industry (tour operators and travel agents), a market that had all but been ignored until 10 years ago. Travel agents can reach potential skiers in their locality and suggest a ski vacation; can overcome objections and obstacles (as they do for a cruise product); can recommend a suitable ski destination based on needs, wants, and budget; and can provide the convenience of one-stop shopping. Tour operators accomplish two critical functions: They bring down the cost of skiing (a major impediment), and they reduce the confusion and complication of booking all the different elements of a ski trip (air and ground transportation, lodgings, lift tickets, lessons, equipment) by packaging all the elements purchased at negotiated rates. Some of the largest ski tour operators include Advance Reservations, Park City, UT; and Any Mountain Tours, Arlington, VA.

Increasingly, ski resorts have formed their own travel agencies and tour operations in order to better reach consumers with one-stop shopping and competitive rates. They have gone so far as to subsidize direct-air services on major airlines, such as American, United, and Delta, into local airports in the competition to get skiers to their resorts in the fastest, most convenient way possible.

Children's programs also present a huge opportunity (the idea is not only to make it easier for parents to ski but also to "hook" the little ones on skiing early so that they will be the skiers of the future). A decade ago, children's ski programs had to fight for recognition within a ski resort; marketing was targeted at single women and young executives. Today, the focus has shifted to families, with emphasis placed on nurseries, day camps, ski school, and family activities. With this shift has come the need of caretakers for infants, of activities directors, and of ski instructors for older children.

Back in the 1950s and 1960s, ski areas were precisely that—places where people went to ski. Now, more and more areas are emerging as true destinations with a full range of nonski activities. Health spas, jeep tours, dog-sledding trips, indoor sports (tennis, racquetball), and ice skating are all now available as ski areas focus on the challenge of satisfying skiers and nonskiers alike.

Ski areas have actively diversified by developing summer activities and programs as well in order to support local communities (which are usually dependent upon the ski resorts), keep people employed, and maintain cash flow year-round. Many, like Stratton, VT, have developed tennis programs; others, like Winter Park, CO, and Mt. Snow, VT, have established themselves as mountain biking centers. Telluride, CO, has opened a golf course and a major spa; Crested Butte, CO, and Loon Mountain, NH, have created comprehensive "Sports Afield" family packages; Attitash, NH, has alpine and water slides and gives gondola rides. Other areas, such as Aspen and Copper Mountain, CO, have cultivated music, dance, film, and cultural festivals; Snowmass, CO, has developed culinary and wine events; Keystone, CO, woos conventions and meetings.

Surmounting Challenges

Other challenges to the ski industry include environmental constraints, which have prompted opportunities for government/public affairs specialists (indeed, the president of Aspen Skiing Company, Bob Maynard, was formerly associate director of the National Parks Service). Also, the ever-increasing cost of insurance and exposure to liability and the decline in leisure time and discretionary dollars present further challenges to be overcome by the ski industry.

Getting In, Rising Up

The ski industry draws people who are committed, even fanatical, about skiing and the outdoors. "You get to ski, to live and work amid incredible scenery, in the outdoors, in pure air, working with people who tend to be active, outgoing, energetic, and delivering a service that makes people feel happy," commented one industry executive.

Like so many prominent executives in the ski resort industry, Paula Sheridan, vice president of communications for Winter Park, CO, started her career as a ski instructor. After seven years, she seized an opportunity to become the first woman on Winter Park's ski patrol. She moved over into "risk management," which involved investigating accidents, interviewing people, and taking pictures. "Then, when I wanted more of a mental challenge versus a physical challenge, I moved over to management as a communications coordinator," said Sheridan, who knew she liked to write. Starting out as an assistant, she anticipated some on-the-job training; three months later, the director left and she had the "sink-or-swim" option of either taking over or facing perhaps 10 more years before she had another chance for advancement.

Ceci Gordon started her career in the ski industry by answering phones and mailing brochures at Mt. Cranmore, North Conway, NH. In less than five years, she rose to director of marketing. "You get your foot in the door and then rise up," Gordon related. "Most companies are not as interested in your background as the type of person you are. You can work 7 days a week, 20 hours a day for 5 months. It requires a person with personality and drive; you can learn marketing, management, and how a lift runs.

"The industry isn't that old—only 50 to 55 years. So many people who started out with a ski area are now managing it," said Gordon, who has since gone on to Cone Communications, a public relations company representing United Ski Industries Association.

Kent Myers, vice president of marketing for Vail Associates, epitomizes another key path into the ski industry—through property management. He started as director of property management for Copper Mountain Resort, CO, and rose up by moving from one ski company to another. From Copper Mountain, he went to Winter Park, where he was director of sales and then vice president of marketing; then to Steamboat Ski Corporation, where he innovated the first direct-air program into a ski resort; and then to Vail, where he also introduced direct-air programs as well as a full in-house tour operation.

Lift line, ski school, and property management jobs are key ways to get into the ski industry. Increasingly, however, ski areas are reaching outside for marketing, sales and finance, hotel operations, and entertainment professionals (one treasurer, for example, came from a jeans company).

Low Pay, Great Benefits

Every ski area has departments in marketing, group sales, and advertising and public relations; a general manager or president; and people in various services, including food and beverage, ski school, ski patrol, guest services, nursery, and day camp. There is usually a maintenance division including a director of lift and vehicle maintenance and a snow-making supervisor. Other departments might include sales or rental management of real estate, hotel operations, retail travel or tour operations, and finance. There also are usually risk management, retail, and clerical positions.

Emerging specialty positions include those in public/government affairs and travel. Some specialties have changed. Food and beverage used to consist of cafeteria-style arrangements; now, many resorts have elaborate restaurants and functions, like sleigh-ride dinners.

Salaries vary considerably from area to area but generally are on the low side (even for the travel industry). For example, a President might make $50,000 to $75,000; Department Director,

$35,000 to $40,000; Assistant Director, $20,000 to $27,000; and Staff Assistant, $18,000 to $20,000 (according to Colorado Ski Country, USA).

Benefits abound, however, including free skiing for the entire family (in New England, employees of one mountain can ski free midweek at any other New England area), reduced-rate day-care, health club membership, and (occasionally) free food. Subsidized housing is sometimes provided for seasonal employees, but housing costs at ski areas tend to be high.

A Competitive Job Market

From time to time, the ski industry runs job expos and aggressive recruitment campaigns. At the start of the decade, however, jobs were very competitive particularly due to an influx of young, out-of-work former professionals who, not being able to find positions in their own fields, decided to enjoy themselves at a ski area and took whatever jobs were available.

One woman, laid off from a marketing position with a Wall Street firm, left New York City and a $900/month apartment for Sugarloaf, ME, thinking to become a lift operator. Instead, she landed a job in the ski area's marketing department (earning $20,000 compared with the $55,000 she earned on Wall Street). "It's a nicer life, a nicer lifestyle," she commented.

She was one of the lucky ones. "There are so many résumés from attorneys, doctors, and real estate people, people who have come here to ski and want to stay," said Jerry Oliver, vice president of administration of Vail Associates. "It is hard to break into industry at middle- or senior-management level because enough of those people stay on. Management jobs pay well; you need three to five years experience in hospitality to be marketable."

Few ski areas have women as general managers or presidents, but women are taking more positions in marketing and public relations, as well as in ski school and ski patrol.

The leading-edge ski companies today include Vail Associates; Ski Ltd., which owns Killington and Mt. Snow in Vermont and Bear Mountain in California; Victoria Ltd., a Japanese company that owns Breckenridge in Colorado and Stratton in Vermont; and another Japanese company, Kamori Kanko, which owns Steamboat in Colorado and Heavenly in California. Japanese ownership has mainly resulted in more capital for development (Stratton, for example, was able to develop its Sun Bowl) with minimal impact (so far) on career opportunities for Americans. Also, Japanese ownership has helped areas attract Asian skiers, putting American ski areas in a better position to draw more of the international market.

Although growth has slowed, new areas are opening. Catamount, near Steamboat Springs, CO, is a ski area that will be about the size of Steamboat and that is being developed by one of the former owners of Steamboat Ski Corporation, in joint venture with Mitchell Engineering Corporation, Houston. Four Seasons in the state of Washington will be one of the only destination resorts in the entire state. Other new areas include Silver Mountain in Silver Valley and Val Bois in Cascade, ID.

"The industry has become more sophisticated," said David Ingemie, president of United Ski Industries Association. "It's still entrepreneurial, but as the industry matures, business practices are becoming more sophisticated in terms of marketing, accounting, strategic planning, opening up new specialties, and tiers of management.

"It's still a career path for ski bums, but for the most part, management is chosen from specialized fields such as real estate, accounting, customer service, travel operations, public relations. It's the kind of business where you either stay a season or two – or a lifetime."

Robert Gillen, assistant vice president of corporate communications for Crested Butte, CO, is one who sees a bright future for the ski industry and for career opportunities for professionals. "The ski bum is on the endangered list. Continued maturation of the ski industry means growing professionalism. There is demand for professionals from business, sales, public relations, advertising, and a lot of flushing out of the hale and hardy ski bums. You have to make a commitment over a few years. You sacrifice income for the view. And you have to work hard – salespeople work 60 to 70 hours a week sometimes."

But you do get to ski. Gillen, who came to the ski industry by way of *Ski* magazine, purchased new ski boots that were easy to get on so that he could be out the door of his office and on the slopes within 10 minutes. He managed to ski 100 days one season.

An Example: Vail Associates

Vail Associates is widely regarded as one of the largest and most forward-looking ski companies in the country. The company generates $100 million in sales, mainly from operating Vail Mountain and Beaver Creek. In addition, Vail Associates now manages Eldora near Boulder and Ski Broadmoor. The company maintains year-round employment of 675, peaking out in winter at 3,500; in summer, the company employs 900. Vail is organized into six major divisions: finance, administration, marketing (public relations, advertising and sales), real estate, hospitality (and travel), and mountain operations.

Vail, like so many ski companies, is developing summer programs to balance out seasonality. It created a music festival and special children's camp, Camp Matawan Village, which attempts to create an Indian experience. It also introduced a "Peak Performance" program of customized plans (similar to Outward Bound experiences) geared to corporate groups.

Besides operating the ski lifts and other ski-related facilities, Vail manages various hotels, condominium units, and homes; has a large real estate brokerage; and handles time-share management. The company now has a full-scale in-house tour company and travel agency, with 30 reservationists on staff in the winter (2 in the off-season), that sell only Vail products. The travel company has people on staff who negotiate with airlines, transportation companies, lodges, tour operators, travel agencies, and ski clubs.

As you would expect considering Vail's premier position, salaries are at the top of the pay scale, along with those of Aspen, Deer Valley, and Killington, as compared with those of Steamboat or Crested Butte. They still would be considered relatively low compared with salaries in other parts of the travel industry, however.

Vail employs 1,100 ski instructors (a career in itself) including 175 who teach only children. In addition, 185 children's caretakers, many of whom are child development specialists, are employed in the nursery and day camp, and oversee some 73,000 children in a season.

Emerging specialties are in areas having to do with children's programs (which, at Vail, like so many other ski areas across the country, are getting special emphasis), as well as adult sports camps. Hospitality is also a developing area. Indeed, Vail is a community of 30,000 "pillows" plus 15 to 20 restaurants. For positions in this area, including those of resident managers and office personnel, Vail looks for people with hospitality (resort) operations experience.

People involved in the technical area of mountain management have the least turnover. Vail employs three people for ski patrol, skier services, and the race department.

Some internships are available, such as for lift operators and for food service personnel. Every year, Vail recruits 1,000 new people to replace about 25 to 30 percent of the staff.

Oliver, who came to the ski industry from another field (theme parks) observed, "The ski industry and the theme park are very similar. Skiing is nature's version of a thrill ride." The theme park influence at Vail is clear: Fort Whippersnapper (Oliver chose the name) provides a themed frontier experience as a training ground for the children's learn-to-ski program.

Contacts and Sources

Apart from regional ski associations, other organizations that can provide information include:

United Ski Industries Association, 8377 B Greensboro Dr., McLean, VA 22102.

Colorado Ski Country, USA, 1560 Broadway, Ste. 1440, Denver, CO 80202, tel. 303-837-0793; represents 27 of Colorado's major ski resorts and keeps a job bank.

National Parks Trade Journal, published by Taverly Churchill, features opportunities for more than 100,000 positions in national parks, ski resorts, scenic lodges, outdoor schools, and worldwide environmental organizations. It is available for $14.95 postpaid from *National Parks Trade Journal*, Wawona Station, Yosemite National Park, CA 95389. Other publications include:

Ski

Skiing

Powder

Snow Country

Tour & Travel News

Travel Weekly

9

Theme Parks and Attractions

Where Fantasies Come True

To appreciate the role that theme parks and attractions play in the travel industry, you only have to arrive at Orlando International Airport, an airport that has tripled in size since opening in 1981 and that now handles 9.2 million passengers a year, and travel up International Drive, where many of the area's 76,360 hotel rooms and 50 theme parks and attractions have sprung up to cater to the 13.6 million visitors who spend $4.6 billion a year. Then, consider that in 1971, the year Walt Disney opened his personal fantasyland, Orlando was swampland and orange groves.

"It has often been my pleasure to tell people where I work and watch a slow smile creep across their face," said Peter Irish, director of association relations for the International Association of Amusement Parks and Attractions (IAAPA), Alexandria, VA. "Even at the association level, the industry has a unique ability to bring joy, entertainment, distraction, and a certain relief from daily cares and concerns to consumers around the world. This is a very rewarding activity."

However, despite the fact that the industry draws about 253 million visits a year, generates about $4.3 billion in sales, and employs more than 250,000 people on a seasonal or part-time basis, full-time career-oriented jobs are in short supply and high demand. Only about 15,000 people are full-timers. Even at Walt Disney World, more of a complete city than a theme park, only about 3,300, or 10 percent, of the 33,000 employees are salaried. Still, for people who do get jobs in the industry, working for a theme park or major attraction is like a fantasy come true.

Theme Parks

Walt Disney really invented the "theme park." Up until 1955 when Disneyland opened, there had been only amusement parks, consisting mainly of rides in a carnival-like atmosphere. Walt Disney, who had two young daughters at the time, sought to create a place where the whole family could experience attractions together. He created themes, a story woven into the costuming, the architecture, and everything connected with an attraction. Instead of a roller coaster, for example, there was "Big Thunder Mountain Railroad," an Old West runaway mine train.

The vast majority of the approximately 600 parks and attractions that comprise the U.S. amusement industry cater to a local market. Of these, about 50 to 100 qualify as destination attractions capable of drawing visitors from regional, national, and international markets. The largest destination theme parks (many of which are household names) include Walt Disney World, Lake Buena Vista, FL; Disneyland, Anaheim, CA; Knott's Berry Farm, Buena Park, CA; Universal Studios Hollywood, Universal City, CA; Sea World of Florida, Orlando; Sea World of California, San Diego; Kings Island, Kings Island, OH; Six Flags Magic Mountain, Valencia, CA; Cedar Point, Sandusky, OH; and Busch Gardens, Tampa, FL.

Often, these destination theme parks are not just included on a trip but are the main purpose for a trip, and they are very much a part of the travel industry. These destination attractions incorporate many travel-related activities including hospitality, food and beverage, and entertainment. They may have a complete travel department that works with the tour operators, airlines, car rental companies, and travel agents, and they may even package their own programs to groups and individual travelers. A major part of their marketing and sales effort is directed toward inspiring tour operators and group organizers to include their attraction.

Though the basic amusement park business is not expected to grow significantly, a proliferation of new and novel formulas is expected. "Amusement parks are amazingly imaginative and will continue to craft new hard ride and entertainment products to attract new segments of the population," said the IAAPA.

Job Categories from A to Z

Probably the most eclectic category of travel, the theme park/attractions industry employs everything from agronomists to zoologists. General categories of employment include general management, operations, marketing, public relations, food service, maintenance, and finance. Particular specialties include engineering, safety, security, MIS, training, and personnel management. Some of the more innovative parks are adding product development and market research specialists.

While there is stiff competition for management jobs, some markets face serious shortages of seasonal workers. The industry has therefore been prompted to adopt a variety of innovative programs including incentives (involving contests and merchandise giveaways); bonuses such as free tickets, subsidized transportation, and gift certificates; busing people in from inner cities; and recruiting senior citizens. Some of the attractions hold job fairs or go directly into high schools to recruit.

Many accomplished executives in the field started out as summer workers, such as Larry Cochran, chief executive officer of Six Flags Corporation, Arlington, TX, and Dennis Speigel, president of International Theme Park Services, a Cincinnati-based management and consulting company to the industry. Speigel, for example, began his career as a ticket taker during the summer at Coney Island Amusement Park in Cincinnati, worked his way up to assistant park manager there, and then went to Kings Island where he supervised general park operations including personnel, rides, food/beverage, merchandise, and games. He then became the vice president and general manager of Kings Dominion/Lion Country Safari, Richmond, VA. In addition to overseeing the planning and construction of the park, he administered a $60-million construction budget and managed the park—all of which gave him the broad background he needed for his consultancy.

An Example: Walt Disney World

Walt Disney World is probably the quintessential theme park (actually three in one–Magic Kingdom® Park, EPCOT® Center, and Disney-MGM Studios). It is both the model and the pinnacle for the industry. The largest theme park in the world, Disney World has become elevated to a vacation destination in its own right (indeed, it is frequently included on lists of the most popular vacation places on the planet) and is actively involved in the travel industry. It has a massive travel company that packages its own product sold to consumers and the trade, a reservations center, and a retail agency. It has a convention services and incentives and meetings department (an expanded activity since Disney World opened its own hotels and can now accommodate large meetings).

The Walt Disney Company has become a major hotel company, operating seven hotels with 15,000 rooms plus a campground and vacation villas at Disney World alone. It is getting involved in building a new vacation-ownership (time-sharing) development.

The scope of what an attraction like Walt Disney World entails becomes clear when you consider that on any night, there might be 50,000 people living in the on-site accommodations and as many as 100,000 people in the park per day (20 million per year). Disney World is a self-sufficient city complete with its own energy plant, waste facilities, and transportation system. EPCOT Center even grows most of the food served in the restaurants. Some 1,500 "back-of-the-house" culinary professionals ranging from assistants to executive chefs are employed to serve the hordes of hungry park attendees.

Disney World employs more than 1,000 entertainers including musicians, performers, and technical support people like set designers. Because theme parks like Disney World employ hundreds, even thousands of entertainers, the theme park industry can be an alternative to struggling for a spot on Broadway. (Steve Martin is just one of many entertainers who went on to fame and fortune after working at Disneyland). The Disney company often sends talent scouts on national tours to recruit entertainers. In the summer, WDW College Entertainment Workshop gives musicians an opportunity to perform in an orchestra at Disney World in Florida or at Disneyland in California (the players are selected during a national tour).

Though the "imagineering" staff (the people who dream up the concepts for rides and attractions) are based in the Burbank, CA, headquarters for the Walt Disney Company, many operations people work in Orlando to ensure that the concepts are actualized. Completion of any given project involves some unusual career paths. For example, nearly 500 people work in horticulture and landscaping; others are woodcarvers and costumers.

The Disney Company also has a noncredit college program whereby students can spend a semester working at the park usually in a job related to their major, such as hospitality. Often, college students who work at Walt Disney World during the summer or a season go on to a career there. Dick Nunis, president of Walt Disney Attractions, is one example. The company also offers a management development program through (what else) the Disney University.

Occasionally, for jobs that require a certain specialization that would have to be acquired elsewhere, people are hired from the outside. The strongest effort, however, is to hire from within.

An example of one who was hired from within is the executive chef at EPCOT Center, Keith Kehoe. Today at the highest position in culinary art, he started at Walt Disney World in 1971 as a burger chef but "was motivated and was obviously talented," an executive related. Kehoe was put into a culinary development program and learned under some top chefs. Now, Walt Disney World has a culinary apprentice program (affiliated with the American Culinary Federation, which sets out guidelines for culinary development) so that budding chefs can become ACF-certified at Disney World.

In general, the Disney company approaches personnel hiring as "show business—you are cast for a role," the executive stated. Hence, the personnel office is called the "Casting Center." The back page of the employment application asks applicants to choose areas of interest, and efforts are then directed to matching talent to available positions.

Attractions—Historical and Otherwise

The attractions industry is more difficult to describe. Attractions are just about everywhere. They range from the natural, like the Grand Canyon, to the manmade, like the Empire State Building, to the historical, like the Alamo, to the supernatural. They can be caves, historic buildings, national parks like Yosemite, shopping centers, theaters–anything that draws visitors. Hundreds of major attractions are members of the National Tour Association, which brings them together with tour operators who influence such a large proportion of travelers.

An Example: Colonial Williamsburg

Colonial Williamsburg in Williamsburg, VA, draws about 1.2 million visitors a year and, in many ways, has become the hub of an attractions industry centered in Williamsburg (similar to what Walt Disney World has been to Orlando). As Colonial Williamsburg developed and drew more and more visitors, other attractions such as Busch Gardens and Kings Dominion, and even other historic attractions like Jamestown and Yorktown, have developed. Today, 9,000 hotel rooms in the area cater to visitors.

Williamsburg had been the capital of the Virginia Colony, which at the time went as far west as the Mississippi River and north to the Great Lakes and was where George Washington, Thomas Jefferson, Patrick Henry, and other founding fathers learned the fundamentals of representative democratic government. After the Revolution, however, the capital was moved to Richmond, and since Williamsburg was not on a river or in a commercial area, had nothing to sustain it. Then, in 1926, John D. Rockefeller, Jr. sought to restore Williamsburg to the days of its greatest glory. He contributed $68 million for the preservation of 88 original structures that had survived to the present time, the reconstruction of another 50 buildings, and the acquisition of additional property to create a protected historic area. What he accomplished then could not be afforded today.

Colonial Williamsburg is not a theme park; it is an institution of education. It is a living history museum, the largest of its kind interpreting eighteenth-century American colonial history, and consists of 400 buildings altogether. (Indeed, 100 of the buildings are occupied, rented out to employees or relatives of employees, which creates an eerie, Brigadoon kind of atmosphere. There are no barricades or locks to keep people out after hours).

Some 4,000 people work at Colonial Williamsburg, including its hotel, restaurants, bakery, and costume shop, in some 850 different job titles that range from typical hospitality specialties (golf maintenance, health and fitness club, and tennis support people) to historic responsibilities. There are 150 people who are historic interpreters plus 15 historic trade apprentices who wear eighteenth-century dress and basically stay in the character of the Colonial Williamsburg resident whom they are portraying.

Most employees, however, are very much a part of the twentieth century, and must deal with contemporary issues in human resources, marketing and sales, information systems, publicity, and personnel. A programs manager for one of Colonial Williamsburg's galleries, for example, is responsible for planning, developing, and implementing various educational programs and special events, as well as media promotions. Considerable sales and marketing activity is directed to the travel market as a source of badly needed revenue, particularly as contributions from government and other funding sources decrease while overhead increases.

Very few entry-level positions are available. While apprentices are technically entry-level, they may take six to eight years to learn their craft well enough to rise to a journeyman's level. Even as apprentices, these people generally have a strong background in their trade and a knowledge of using eighteenth-century tools. Many may have been hobbyists who practiced their craft at home, before being recruited by Colonial Williamsburg through a national search, frequently through advertisements in specialty magazines.

Colonial Williamsburg tends to draw people who are very committed to the history and culture of the time; there is little movement from one historic attraction to another and little turnover of positions. Many other people are drawn by the opportunity to work in such a special attraction and to deal with people.

"We try to focus people into jobs they are qualified for, but people can move over into something else," said Lynn Bloch, director of employment. "But it usually takes a year to adjust to this different work environment."

Colonial Williamsburg mainly hires from the immediate area (relocating fewer than a dozen people a year). It offers a day-care facility as a means of attracting and retaining employees and "because we felt it was the right thing to do."

Colonial Williamsburg has its own Jobsline, 804-220-7129

(available 24 hours daily). (Contact Colonial Williamsburg Foundation, P.O. Box C, Williamsburg VA 23187.)

Cultural Tourism

Broadway theaters, Radio City Music Hall, the Metropolitan Museum of Art, and Lincoln Center are all in the cultural tourism business. More than half of the summer theater-goers in New York City are from out of town, and advance bookings from incoming visitors help keep shows going in the early months and sustain them through their runs. Cultural attractions in New York City have been found to be a key motivation for the city's 17 million visitors to make a trip there. Exhibits like "King Tut," "Impressionist Painters," and "Van Gogh" at the Metropolitan Museum of Art draw tourists from throughout the world. Opera festivals are the basis of many tour programs, such as Dailey-Thorpe of New York, and festivals like Tanglewood and Spoleto lure countless visitors.

At the same time, cultural institutions, facing critical funding cuts from government and private sources, have looked to the travel industry to help increase their revenues from attendance and have become more deliberate in their dealings with the travel industry. The New York City Opera, the Museum of Modern Art, Carnegie Hall, and the Brooklyn Museum have gone so far as to have travel industry specialists on staff who are responsible for developing packages and marketing programs.

Just how important a market cultural tourism is was demonstrated by a study by the Cultural Assistance Center and Port Authority of New York and New Jersey.

1. The study showed that 1,900 arts institutions entertained an annual audience of 64 million people in the metropolitan area, 13 million of whom visited from outside the region. Of the visitor audience of nearly 13 million, more than 42 percent, or nearly 5.4 million, came to the region specifically for the arts and stayed an average of two days. In addition, another 15.6 percent extended their stay by an average of two days in order to attend cultural events, which represented enormous incremental revenue to the localities.
2. It demonstrated that 16 percent of the arts-motivated visitors purchased a package tour, spending an average of almost

$75 for the package; 80 percent of the tours included transportation.

3. The study estimated that $1.6 billion was generated by the expenditures of visitors who come primarily for or extend their stay for arts and culture and from the portion of the proceeds of touring companies that is returned to the metropolitan economy.

Promoting tourism at cultural institutions is a whole new field for travel professionals. Besides employing travel professionals to draw visitors into their cultural institutions, many theater and dance companies and even art shows are utilizing the services of travel professionals to coordinate their tours.

Contacts and Sources

Apart from local convention and visitors bureaus and chambers of commerce, other organizations that can provide information include:

International Association of Amusement Parks and Attractions (IAAPA), 1448 Duke St., Alexandria, VA 22314, tel. 703-836-4800; provides an international student exchange program that sends students from one country to work on a temporary basis in amusement parks in another (students must demonstrate sufficient linguistic skills and meet other requirements of the program); also provides a growing number of training and educational materials; and publishes the most comprehensive annual guide to the industry, *International Directory and Buyer's Guide.*

National Tour Association (NTA), 546 E. Main St., Lexington, KY 40508, tel. 606-253-1036.

Leading trade publications include:

Funworld (published by IAAPA)

Amusement Business

Park World

Splash

10

The Airline Industry

Airline Industry Overview

President Jimmy Carter's signature on the Airline Deregulation Act of 1978 was like a gunshot signaling the start of the most frantic air race in history.

After decades in which the airlines operated much like utilities with protected routes and regulated pricing, they were thrust into a free market in which they could enter and exit routes virtually at will and charge as much or as little as the market would allow. For the first time, the way was clear for new carriers to rush in with innovative services, fares, and corporate structures that might better suit new and changing markets while those that could not compete effectively were left to fail.

And rush in they did. Bold, innovative carriers took on the established giants like modern-day Davids and Goliaths. In the past, the airline industry had always attracted risk-takers and those with a spirit of adventure (the old barnstorming image), but now risk comes not so much from flying as from the business itself. Risk affects entrepreneurs and employees alike; new as well as old carriers may fail or be swallowed up.

Prior to 1978, only 36 carriers were certificated by the Federal Aviation Administration (FAA), of which 20 are still operating. If all the carriers that have been certificated since 1978 were still operating, there would be 200 carriers today. But, in 1990, only 133 were actually operating. Even the largest and oldest carriers are not immune to failure, as the demise of Eastern Airlines proves.

At the start of the decade, there were only 13 major carriers, which prompted new fears that deregulation has produced less competition – an oligopoly of sorts – instead of more and renewed the debate over the need for governmental regulation. Indeed, it is estimated that three "mega-carriers," American, United, and Delta, control more than 60 percent of the market and that each virtually monopolizes travel at its major hubs.

Intense Job Competition

There were 330,000 employees working for U.S. scheduled airlines in 1978, just prior to deregulation. By 1989, a total of 506,728 people were employed by the airlines, with another 300,000 indirectly employed by entities serving the airlines. Payroll totaled $30 billion. Despite the growth of the industry, competition for jobs is probably more intense in this segment of the travel industry than in any other. Finding a job, therefore, takes considerable resourcefulness.

Deregulation opened up career opportunities with the scores of new carriers and new types of services that were spawned. And, by radically changing the structure and economics of the industry, deregulation also changed the volume, nature, and even location of employment. Competition brought a sudden demand for marketers. Proliferation of fares and services, all changing at mind-boggling speed, forced a shift toward computerized information and reservations systems, creating demand for computer experts as well as analysts and yield management experts. (There were 117 million ticket price changes up until August of 1990, averaging 70,000 a day; then, when Iraq invaded Kuwait, fare changes soared to more than 1 million to 2.5 million a day). The profit/loss quagmire that the carriers found themselves in fostered a need for a new breed of financial whizzes.

Cost efficiency became the key to survival in the new environment. The major airlines (carriers doing more than $1 billion in revenue a year), which essentially had always flown point to point (city to city in a line), found that they could operate more cost-effectively with a hub-and-spoke system, funneling traffic from secondary cities to a central station (hub) for connecting flights. Almost overnight, cities like St. Louis, Dallas, and Atlanta that had had only limited air service became major hubs, vastly increasing the number of reservationists, station personnel, and maintenance people located in these centers.

The hub-and-spoke system also proved a windfall for regional and commuter carriers, particularly those that entered into partnership with the major carriers. The 150 regional and commuter carriers, which generated $3.5 billion in sales in 1990, saw their passenger counts grow by 170 percent during the 1980s, according to the Regional Airline Association, while the major carriers lost a substantial share of the domestic airline traffic (much like network television lost share to cable operators).

Roller-Coaster Profits and Losses

The airline business can be like a roller coaster, with one year of astronomical profits and the next of spectacular losses. The U.S. scheduled airlines scored record operating profits of $2.3 billion in 1984, but just four of 36 airlines (United, American, Delta, and USAir) accounted for 60 percent of the amount. In contrast, 1990 produced a record loss of $2 billion on total operating revenues of about $70 billion despite record passenger traffic, according to the Air Transport Association. In just the first quarter of 1991, with the world embroiled in the Persian Gulf War, the airline industry lost another $1 billion.

The airline business is not unlike a three-dimensional chess game in that the key strategic element – the aircraft – can be moved quickly and fairly easily. You are selling both a service and a price-sensitive commodity. An airline seat is one of the most perishable products in the world: Once the airplane pulls away from the gate, the seat – the airline's product – is gone forever. There is no opportunity for a "mark-down" sale later, to get rid of excess inventory. This fact puts intense pressure on planners to predict demand, decide on how much capacity (how many seats) to offer, and determine a price that will attract enough people to cover costs and make a profit (the yield management field is one of the principal growth areas in aviation). In fact, demand shifts depending upon the time of day, day of week, and season of year (which is why there are so many different fares between two points).

Then, just when you think you have your market figured out, you have to predict what the competition will do, and the competition is changing all the time. Unlike hotels and factories, which take years to plan and build and cannot be moved from place to place, an aircraft can be shifted almost at will so that the competitive environment facing the airlines changes constantly. One moment five carriers may be offering 1,000 seats altogether to Honolulu, a market that may have demand for 1,200 seats. Everyone is doing well until five more carriers, perceiving an opportunity, jump in, doubling the number of seats available for sale per day. Then, all of the carriers are forced to cut fares sharply, increase advertising in order to attract passengers, and probably operate at a loss.

Moreover, the airlines have to work within parameters. An airline may have an aircraft fleet that works most efficiently on a certain length of flight and that has a certain number of seats. The transcontinental (New York–Los Angeles) market may thus be so critical for the carrier that the carrier may resort to "kamikaze" pricing (offering tickets below cost) in order to protect the market from predators.

Airlines are vulnerable to any number of conditions. Fuel is the second highest expense for an airline after personnel; a penny change in the price can save or cost a major airline millions of dollars. In 1990, Iraq's invasion of Kuwait and the Persian Gulf War sent fuel prices soaring from 60 cents to $1.40 per gallon; every penny change in the price cost U.S. carriers $150 million (airlines spent $7.8 billion on fuel that year) and contributed heavily to their $2-billion loss.

Changes in the value of the dollar against foreign currencies and interest rates also have dramatic consequences for profits and losses. Strikes, accidents, terrorism, and economic declines all seriously impact on demand for the airlines' services. Indeed, the Persian Gulf War, besides sending fuel costs skyrocketing, caused fear of terrorism and, coupled with a recessionary economy, sounded the death knell for Eastern Airlines, thrust Pan Am into bankruptcy, and caused TWA to teeter.

The market for airline travel divides into two roughly equal parts: (1) nondiscretionary travelers, primarily people who have to travel for business purposes and who are not as much concerned about price as convenient schedules and good service, and (2) discretionary travelers, people who travel for vacation or pleasure or to visit friends and relatives, and who are very much swayed by price and can choose to travel or not. By balancing out these two markets–business travelers and leisure travelers–through calculated use of fares, schedules, and routes, airlines can increase their load factors (the percentage of seats occupied by paying passengers) and maximize the utilization of their fleets, both of which are critical for achieving profitability.

Continued Growth in Air Travel

Despite periodic reversals and the consolidation process that is going on among airlines, the airline industry as a whole continues to expand. Once, air travel was a luxury; today, airlines are the largest common carrier. With improved technology, the rise of low-cost airlines, and the proliferation of discount and promotional fares, the cost of airline travel has come down dramatically over the decades. Air travel now competes with bus, rail, and even private automobile in terms of all the expenses associated with a trip. More than 90 percent of all public transportation (air, bus, or rail) is on airlines, according to the U.S. Travel Data Center.

Air travel is also expected to increase because of changing demographics (particularly the maturing of the Baby Boomers into their peak earnings and travel years), migration of family members to other parts of the country, and higher standard of living and increased leisure time. A growing, increasingly global economy means more business travel as well.

In 1990, U.S. carriers handled a record 466 million passengers, according to Department of Transportation figures (compared with 275 million in 1978, the year that deregulation was initiated). Moreover, surveys have shown that three out of four U.S. adults have flown at least once in their lives (compared with two out of three in 1980).

Finally, the FAA forecasts that the U.S. aviation industry should average 5.2 percent growth in revenue passenger miles systemwide (domestic and international) between 1992 and 2002.

Hiring Trends

The major forces affecting the travel industry–deregulation, consolidation, technologization, and globalization–are nowhere as apparent as in the airline industry and directly affect hiring trends.

Deregulation reshaped airline economics and put pressure on marketing and sales; competition then fostered consolidation in terms of mergers, acquisitions, and failures. Now, globalization is producing alliances and outright ownership of U.S. airlines by flag carriers of other nations. More sophisticated computerized reservations systems give airlines the edge to managing their product and delivering it to the user, resulting in a demand for computer specialists.

The roller-coaster pattern of profits and losses in the airline industry against a backdrop of economic cycles is reflected in its hiring (and firing) patterns. Between 1980 and 1982, a period of back-to-back recessions in the United States, the airline industry hired only 1,860 jet pilots and only 8,000 flight attendants; then, with the economy rebounding and expanding in 1983 to 1985, the industry hired 14,700 jet pilots and more than 30,000 flight attendants, according to Airline Economics, Inc. Hiring dwindled again in 1990 when only 7,700 pilots were hired.

"People interested in the airlines must be aware that it is an extremely volatile business," asserted Fran Hamilton, manager of central employment for TWA. "With deregulation, companies come and go; jobs come and go. This isn't the place for a person who needs security."

Being successful in the airline business, she advised, depends on much more than "love people, love travel. A person must be flexible and resilient–someone who can handle nonroutine and unpredictable situations. There are a lot of technically qualified people who don't succeed because they can't handle the environment. The cultural environment is more significant than technical qualifications."

Employees are frequently asked to relocate. "An airplane can go anywhere," Hamilton explained. "In deregulation, airlines have to respond to keen competition. There is no way of anticipating how long the carrier will be in a market. Routes, schedules, fares, capacity are all shifting fast, and individuals are affected."

Despite the insecurity, there is no shortage of people wanting to plunge into the airline business.

"There is an aura to the airlines, a special feeling you have even after you join, even among the administrative and accounting people that never see an airport," said USAir's director of personnel services.

Moreover, compensation rates tend to be high compared with most travel industry jobs, and airline employees usually have coveted travel benefits on their own and other airlines.

One of the reasons that jobs are hard to get is that few people leave the airlines voluntarily. Many jobs are unique to the airlines, such as pilot, and salaries are largely based on seniority. A pilot earning six figures at one airline would face a substantial drop in salary by moving to another.

Largely because the attrition rates are so low, advancement at an airline depends upon how swiftly it is growing–in routes or fleet. Hamilton noted that at TWA "it is possible to jump into a responsible position, but that's not likely to happen fast. The competition in the organization is keen. Movement in management ranks is slower." An up-and-coming carrier or even a strong regional or commuter carrier may well offer a faster track up the career ladder.

Job Opportunities

Though deregulation has created new demand for marketing, computer, and financial professionals, it is still the pilots, flight attendants, customer service representatives, reservationists, mechanics, and engineers who account for the vast majority of positions.

Individual airlines vary tremendously in terms of the management style, work environment, and career opportunities they present.

The airline business is probably the best-paying segment of the travel industry. Annual compensation per airline employee (including salary) ranges from about $12,000 for a new flight attendant to more than $100,000 for a senior airline captain. Senior-management executives are also well compensated compared with other travel counterparts. Some examples include:

Corporate Account Manager, $38,000
Manager of Agency Sales, $38,000
Resident Sales Representative, $40,000
International Pricing Analyst, $40,000
Supervisor–Passenger Services, $45,000

Manager–Customer Service, $50,000
Leisure Market Development Manager, $50,000
Regional Marketing Manager, $55,000
Director–Yield Management, $65,000
Vice President–Cargo Marketing and Sales, $90,000
Vice President–Passenger Sales, $92,000
Regional Vice President, $102,000

However, after the incredible expansion of the 1980s, the industry started off the 1990s with a sudden, dramatic consolidation, resulting in vigorous downsizing of the labor force. As a result, the labor market was glutted with high-paid, experienced professionals, which forced salaries down. One foreign flag carrier launching a new service out of New York, for example, was offering to pay only $40,000 for a marketing manager with 15 years of experience including five years in the airlines. Such a period of retrenchment should last until the middle of the decade when opportunities should rebound.

Three main job categories of airline personnel are: flight operations; maintenance and engineering; and administration, sales, and marketing. Each category and its accompanying positions are discussed separately in the following subsections.

Flight Operations

These positions require FAA certification:

Captain. Commands the aircraft and is responsible for the safety of its passengers and cargo.

Copilot. Assists or relieves the captain in the operation of the aircraft.

Second Officer/Flight Engineer. Assists in flight operations and sees that the mechanical and electronic devices of the aircraft are in perfect working order.

These positions are extremely limited and competitive. Often, the carriers' requirements for flight time and equipment necessitate a military career. In addition, airlines prefer individuals having a college degree or equivalent. The necessary flight time can sometimes be earned by working with private or corporate aircraft. Newer, smaller carriers generally do not require the same amount of experience as the major carriers do.

Cockpit jobs are the most glamorous (though the flying assignments to exotic points in Europe and Asia are few and far between, and short hops around the United States are more typical) and well paid (salaries can reach $165,000), but they are also the jobs that exact heavy demands on lifestyle. "You get up early, wait around the airport, sleep in midday in a strange hotel," said a spokesman for the Air Line Pilots Association (ALPA), which represents 43,000 pilots at 44 U.S. commercial airlines. "Pilots tend to be health conscious: You have to take medical exams once or twice a year, and your career can end with a wrong swiggle on an EKG."

There is an oversupply of pilots now, exacerbated by the collapse of Eastern Airlines, which left about 7,000 pilots unemployed. ALPA calculated an 8 to 9 percent unemployment rate, which is "terrible when you consider that if you want to stay in your career classification, there is no place else to go. It's not like computers; the skills of a pilot are not transferable."

Seniority is precious; it not only affords the highest pay and preference for aircraft, routes, and schedules but also ensures the highest position and privileged status when a carrier has to furlough pilots. Consequently, people usually stay at an airline until their mandatory retirement age of 60. This is not a burnout field; pilots are passionate about flying and do not leave their positions unless forced out for medical reasons or by furlough.

Historically, airlines have been reluctant to hire pilots in their thirties because of the enormous investment in training. In the 1980s, however, when pilots were in large demand, carriers did hire older people, even some in their fifties as well as some women (about 1,000 pilots are women).

The military used to be the primary source of airline pilots, but it is less so today. Currently, many pilots start as private pilots and become instructors in order to log the hundreds and hundreds of hours needed to qualify for an air taxi operation and then for small regional or commuter airlines. After a few years and accumulated flight time, they can go on to larger regional carriers and finally to the major ones. The career path is made easier due to strong alliances, even ownership relationships, between the major and regional carriers (American Airlines, for example, owns American Eagle).

Although cockpits have become increasingly computerized, flying itself has not been made any easier. Automation reduces much of the work load, even enabling airlines to eliminate the third person in the cockpit, the flight engineer. However, due to overcrowding at the airport and in the sky and to pressure by airline companies to increase efficiency, flying has become more difficult.

The best source for cockpit jobs is the Future Airline Professionals Association (FAPA), which publishes a *Pilot Directory of Employers* with salary information, projected demand, requirements, and contact information.

According to FAPA, 123 airline companies, with combined fleets of 6,301 aircraft and a total of 68,447 pilots, hired more than 7,700 pilots in 1990 at an average annual starting salary of $23,381. Despite the slow start to the decade, FAPA projects that airlines will hire 52,000 to 62,000 pilots by the year 2000. The directory also lists opportunities for 45 helicopter operators and 289 Fortune 500 companies maintaining private planes. Another good source of where jobs are is the Air Line Employees Association (ALEA).

Flight Attendant. Responsible for the safety and comfort of passengers during a flight.

Most travelers fail to appreciate the great responsibility for passenger safety that flight attendants have and the intense training that these key flight crew members must undergo. American Airlines, for example (which looks for public contact work experience and an educational background in English, psychology, public speaking, first aid, language, and home economics when evaluating candidates), gives a five-week training program at American's Learning Center, Fort Worth, TX. Immediately following training, new flight attendants are assigned to a U.S. city (such as New York City or Chicago). Seniority determines flight assignments.

Being a flight attendant is more of a career now and one that is no longer confined to women. Whereas stewardesses (as they were called) used to have to resign after marriage and/or pregnancy, today many married women and even mothers continue to fly. While it is possible to work out schedules that allow you to be home almost every night, many flight attendants prefer the excitement of long-distance travel.

When TWA was hiring flight attendants recently, an ad exulted how "a career in the sky is like none on earth." Its minimum qualifications stated that you have to be at least 18 years old, a high school graduate, and between 5'2" and 6'2"; have weight proportionate to height, and vision correctable to 20/50 or better; be a U.S. citizen or have a permanent-resident visa, be willing to relocate; possess excellent communications skills; and be able to attend tuition-based training.

The airlines employ 95,489 flight attendants. In 1990, some 14,176 flight attendants were hired at an average starting salary of $12,000. FAPA projects that 100,000 flight attendants will be hired by the year 2000.

Operations Agent. Computes the weight and balance of the aircraft so that baggage and cargo can be properly loaded to balance the aircraft; also schedules aircraft work crews and coordinates information for the passenger service employees, provisioning department, and flight crews. About 8,500 operations agents are employed by U.S. scheduled airlines and earn salaries of $14,000 to $33,000, according to ALEA.

Flight Dispatcher. Authorizes all takeoffs of aircraft and monitors a flight's progress to the destination by radio, also helps control the entire daily flight schedule of an airline, taking into consideration weather as well as problems with aircraft, flight crews, destination runways, and passenger/cargo/fuel loads. Prerequisites for training positions are college mathematics, physics, and meteorology. The 5,400 dispatchers currently employed earn salaries of $22,000 to $45,000.

Meterologist. Prepares weather reports for flight personnel and for airline operations and traffic departments.

Maintenance and Engineering

Maintenance is another huge personnel category for the airlines. According to FAPA, there are 73,000 maintenance professionals; during 1990, 9,404 mechanics were hired at an average starting salary of $12.75 per hour. FAPA projects that 46,000 maintenance technicians will be hired by the year 2000. Maintenance jobs include the following.

Airline Maintenance Inspector. Checks the work done by mechanics and other specialists and must give final approval before the aircraft is released for operation.

Airframe and Power Plant (Engine) (A&P) Mechanic. Works with skin and frames, engines, propellers, brakes, and wheels and is responsible for the proper mechanical functioning of the aircraft. Salaries range from $18,000 to $45,600; a certificate from the FAA or the military is required. There are 48,000 certified mechanics with U.S. scheduled airlines.

Instrument Technician. Installs, tests, repairs, and overhauls all aircraft, engine, and navigational instruments. A certificate is required.

Radio Technician. Installs, maintains, repairs, and tests all aircraft radio equipment.

Other maintenance jobs include machinists, sheet metal workers, carpenters, electricians, painters, electroplaters, drill press operators, upholsterers, and various types of mechanics. Skills required for certification may be developed at privately owned and operated FAA-approved schools.

Airline Engineer. Works closely with aircraft manufacturers, such as Boeing, McDonnell-Douglas, and Lockheed, to develop equipment suited to the airline's particular type of operation; is often involved in the design of aircraft and aircraft accessories and in improving maintenance and overhaul procedures; may be responsible for safety oversight.

Administration, Sales, and Marketing

Administrative, sales, and marketing departments offer some of the best entry-level positions with the least requirements for education and prior experience or accreditation. However, the competition for jobs has allowed the airlines to stiffen their requirements, and those who have completed a travel and tourism program at a college or vocational school generally have a better chance at employment.

Reservations Agent. Sells reservations and other travel products, such as tours, hotel accommodations, and car rentals; operates computer reservations equipment; and assists passengers in solving their travel needs. About 54,000 airline reservationists in the United States occupy the better part of a day sitting in front of a computer screen with a headset on, talking over the telephone to consumers and travel agents, making and changing reservations. American Airlines looks for individuals with a high school degree or equivalent, two years of college or business experience, and an aptitude for telephone sales and excellent telephone technique. Salaries range from $12,064 to $38,600, according to the ALEA.

Ticket Agent. Sells tickets to airline passengers at the airport and at city ticket offices. At American Airlines, this agent also promotes and sells air travel, gives air travel and tour information, makes the flight and tour reservations, computes fares, prepares and issues tickets, routes baggage, and prepares cash reports. There are about 20,000 ticket agents in the United States. Starting salaries range from $10,000 to $16,000; at the tenth year of service, they range from $15,000 to $28,000, according to ALEA.

Airport Operations Agent. Performs agent duties in airport operational areas; meets and dispatches flights, lifts tickets, administers seat selection, coordinates boarding and post-departure procedure, handles baggage service, and maintains a high level of customer service with passengers.

Passenger Service Agent. Provides service to passengers primarily at the ticket counter or passenger boarding or baggage claim areas; assists passengers by providing information, arranging for ground transportation, and giving directions; when necessary, may fill in for reservations or ticket agent.

Fleet Service Employee. Loads and unloads air cargo and baggage on the aircraft and makes certain that baggage gets to the proper destination. Good physical condition and ability to work outdoors in every kind of weather are required; previous experience with equipment (belt loaders, container lifts, heaters, aircraft pushback tractor, and deicing equipment) or in freight handling is a plus. There are about 32,000 fleet service employees whose salaries range from $12,000 to $38,000, according to ALEA.

Sales Representative. Promotes and sells an airline's various passenger and cargo services mainly to travel agencies and to corporate accounts.

District Sales Manager. Administers city ticket and reservations offices and promotes and develops airline passenger and cargo traffic in the district in accordance with the company's goals and policies.

District Operations Manager. Is in charge of ground and flight operations at an airline station and supervises all the people involved.

Freight Airport Operations Agent. Processes routing and rating of shipments and contacts customer on arrival of shipments and arranges for delivery.

Freight Telephone Sales Representative. Quotes rates and patterns of service and completes necessary shipping documents.

Fleet Service Clerks. Cabin service clerk cleans cabin interiors and replenishes cabin supplies; line cargo clerk handles loading and unloading of baggage, freight, and mail on passenger aircraft; air freight clerk handles loading and unloading of freight in specialized equipment on jet freighters.

The Air Line Employees Association, a union that represents ground employees including reservations agents and clerical, office, fleet, and passenger service employees, is a good source for these jobs. ALEA offers a job opportunities program consisting of monthly bulletins for 16 different career categories including qualifications, requirements, and contact information; a magazine published six times a year; and a directory of aviation-related schools and colleges.

Apart from the specific positions previously described, headquarters and regional sales offices employ people in public relations, personnel, accounting, insurance, and finance; secretaries, typists, clerks, and receptionists are also employed.

Marketing departments employ research analysts, whose job is to prepare detailed statistical analyses and reports that relate to items such as the rate structure and tariffs, traffic problems and trends, or the number of passengers and amounts of mail and freight carried.

Management/Specialty Positions

Most carriers have a policy of filling management/specialty positions from within. At American Airlines, for example, promotional opportunities include those of crew scheduler, executive secretary, foreman, industrial engineer, inspector, instructor, passenger service manager, personnel representative, programmer/analyst, purchasing agent, and statistical analyst and supervisor.

The three broad job categories for airline personnel mask the diversity and range of specializations. For example, an incentive sales representative specializes in working with coordinators of travel prizes, a travel industry liaison works with travel agents, and an interline salesperson coordinates with other airlines on mutual exchange of tickets and is responsible for reduced-rate travel of airline and travel agency personnel. Other speciality areas include aircraft purchase and sales, charters, freight/cargo, insurance, properties and facilities, purchasing, labor relations, and community and environmental affairs.

Many airlines also have sizable tour operations. TWA, for example, has TWA Getaway (now operating as a separate entity); American Airlines has FlyAAway Vacations; United has United Vacations. These entities employ many of the same kinds of professionals as tour companies do, including product development, operations, and marketing and sales professionals.

Computer Reservations Systems

Perhaps the most significant change in the airline industry is computer technology and the employment opportunities the computer has generated. Several carriers own outright or have stakes in sophisticated computer reservations systems marketed to travel agents and used by other airlines and travel suppliers (hotels, car rentals, tour companies). These systems include Sabre (American), Apollo (United), Worldspan (Delta and TWA), and SystemOne (formerly Eastern Airlines). These computer operations have become profitable businesses in their own right, and huge computer centers are staffed by computer programmers, technicians, and sales and marketing people.

Haute Cuisine at 25,000 Feet

The notion of serving haute cuisine at 25,000 feet (the task of the in-flight meal service) may seem very attractive for someone aspiring toward the culinary arts. However, most of the meal service is provided by a few major companies on a contract basis. American Airlines is one of the few airlines that has its own in-flight kitchen operation, Sky Chef, and these workers, whether they are the salad makers or the master chefs, all have flying privileges (whereas nonairline catering people do not). Most of the work is performed on an assembly line basis, but the kitchens do employ a few top chefs who have the awesome task of preparing enticing meals by the hundreds to be served hours later. Some airlines employ a food service person to create the menus, which are then prepared by the kitchens. KLM went so far as to hire a renowned chef to create specialities for the airline.

Getting In

The airline business is one area of the travel industry where you should be discriminating about where you take a job (if possible). In most other areas, the object is simply to get in; moving up or over is relatively easy. But in the airline industry, if you are laid off or if the airline fails, getting a new job will be difficult because you will be competing with literally tens of thousands of experienced airline professionals who also have been laid off. You are better advised to take a job with a sound, growing commuter or regional airline than with an ailing major carrier.

Each carrier presents a different work environment (work conditions range from plush to World War II-salvage bunkers) and a very different outlook for advancement opportunities and security. The age and size of a carrier are not necessarily indications of vitality.

You can get leads and insights about airline companies from trade publications and the financial pages of newspapers or magazines. It is also helpful to review annual reports and literature by and about the companies, as well as the directories published by FAPA.

Salary is important, but many airlines now offer employees stock options and profit sharing in lieu of salary hikes. It is also important to consider the benefits package. If travel is important to you, find out what the travel benefits are and whether the airline has interline privileges (entitling personnel to travel on other airlines at very little cost).

Examine the job itself and the opportunities the company offers for advancement. Look at the background of the company (particularly its human resources policies and past record on layoffs) and its future plans. Find out how many cities and what cities it serves, what kind of fleet it has, what its fleet purchase plans are, who is backing the company, whether it has joint marketing arrangements with other carriers, and what its relationships with other travel entities (particularly travel agencies) are. Consider whether the airline is having difficulty with unions or staff and whether a strike is looming. Look at the airline's share of the market and whether its share has been growing. Consider its profitability.

The most active job categories at the entry level are reservations, secretarial, and airport positions. For reservationists, airlines generally look for people with travel and training acquired at a travel school, a travel agency, or another airline. They seek some kind of relevant experience, particularly some familiarity with an airline computer reservations system. Reservations people have some mobility within a company, primarily to automation support, sales, customer service, training, and marketing.

Secretarial jobs, generally full-time, also offer a means of getting in and moving up in a company, particularly into sales representative, quality control, and training positions. However, though most airlines make an effort to promote from within, there is understandable concern, particularly among women, of becoming trapped in entry-level positions like secretarial and reservations jobs.

"Anyone who enters the airline industry in entry level could be trapped for some time because there are so many experienced people also looking for positions," said TWA's Hamilton. "The opportunities are not as plentiful as they used to be. It used to be a reservationist could become a supervisor in one year. Now, we point out to new hires that we can't promise a lot of quick movement."

And, while it is common to think of jobs like reservationist and passenger service agent as steppingstones to other positions, 90 percent of the people employed in these positions, as well as in clerical, fleet service agent, and ticket counter agent positions, are content to spend their entire career in these jobs, asserted ALEA.

There are 200 applications for every opening. "We get 1,000 per month from flight attendants alone," said one airline's hiring executive. "One year we saw about 8,000 candidates for flight attendants and hired 330, or 4 percent. This is the most selective area."

One way into the business is to start part-time (in fact, a much greater proportion of jobs throughout the airline industry are part-time, perhaps 15 to 25 percent, because there is such fluctuation in schedules and traffic and part-timers are more cost-effective for the airline). Often, part-time jobs lead to full-time positions.

Compensation is fairly good compared with most other travel industry jobs, and airline employees have travel benefits. Several of the major carriers, however, in order to be competitive with newer airlines that have a much lower salary structure, have introduced two-tier structures with the lower pay levels going to new hires.

Regionals Offer Faster Track

Regional airlines may present more career opportunity than major carriers will. The 150 regional airlines, which provide scheduled, short-haul air transportation between small and medium-sized communities and the nation's hub airports and generate about $3.5 billion in sales, accounted for 55 percent of new jobs for pilots in 1990.

Regional airlines, which employ about 20,000 people, not only pose more opportunity for entry level, but, in recent years, they also have offered a healthier pattern of growth and stability. Over the past decade, the regional carriers have been growing and taking a greater share of traffic; they now account for about 30 percent of all domestic traffic.

Another advantage of regional carriers is that they provide more opportunity to be a "jack-of-all-trades." "You're more likely to have hands-on experience," said one executive. "The majors are more specialized."

Getting in at a regional carrier can be more than just being in the right place at the right time; you can "make it happen." By being alert to when carriers enter a market or when they are about to be certificated, you can approach them before they are flooded with applicants. If possible, call upon people you know within the carrier. Also, getting a job at a regional airline, of course, is easier if you have some experience or training in the travel industry, such as from an airline or a travel school that teaches reservations systems. "Occasionally, when we enter a new market, we will hire locally," said an executive, "but generally you need some skill or training or have to know somebody."

Some people regard the regional carriers as steppingstones to the major carriers, but many step up and then find themselves laid off. Staying at a regional carrier may present greater advancement opportunity.

While not all regional carriers have interline arrangements with other carriers, they may offer free-flight privileges on an airline in some cases. They may also have pass agreements with major airlines.

Compensation in terms of salaries, though somewhat lower than the major airlines, is decent. A sales manager, for example, earns $15,000 to $40,000; a station manager, $15,600 to $37,000; and a vice president of operations, $30,000 to $90,000.

Working for a Foreign Flag Carrier

Foreign flag carriers offer more limited opportunities—but opportunities nonetheless. Salaries are comparable with those of other aviation companies.

International carriers offer positions in middle management, but most senior-management positions are held by foreign nationals. The exception is the second in command, who is usually an American (because he or she knows the market). Department heads, except for public relations and personnel, also tend to be foreign nationals, but all departments usually have U.S. nationals under them.

Station heads may be foreign or American. Reservationists and sales and marketing staff members are typically American. Reservations usually is the entry point for Americans. Few Americans are employed by the foreign airlines abroad.

It is not imperative but is definitely beneficial to have foreign language capability in order to rise. However, some positions may require foreign language (such as reservations).

Jonathan Hill: Glasnost and Geopolitics

One of the more fascinating aspects of working at an international flag carrier is the possibility of becoming caught up with geopolitics and geoeconomics. Jonathan Hill, for example, personally lived *glasnost*. Joining Aeroflot, the world's largest airline, as marketing manager, USA, just as relations between the United States and Soviet Union were reaching an all-time high, Hill also suffered when the Soviet government cracked down on regional independence movements, prompting a renewed chilling in U.S.–Soviet relations.

An airline is a country's lifeline and its pipeline to the world. It is not only a mark of prestige but also integral to its independence and defense. Consequently, Hill's position is a vital one, and he has met with people at the highest rungs of government. Hill (whose parents met fighting over a passenger when his father was at United and his mother worked at American) has the distinction of being the lone capitalist in an organization struggling in that direction. "It's been a priceless experience," he declared.

Contacts and Sources

Sources of information and leads for potential employers include:

International Air Transport Association (IATA), 2000 Peel St., Montreal, Canada, H3A 2R4, tel. 514-844-6311; represents 166 members and 35 associates worldwide; offers an IATA diploma in airline management; recently opened a training center in Miami, FL, tel. 305-592-4878.

Air Transport Association, 1709 New York Ave. NW, Washington, D.C. 20006, tel. 202-626-4000, has a career pamphlet listing airline member contacts (send self-addressed, stamped envelope).

Future Airline Professionals Association (FAPA), 4959 Massachusetts Blvd., Atlanta, GA 30337, tel. 800-JET-JOBS; offers "Pilot Directory of Employers" ($23), "Flight Attendant Directory of Employers & Salary Survey" ($22), and "Maintenance Directory of Employers" ($17); lists regional and commuter carriers; also includes opportunities at international carriers in its directories.

Air Line Employees Association (ALEA), 5600 South Central Ave., Chicago, IL 60638–3797, tel. 312-767-3333; offers a job opportunities program of monthly bulletins for 16 career categories ($40 annual fee) as well as a directory of aviation-related schools and colleges.

Regional Airline Association, 1101 Connecticut Ave., NW, Ste. 700, Washington, D.C. 20036, tel. 202-857-1170; publishes a helpful annual report.

Federal Aviation Administration (FAA), Department of Transportation, Washington, D.C. 20591; provides an approved list of privately owned and operated schools where maintenance professionals may obtain certification.

Trade publications include:

Aviation Weekly

Travel Agent

Travel Weekly

Commuter Air International

Commuter/Regional Airline News

Regional Aviation Weekly

11

The Car Rental Industry

Car Rental Industry Overview

"Once car rental gets in your blood, it stays. There are a lot of 'retreads' in the business—people who go from company to company," declared one car rental executive.

Like many people in the car rental business who are not otherwise driven by some fascination with the automobile, Robert Coffey stumbled in but soon found himself caught up in the dynamics of the industry and has never left. Coffey had been working for Pan Am for five years when he became one of the casualties of the "blood bath of 1974" in which thousands of airline personnel lost their jobs. His boss at Pan Am, however, had a friend in top management at Avis Rent a Car System who offered him a position.

"I was complacent," Coffey related. "I thought the airline business so dynamic—a fleet of 150 airplanes going to hundreds of points all around the world. You knew where they were going. Then I realized that Avis had 65,000 cars in its fleet, and that customers may tell us they will return a car to one place and wind up in another. The whole prospect of keeping track became exciting.

"I found the car rental business one of phenomenal change – the capacity of the product changes daily in each city. There are new cities to open, new marketing opportunities, new people to meet, new places to go."

Coffey has since been in the business nearly two decades, moving from Avis to Alamo Rent A Car, most recently as vice president-market planning, "and it is more exciting every day."

Car rental does not have the glamour (or prestige) of the airlines; many come to it after they cannot get jobs in the airlines. But people fail to appreciate the dynamics and the challenge of the business and the fact that it offers much the same people contact, high technology, and excitement of airport activity as the airlines.

The car rental industry exploded in growth during the 1970s and into the 1980s when there was a frantic scramble for car companies to obtain coveted on-airport locations. The airport was where the real growth of the business was taking place as airline deregulation caused people to leave their personal cars home and take airplanes instead, leaving passengers with a need for rental cars at their destinations. The car rental industry doubled in size during the decade, averaging 10 percent growth a year and outpacing most other segments of the travel industry.

Car rental is nearly a $10-billion business, employing about 150,000 to 200,000 people. There are several thousand car rental companies in the United States (350 in southern Florida alone), the vast majority small "Mom and Pop" outlets, and together they operate at 20,000 locations. The 10 largest companies are Hertz, Park Ridge, NJ; Avis, Garden City, NY; Budget, Chicago; National, Minneapolis; Alamo, Ft. Lauderdale, FL; Dollar, Los Angeles; Thrifty, Tulsa; Value, Deerfield Beach, FL; General, Hollywood, FL; and American International, Boston. These companies account for more than 6,000 locations and control about 80 percent of the business.

Companies differ markedly in style, in their position in the market, in market niche, and to some degree in the kind of services they offer. Foremost Euro-Car, Inc., based in Van Nuys, CA, and Interrent Car Rental System of Los Angeles specialize in arranging lease/purchase deals for Americans in Europe. Other companies specialize in fly/drive programs in Europe. Some companies specialize in renting recreational vehicles. In some highly competitive leisure markets, the car company can become extremely creative. In Hawaii, the Budget franchise came up with a discount coupon book at restaurants and attractions as an additional inducement to customers. Still other companies, such as Carey International, specialize in car and driver arrangements.

Intense Competition

Like the hospitality industry, the car rental business has huge growth prospects and affords excellent advancement opportunities as well as the chance to take on tremendous responsibility early on in a career. But unlike the hospitality industry, where hotels take years to plan and construct and where capacity is fixed, car rental companies (like airlines) can shift their supply and adjust prices to meet demand virtually at will. This flexibility allows them to react quickly to competitive threats.

Consequently, the car rental business is one of the most intensely competitive of all travel businesses. Every detail is shrouded in secrecy; executives do not divulge, for example, the number of cars in any one location because it would betray valuable information to the competition. Car rental is a commodity business where the commodity—the car—can be moved instantly to tap into demand.

Service and price rule here (as with the airlines), but the two key elements that contribute to the specialness of the car rental business can be summed up as fleet and finance. Fleet utilization is the name of the game in car rental, and this means logistics. Contributing to this dynamic is that a company may not have gauged demand correctly and can place too much of its fleet in a location.

"There is a substantial logistics problem in getting the fleet to the right place at the right time," a Hertz executive stated. For example, when Hertz was faced with a problem of moving cars out of Florida and back into the Northeast after peak season, it solved the problem through substantial price incentives: Floridians were offered a car for a week plus two return air tickets to Florida for only $129.

Car rental companies are intimately linked with the airline business (80 percent of industry revenues come from airport locations). While some were helped, others were hurt when deregulation changed the airline pattern to a hub-and-spoke system. All car rental companies, however, are affected constantly by shifting demand for air services, which is often helped along by aggressive pricing by certain carriers.

Besides logistics and demand, fleet utilization also involves the kinds of cars rental companies offer. A car company has to anticipate the design, size, and fuel economy of cars that people will want to rent (if fuel is plentiful, people want to drive bigger, sportier, faster cars; if scarce, they shift to downsized vehicles). The company also must consider what cars people will want to buy 18 to 24 months later (rental companies have to sell off their used cars).

"There's so much to consider," asserted Coffey. "You even have to figure the impact of such things as teleconferencing [satellite transmissions that enable meetings participants to be in different locations and that will likely cut down on the amount of airline travel], or will people want cellular phones, and how the cost of airfares may or may not stimulate air travel."

Moreover, many car rental companies are also in the franchise business, which adds yet another dimension to business operations.

In their highly leveraged, capital-intensive business, car rental companies borrow heavily each year to finance a new stock of cars. A point change in interest rates can mean $5 million to the bottom line of a major company like Avis. The intense competition among companies has also put pressure on pricing, which means equal pressure for raising productivity. "If you're positioned properly and have read from the crystal ball correctly, you make money," an Avis executive quipped.

Largely due to the high rate of borrowing to finance the fleet and because car rental companies generally earn a high rate of return, the two largest in the field, Hertz and Avis, have been plums in takeovers by major conglomerates. Since Hertz was founded in 1918, it has had many owners including RCA and United Airlines. Avis had been owned by ITT, then was publicly owned, then was acquired by Norton Simon, which was bought by Esmark, then was acquired by Beatrice, followed by Westray Capital, and, in 1987, by its employees in one of the nation's largest ESOPs (employee-sponsored ownership plans).

Major car rental companies have a second business equally important as the rental side – selling the used cars. The companies have to predict two to four years in advance what customers will want to rent as well as to buy; frequently, the two wants are not the same. A change in gasoline prices can render a whole fleet obsolete.

Over the past five years, however, major car manufacturers including Ford, General Motors, Chrysler, and Volvo have stepped in to take substantial ownership interest in several of the major car rental companies. They have changed the complexion of the car rental industry by way of a buy-back arrangement that reduces the risk of disposing of used cars and makes it possible for renters to have new cars each year (a competitive edge). In exchange, the rental companies usually have to acquire car models of the manufacturers' choosing.

A relatively new company, General Rent A Car, based in Hollywood, FL, was financed by Chrysler (which also has interests in Thrifty, Dollar, and Snappy). Ford has a substantial interest in Budget and Hertz (with another 20 percent owned by Volvo). General Motors has stakes in Avis and National. Mitsubishi purchased a majority interest in Value Rent A Car (the first Japanese company to acquire a U.S. car rental company).

Commercial and Leisure Renters

The backbone of the car rental business is the commercial renter – the business traveler. Signing up commercial accounts and enticing them with corporate rates, frequent traveler programs, and other incentives are prime activities.

The growth side of the business, though, has been the leisure renter. Car rental companies have created a new form of travel package – fly/drive (a combination of airline travel and car rental). Negotiating with airline and tour operator partners in order to be included in their packages and currying the loyalties of travel agencies through incentives and promotions are key responsibilities for car rental marketing and sales departments.

The leisure business is likely to expand markedly due to the growth of airline travel, particularly when discounts and low fares abound. The maturing of the Baby Boomers into family units will also help since fly/drives offer more appeal and convenience than do very long trips with the family car.

One of the central changes in the car rental business is that "the customer" is no longer the car renter but the travel agent or the corporate travel manager who has to be presold to choose a particular car rental company. Fifteen years ago, few travel agents booked car rentals and only 10 percent of the industry's revenues were generated by agents. Today, about 60 percent of the industry's revenues come through agents (car rentals are now the second largest source of agency revenues after airline tickets). The change reflects dramatic shifts in marketing, commission structure, and computer reservations systems.

"Increasingly, this is becoming a technology-based industry with global computerized data communication networks," commented an Avis executive. "The only way to survive is to be quick and accurate."

People Power

The largest category of people power in the car rental business are the rental sales agents. They work the counter and have considerable responsibility in determining whether a customer is fit to take possession, however temporarily, of an $18,000 vehicle. The counter agents are sent for two weeks of training before they can assume a position.

Handling people proves to be the challenging and even creative aspect of the job. "Someone who has been on an airplane for six hours has not had control of his life – where he sits, where his bags wind up, what he eats, who sits next to him. The first time he retakes control of his life is at our counter, where he asserts himself," said an Avis executive.

What do car rental companies look for when hiring counter agents (or rental sales agents)? They prefer someone with good communications skills, someone who is adept at dealing with people, someone who enjoys challenge and is not timid, someone who can make judgment calls.

The second-largest category are the service agents. They clean and prepare the cars. If "love of cars" is your motive for entering the car rental business, this position can best realize your objective. Service agent positions, however, are more assembly line in nature since they involve repetitive tasks and little decision making.

The third-largest category are the "shuttlers." These people move cars from one location to another. Other entry-level positions in a rental outlet include bus drivers, service mechanics and helpers, and clerical support workers. The number of office positions varies largely by location.

Salaries at entry level are slightly better than minimum wage, but there are bonuses for everyone in the field based on performance.

Management positions include those of the shift managers (outlets are open 24 hours a day), the assistant city manager, and the city manager, who is in charge of a facility. The city manager also has marketing responsibility. Every city develops its own marketing contacts, including contacts with airline managers, local travel agents, and tour operators. The city manager tries to get group business and may participate in sales blitzes throughout the country (for example, the Miami city manager may come to talk with New York City travel agents).

Aspiring to a management position is a realistic goal for rental agents. A typical career path might be from rental agent, to "lead agent" (who answers customers' questions) or quality assurance supervisor (who talks to customers to find out how the car performed and assists customers generally), to shift manager, to station manager, and then to city manager. From city manager, a person can move up to division manager and then to regional vice president or can move into general financial management.

Headquarters positions include those in operations (personnel, car control, fleet control, fleet utilization); fleet administration (making deals to buy and sell cars); sales and marketing; reservations; and finance (accounts payable/receivable, data processing). Alamo, for example, employs about 400 people (out of 2,000 people systemwide) in its headquarters in personnel, car control, fleet control, fleet utilization, fleet administration, marketing, reservations, and finance.

The marketing function (planning, forecasting, designing the product, pricing, and physically selling the product) generally is consolidated at the national level, but there usually are marketing managers in each region. Marketing specialists are the individuals who try to negotiate alliances with airlines, tour companies, and hotels. Sales programs are also established at the national level, but in major markets companies usually maintain sales offices that have sales representatives who call upon commercial accounts and travel agents.

Technology is a growing part of the car rental business. Avis, for example, a company that made early inroads into computer systems, has 400 computer specialists and maintains a training department just for this "special breed of cat." The computer specialists are divided between Avis's world reservations center in Tulsa, OK, and its Garden City, NY, headquarters, where the mainframe is located.

Among the top management positions for car rental companies are the fleet acquisition/positioning specialists, fleet coordinators, accounting people, and controllers. There are also specialists who negotiate with airlines and tour companies. While there are quite a few of these senior-management specialty positions, there are not very many positions as compared with the legions of lower-level jobs. Therefore, many people at the management level move from company to company or from city to city in order to advance. Some examples of specialties and salaries include:

Automation Training Manager, $44,000
Director of Sales and Marketing, $60,000
Regional Vice President of Sales and Marketing, $60,000
Vice President, Travel Industry Marketing, $150,000

Getting In

To get leads for jobs in the car rental industry, start with the local *Yellow Pages.*

It is best to apply at the district office or head office for the area in which you wish to work.

The oldest and largest car rental company with 4,500 outlets worldwide, Hertz is considered one of the best training grounds for the industry since there is much movement from company to company. Hertz employs some 19,000 people in the United States. While most of the hiring is done at the local level, the company does have training and development programs at the corporate level.

Avis has a new hire program for incoming rental sales people, which involves training at one of seven major training centers for two weeks. The training familiarizes the individual not only with the computer but also with how to rent a car without it and, even more importantly, with how to handle situations such as qualifying a customer, computing a rate manually, and dealing with travel vouchers and travel agents' commissions. The myriad details are what make the job interesting (not to mention the people contact and the airport activity).

A multinational company like Avis affords only a few opportunities for Americans abroad; most of these positions are filled locally. However, your chances of being posted abroad are better if you have foreign language capability.

New demands have been placed on the car rental industry to comply with environmental rules and regulations such as the Clean Air Act of 1990. These demands may open opportunities at car rental companies for legal and engineering professionals.

Contacts and Sources

American Car Rental Association, 927 Fifteenth St., NW, Ste. 1000, Washington, D.C. 20005, tel. 202-789-2240; is mainly a lobbying group with 500 members.

Trade publications include:

Auto Rental News

Travel Agent

Travel Weekly

Business Travel News

12

The Motorcoach Industry

Motorcoach Industry Overview

The motorcoach industry, though one of the most uncelebrated areas of travel, is poised for some exciting changes and expansion. Still wrenching itself from under the weight of unflattering stereotypes of the bus and its customers, the motorcoach industry affords unlimited creativity and challenge as it seizes the opportunities of a marketplace only recently freed from regulation and branches out to new types of customers and services.

Languishing in the decades after World War II as the nation's resources went toward building a highway system to support private automobiles and the airlines skyrocketed in popularity, the motorcoach industry was revitalized with the energy crisis of 1973. It was then that the nation was reminded about the essential service, the fuel efficiency, the flexibility, and the economy of the bus.

When gasoline supplies returned, attention all but vanished again until the federal government lifted the constraints that had been imposed since the Interstate Commerce Commission Act of 1935. The industry became free to address the problems of an archaic product and could develop new products to fit current needs.

While the bus business was regulated, existing companies operated under a kind of government protection, with their routes like franchises and their profits virtually assured. The companies generally could charge customers what they liked, and though they usually had authority to operate both point-to-point (scheduled) service as well as charters, long-haul scheduled service was the mainstay of the business. Many companies were family businesses, operated by third and fourth generations of the founders, and had little incentive to innovate or respond to changes in the marketplace.

Immediately following deregulation in 1983, however, thousands of new companies obtained operating licenses. There were 1,500 companies in 1983; today, 3,000 to 4,000 companies employ about 51,000 people and offer bus service in one form or another. However, only 452 provide scheduled service; charters and tours have become a critical component of the business, accounting for almost 40 percent of all bus passengers and revenue.

In the 1940s and 1950s, the heyday for bus operators, relatively few families had a car; air service was nonexistent or prohibitively expensive, and even the railroad served limited numbers of communities. Things have changed dramatically over the years: Cars have become ubiquitous (now even many 16 year olds have their own); air travel has become much more available and affordable; and rental cars fill in any gaps. Consequently, the bus industry has been fighting an uphill battle to maintain its customer base.

Nonetheless, the intercity bus industry still serves more communities (one estimate is 13,000, compared with only about 200 airports for scheduled service) than any other common carrier. In 1989, the industry carried 119 million revenue passengers including 40 million charter and tour passengers. The intercity bus industry generated some $1.8 billion (compared with $2.3 billion in operating revenues in 1984), of which $593.3 million came from charters and tours.

Buses still perform a valuable service in providing low-cost point-to-point transportation, particularly from the thousands of communities not readily accessible by air. It is difficult, however, for bus lines to compete with airlines for speed and competitive rates and particularly with personal automobiles. For the industry to survive, it must find ways to provide widespread, quality service at low fares ($21 is the average fare).

Greyhound Rising to the Challenge

Greyhound, still the largest single bus company and the only one providing a truly nationwide network of regular-route passenger service, epitomizes the challenge facing the motorcoach industry. Greyhound typically carries 30 to 35 million passengers in a year and offers service between 38,000 city pairs.

In 1987, Greyhound acquired Trailways Lines, the largest operator in the Trailways System, which gave Greyhound service to 400 cities that Greyhound had not previously served. For three years, the merged company recorded increases in passenger service. Then, in 1990, Greyhound was devastated by a brutal strike by its drivers and forced into Chapter 11 bankruptcy. The company emerged from Chapter 11 on Oct. 31, 1991 and, at the same time, became a public company, with 95 percent of stock held by equity shareholders including creditors and 5 percent by employees under an ESOP (Employee-Sponsored Ownership Plan). The company decided to focus almost entirely on regular-route passenger service and pull back from the charter side (though it still maintained about nine sales offices around the country).

"We think there will always be a demand for high-quality, low-cost ground transportation," a spokeswoman explained. "It will never again be like the 1950s—there have been too many changes in demographics, standard of living, high-technology airplanes, and faster, safer, cheaper air service. But we're still returning to basics. We've chosen not to compete with smaller bus companies doing charters—the operating cost for us is too high.

"Our challenge is to see ourselves as a customer service, rather than a transportation company," she said. "That means that our primary concern is helping passengers get to their destination, rather than moving a bus. We are focusing more on quality service and customer needs." This focus has translated into more customer service and quality control positions. Also, by seeing point-to-point travel in a new light, Greyhound can address marketing issues aimed at winning back passengers and gaining new converts.

The further challenge is to provide quality service at low cost (the average ticket is $35, and it is possible to travel across the country for $69) and to provide comprehensive service through a variation on the hub-and-spoke pattern of the airlines by funneling people in and fanning them out. These measures require improved yield and fleet management, necessitating computerized controls.

Thus, the bus industry, like the airline industry, will be focusing on innovations in marketing and sales, yield management, customer service, and computerized reservations and fleet management systems, all of which spell new professional opportunities. "It's more challenging and interesting than I had imagined it would be," commented one manager.

Out of 7,700 employees, about 1,000 are managers. "The Greyhound manager must be a very strong, nonbureaucratic, broad-based manager who can deal with all kinds of customer service, bus control, and driver issues," said Ted Knappen, senior vice president. "Airlines are encumbered by more levels of specialization; our managers are generalists—people with practical, hands-on general-management experience."

Tours and Charters

Tours and charters have proved to be one of the more profitable areas of the bus industry, and most of the companies (Greyhound is a notable exception) are rushing into this area. This trend is vastly changing the professional makeup of the industry, shifting the emphasis from operations to sales and marketing. "For the first time," an American Bus Association veteran noted, "companies are going outside the family unit. They are hiring people with hotel sales experience who know how to package and sell tours." Many people are coming into the tour and charter side of the business from travel agencies as well as hotel sales.

The National Motorcoach Marketing Network, born in 1983 from deregulation, epitomizes the new direction in which the industry is heading, and the new emphasis on marketing. A consortium, or marketing alliance, of 30 of some of the largest motorcoach companies, the National Motorcoach Marketing Network represents the largest charter entity in the country. Collectively, its members account for 1,500 coaches covering virtually every state. In 1990, the group tallied 14 million charter and tour customers generating $1.1 billion in tour sales.

The network is able to wage marketing efforts that independent companies cannot afford on their own and, in so doing, has been able to tap into new markets for coaches beyond the mainstay senior-citizen market. These markets include military personnel (the network is an official carrier for the Department of Defense and in 1990 carried 22 percent of all military groups); student bands and sports teams (it is the official carrier for National Junior Achievement); festival groups; inbound visitors; travel agency-generated groups; and corporations and associations.

In addition to a national marketing effort, the network is able to offer members access to maintenance centers nationwide and guarantee payment for repairs, as well as access to a one-stop booking center. It publishes an in-bus magazine, *Byways,* similar to the airlines' in-flight magazines.

High-Tech Equipment, Unpretentious People

Some people tend to think of a bus as a rumbling, smokey, dirty vehicle in a dingy terminal in a decrepit inner city. The present reality, however, is vastly different from this worn stereotype.

New, slick, high-tech buses incorporate many of the amenities of airline compartments and go beyond the airlines in terms of wide windows and roomy seats (some buses even have in-bus movies). Tours are being designed to appeal to every interest and degree of travel experience (see the section on domestic tour operations in Chapter 4). Those who work on the tour side say they find the bus business as interesting and exciting as any position in tour operations. Innovations in fares, negotiated programs with other travel suppliers, and distribution (computerized reservations and ticketing) are also making the business more interesting—as well as profitable.

The motorcoach industry tends to attract people who are "very unpretentious, warm, and friendly," commented one veteran. "There is comradery—people enjoy the business. Some owners think nothing of taking tours out themselves."

The industry also tends to attract individuals who are mechanically oriented, enamored more by the vehicle itself than by the notion of travel (much the same as airline people who are in love with a "silver bird").

Jobs in the motorcoach industry are similar to those in the airlines but have less specialization. Entry-level positions include driving, working as an escort, or dealing in sales and service to customers. Positions in operations include mechanics, maintenance personnel, supervisors, parts/purchasing personnel, drivers, dispatchers, schedulers, and general managers. Drivers are paid an average salary of $23,500. Clerical positions include those involved in payroll and in keeping track of different states' bus regulations. The motorcoach companies also employ tour directors, sales managers, advertising executives, tour planners, and people who prepare company brochures.

One of the special appeals of working in the bus business is that, because the businesses tend to be small (many are family owned and operated), they are more personal. "For somebody who wants to work in the travel industry, the bus business may be one place to fulfill what you want to do," said one veteran. "It may not be as glamorous as the hotels, but is another way to fulfill one's dream."

An Entrepreneurial Business

Except for the largest companies like Greyhound, bus companies tend to be small and entrepreneurial; few companies generate more than $20 million in revenues. However, job mobility is limited either because the organization is so small or because top positions are kept within a family. Moreover, opportunities to rise are shifting away from operations people to those in sales and marketing. "As sales experience and marketing become the most important aspect to a company, these people will rise to the top," said a motorcoach executive.

Bus businesses are also finding that they have to diversify. As scheduled service continues to become less of a critical factor, the bus companies are moving into enterprises as feeder service to airports (in place of car rental), package express, commuter services, and, of course, tours and charters. Thus, the industry is still quite entrepreneurial. (You can start a bus company with about $100,000 – $50,000 for a bus, the rest for licensing, insurance, ICC authority, advertising, and salaries.)

An Example: Shuttlejack

When Ray Sena graduated from Harvard Business School more than a decade ago with his master's degree, he informed his father, who owned a small bus company, that he wanted to go into his father's business. His father refused. "He didn't send me to Harvard to run his business," Sena said. "He wanted me to have a glamorous job." Undaunted, at age 29, Sena set up his own bus company, Shuttlejack, in Santa Fe, NM, with $200 he borrowed from his wife. He has since become a millionaire and bought out his father's company.

Sena agreed that the bus business lacks glamour. "It is a low-technology industry." What attracted him to it was the vast opportunity the industry presented, but he acknowledged that "things have to be done differently from the past. Up until 1980, about 65 percent of bus transportation was dominated by Greyhound. It was a regulated industry until then. Greyhound was profitable for decades without having to compete. Since deregulation, the market has changed, but [companies like] Greyhound didn't. There is great opportunity for those with a different perspective. [Large companies like Greyhound] are dinosaurs in a dying age."

Shuttlejack offers a mixture of point-to-point, group, and charter services. "Groups and charters is a growth business, though not necessarily profit-making," Sena said. "It gives good cash flow, but marketing costs are high." The company sells direct and through travel agents.

One way in which Shuttlejack has been innovative is in marketing its tours. "A bus company might want to run a Pueblo Indian tour of the Southwest or a New York City–to–New England fall foliage trip," said Sena. "Usually, they run an ad and take the general public. We would do it differently. We would go to a foundation like the New York City Ballet and offer to do the tour as a fundraiser, giving them 20 percent of the cut, like a travel agent. Then we only have to convince one person to get hundreds of passengers."

In another instance, Sena ran tours to Kansas "when no one else did–showing wheat to Japanese farmers, marketing the trip through a Japanese cooperative. There is nothing in Kansas, but they wanted to see agricultural products and equipment." He brought another group from Japan to New Mexico to observe solar energy and nuclear power installations. "The Japanese love seeing Indians, too."

Shuttlejack operates in Albuquerque, Santa Fe, and Dallas, and it is expanding in these cities as well as adding others. The company employs about 100 people. The key job categories include bus drivers, maintenance personnel, mechanics, repairers, bus washers, marketing and sales representatives, managers, and executives.

"Few look for a career in the bus business. Usually, we steal from the hotels – this is a similar service. We offer more money. It can pay well." Sena pays his managers $65,000, "a lot for this kind of business."

Shuttlejack does its own tours and employs a tour planner who had worked for AAA Worldwide and was an amateur historian and expert tour planner.

Sena does not necessarily look for experience when he hires, however. "I have mixed feelings. There is a lot of carryover from the 'dinosaurs.'" He recalls having hired a 14-year veteran of a major bus company whom he fired after a year. "He had six months of experience after 14 years."

He strives for a mix of experienced people with those who are innovative, creative, energetic, and not blinded by tradition. Among the qualities he looks for in a new hire are a "willingness to learn, to change, to innovate, [to] be creative, to accept responsibility above and beyond what's assigned; willingness to experiment; willingness to accept criticism when wrong."

Among the positions are mechanics (they can have a great future, rising to a $60,000 salary and becoming superintendent of maintenance); operations jobs such as dispatcher (frequently bus drivers are promoted to this position); and sales representative, who calls upon organizations such as churches, schools, convention planning companies, and travel agencies. Marketing people are frequently drawn from the ranks of tour escorts.

"To upgrade the status of the industry," Sena said, "we need people who are more consumer-oriented, who can take a marketing position." For marketers, Sena looks for people who have already worked in a service business, such as MacDonald's or a hotel. "Part-time experience while going to school is good."

Like so many of the travel industry segments, this one has its own captivating magic. "Once you get diesel in your blood, you can't get it out," said Sena. "People tend to stay in the business. There is a clubby atmosphere."

Contacts and Sources

American Bus Association, 1015 Fifteenth St., NW, Ste. 250, Washington, D.C. 20005, tel. 202-842-1645; publishes a monthly magazine called *Destinations* as well as an annual report; conducts annual conferences, which are sources of leads for jobs. Another industry publication is *Bus Ride*.

National Tour Association (NTA), 546 W. Main St., Lexington, KY 40508, tel. 606-253-1036.

National Motorcoach Marketing Network, 10527 Braddock Rd., Ste. C, Fairfax, VA 22032, tel. 703-250-7897; publishes a membership directory and will refer résumés.

United Bus Owners Association, 1300 L St., NW, Ste. 1050, Washington, D.C. 20005, tel. 202-484-5623.

13

The Cruise Industry

Cruise Industry Overview

Until recently, those who would have quested after the glamorous life aboard ship as depicted on the popular television show *Love Boat* might have found opportunities extremely limited. But all this is changing. The cruise industry, still technically in its infancy, is undergoing phenomenal growth as more and more people discover this vacation alternative.

Indeed, the industry tripled the number of cruise passengers between 1970, when only 500,000 people cruised, and 1984, when the number swelled to 1.76 million passengers, who generated $1.2 billion. Cruiselines achieved this growth largely by repositioning the concept of "cruise" away from the notion of a mode of transportation to that of a destination/resort product. Since then, scores of new packages and programs have successfully tapped new cruise customers. During the 1980s, the cruise industry grew at an average rate of 10.5 percent a year; by 1990, it carried 4.6 million North American passengers, who generated $5 billion in revenue.

The industry expects the volume to triple again to 10 million passengers by the year 2000. The result will be 50 more ships (for a total of 200) and about 30,000 more jobs (to 78,500) by 1994. Presently, about 10,000 Americans work for the cruiselines while another 20,000 indirectly obtain income from the passenger-ship industry.

Not too long ago, great ships like the *Queen Mary* were the main form of intercontinental transportation. Fortunes sank when High Society (the mainstay of the cruise-going public) became the jetsetters. The industry struggled along until the aura of *Now Voyager,* where Bette Davis is pictured as a debutante who falls in love while on a long-distance sail to South America, gave way to "Love Boat," where it seems whole boatloads find their true love. It was then that vast new groups of people began to see themselves cruising, too. Consequently, instead of competing with the airlines, the shiplines became their partners and now compete instead with destinations, resorts, and other vacation alternatives.

Tip of the Iceberg

Despite the impressive growth rate, Cruise Lines International Association (CLIA), a marketing organization, estimates that only 5 percent of the American population (12 million) has ever taken a cruise but projects another 65 million Americans are potential cruise passengers (of which 38 million have indicated a definite or probable intent to cruise within the next five years). In dollar terms, CLIA estimates the potential cruise market as worth $30 billion to $80 billion.

The two key reasons why the cruise industry has hit only the tip of the iceberg in getting its fair share of the market are (1) lack of awareness of the range of products and prices available and (2) fear and other misconceptions about cruising. One typical misconception is that cruises cater to wealthy senior citizens. Thus, key markets for potential cruise-goers are younger people, aged 25 to 39; Baby Boomers; people with moderate incomes; couples with children (the family market); friends or relatives of current cruise clients; and clients who have taken a resort vacation in the past.

Two factors are tremendously encouraging for the cruise industry. First, the cruise product has one of the highest rates of satisfaction and repeat business (85 percent say they are very satisfied and 74 percent say they will take another cruise within five years). Second, CLIA, which has targeted its promotional efforts to potential first-time cruisers, estimates that half of all current cruisers are first-timers, compared with only about 38 percent a few years ago. Because of the high repeat rate and the success in tapping first-timers, CLIA projects 10 to 15 percent increases in passenger counts a year.

"Let's Make a Deal"

CLIA's 37 members (up from 26 in 1984) operate about 125 vessels ranging from superyachts to superliners and claim to account for 90 percent of all the cruise business. As it is, though, the industry has experienced tremendous increases in cruise capacity that far outstrip the increase in passengers. During the 1980s, some 40 new ships were built; in 1990 alone, 14 new or refurbished ships added almost 11,000 new berths, an all-time record high. Carnival Cruise Lines, one of the fastest-growing lines, was faced with the problem of virtually doubling the number of passengers it had been carrying just to keep up with the increased capacity it brought on with its *Holiday, Jubilee,* and *Celebration* ships.

The growth in capacity has not just been from the existing lines. Many new lines have been launched, such as Premier, the official cruiseline of Walt Disney World, based in Cape Canaveral, FL; Ocean Cruise Lines, Ft. Lauderdale; Seven Seas Cruise Line, Vancouver, B.C.; Seabourn Cruise Line, San Francisco; Crystal Cruises, Los Angeles; Crown Cruise, Palm Beach, FL; Club Med Sales, New York; and Diamond Cruises, a subsidiary of the Radisson Hotel chain. One of the newest lines, Windstar Cruises (now part of Carnival Cruise Lines), has a fleet of four-masted ships with computer-directed sails.

The cruise business is further complicated by the extremely high overhead expenses attached to the ships. "This is a capital-intensive business," stated Robert Dickinson, senior vice president of sales and marketing for Carnival Cruise Lines. "All costs are fixed except food—the fuel consumption is the same for one passenger as 1,200." Whereas a hotel can break even with only 55 to 60 percent occupancy, and an airline at 60 to 65 percent, a ship has to go out 80 to 90 percent full just to cover costs.

Pricing is essential in drawing in new cruise passengers. "We are very price-sensitive. If you have 1,000 passengers, you can spread the fixed costs and make a profit. If you expect only 80 percent occupancy, you have to take the fixed costs and spread them over the smaller number and charge more."

"With that kind of pressure to produce passengers, passengers will be produced," said an industry expert.

This zeal to stimulate new passengers and take a greater share of the existing market has produced a discount pricing situation much like the airlines that frequently has seemed like "Let's Make a Deal." Always deregulated, cruiselines are also responding to the problem with new products and facilities to appeal to virtually every age bracket, taste, and budget – singles, married couples, families, retirees – as well as becoming extremely aggressive in their marketing and sales strategies.

A decade ago, when a wider spectrum of the public began to picture itself cruising, cruiselines instantly responded with more trips of shorter duration – lower-cost trips that would appeal to a more youthful, active market and reach across more income levels. Cruises were introduced ranging from an overnight "cruise to nowhere" for as little as $69 per person to wide selections of three-, four-, and seven-day itineraries.

On-board amenities were also changed to accommodate lighter dining selections, health clubs, computer rooms, and video game rooms. Cunard went so far as to install an entire "Golden Door" health spa on the *Queen Elizabeth II.* Moreover, the lines added more ports into itineraries and developed themed and special-interest cruises to further tap into specialized markets. Big band music festivals, opera performances, and financial planning seminars are but a scant few of the diverse subjects featured on cruises.

These efforts have been enormously successful in broadening the market. A recent study showed that 48 percent of all cruise passengers earn less than $25,000 annually, that nearly half are under 45 years of age, and that 10 percent are younger than age 25. The great surge in singles and families has helped expand the cruise "season" to year-round.

Most of the effort in the cruise industry is being focused on positioning ships as floating, all-inclusively priced vacations. However, the industry is also aggressively pursuing commercial business in the form of conventions, meetings, and incentives (travel awards won by people who meet a sales target or some other preset goal).

Getting In, Rising Up

The changes just described have enormous implications for the kinds and quantities of jobs available in the cruise industry. In contrast to the airline industry, which offers a very limited and specific kind of service, cruiselines have a very diversified and dynamic product, which creates an excitement that is distinct to this segment of the travel industry.

Most of the career opportunities available to Americans in cruiselines are in marketing and sales, computers and reservations, and operations. There are relatively few positions aboard ship because most of the lines are of foreign registry and employ crews from Greece, Italy, Portugal, and the Philippines.

Apart from the conventional areas of marketing, sales, and operations, "the industry is extremely eclectic in terms of its [hiring] needs," one expert declared. "There are many different kinds of people getting involved." Jim Flynn, a former golf pro, for example, became a cruise director for Premier Cruises. He started giving golf lectures aboard ship and went on to organize all of Premier's programs.

The cruise industry also hires entertainers for on-board performances, people to publish shipboard newspapers, training specialists to conduct seminars for travel agents, and doctors. Child-care professionals are much in demand as many of the lines reach out to the family market (Cunard's *Queen Elizabeth II* features an English nanny aboard ship).

The trend toward themed and special-interest cruises has also vastly expanded employment opportunities. One line has a series of celebrity cruises such as a basketball hall of fame cruise, a news cruise, a chocolate lovers' cruise, and a Halley's comet cruise. In addition to the extra people who are hired on to fulfill the theme or special interest, there are entire staffs devoted to dreaming up new ideas and booking the entertainers and celebrities.

Cruiselines have traditionally hired abroad—in Europe, the Mediterranean, and Asia—for most of the on-board positions (entry-level spots for movement into management) because wages were lower and because of the notion that Americans are unwilling or unable to provide the high level of service. "The average American sees *Love Boat* and thinks that working on a ship is an adventurous idea," said Michael Trubenbacher, manager of hotel operations for

Regency Cruises. "The reality is 12- to 13-hour workdays, no days off for a 6- to 8-month contract, living four to a cabin where you live and breathe your fellow worker. It's not glory and glamour." However, with standards of living rising and cruiselines facing shortages of skilled workers, Americans now have more of a chance.

Actually, even the on-board positions can pay well when gratuities are factored in. A waiter can earn $2,500 to $3,000 a month, for example. (Typically, waiters are recruited from Europe or the Mediterranean and, after a few years, "retire" to open their own restaurant.) One position in high demand is the maître d', which on a ship is more of a European-style banquet manager. The maître d' has to organize 400 to 500 people in a dining room, and the position pays well. Entertainers can earn $500 to $3,000 a week, depending upon their reputation.

Cruise companies recruit many of their people from hotel schools and hotel companies since the businesses are much alike. Indeed Cunard, which has a hotels and resorts entity, is moving to increase mobility between the two areas, and Carnival Cruise Lines also opened up a resort.

Working aboard ship, however, is almost a necessity in order to make a career in cruiselines. It is difficult even for a hotel manager to move directly over to a comparable position for a cruiseline. Moreover, "the cruise industry is a small family; we trade amongst each other," said Trubenbacher.

Once you get above entry-level jobs, cruiselines pay relatively well (on the level of airlines and hotels), and many positions afford an opportunity to travel—certainly on the cruise ships and frequently in a sales and marketing capacity. Some examples of specialties and salaries include:

Hotel Director Assistant, $30,000
Agency Marketing Manager, $30,000
Executive Account Manager, $40,000
Entertainment Manager, $50,000
Vice President–Passenger Service, $70,000
Vice President–Sales, $70,000
Vice President and General Manager, $130,000
President and Chief Executive Officer, $150,000

There is also considerable advancement potential. "The cruise industry," stated Carnival's Dickinson, "has not been very rich in management. This is still a largely entrepreneurial business, and there is a dearth of professional management talent. This creates a lot of opportunities." Indeed, many of the American executives of cruiselines have come out of the airlines.

Jobs are "no harder or easier to get than anywhere else – it is largely whom you know," he said.

Entry-level jobs are mainly in reservations and telephone sales. "In the process, you learn product, know product and people, and deal with travel agents from all over the country," said Dickinson. From a reservations position, "you can move quickly, if you are good, to a supervisory position in sales, in groups, air/sea department, or marketing. A lot depends on individual attitude, motivation, and ability to grasp new ideas and grow." Opportunities are greatest at the chief ports of call where shiplines are generally headquartered – Miami, Port Everglades (Ft. Lauderdale), Port Canaveral, Los Angeles, Vancouver, New York, St. Petersburg, Palm Beach, San Juan, and San Diego.

An Example: Carnival

Robert Dickinson is one of the pioneers of the American cruise industry and has probably done more than any other person to transform cruising from a transportation service to a vacation and to popularize this form of travel. Yet Dickinson came to the cruise business by a convoluted route. Raised in the Midwest, he "had no perspective and no experience," as he explained, and cruising was hard to learn. Moreover, his background was in finance and not in sales and marketing. Now, he is senior vice president of sales and marketing for Carnival Cruise Lines, the largest cruise company in the world.

Dickinson, who sold industrial tires while a university student, started off his management career with Ford Motor Company, next went to RCA Corporation, and then found himself at American International Travel Service (AITS), a travel company tapping the new field of charter travel. AITS boldly went out and bought its own cruise ship, which became the embryo for Carnival Cruise Lines.

"Cruising has been the fastest-growing segment of travel. It's where the action is. It is still in the embryonic stages. Contemporary cruising has only existed since the 1960s, whereas the hotels, the airlines are more established. The problem in the industry is not overcapacity; it is underdemand. As an industry, we have done a poor job of marketing our product as a vacation. The biggest change in the industry is in the marketing aspect, and also the product."

Carnival has nine ships in its fleet including the 2,040-passenger *Ecstasy* superliner. In addition to Carnival, the line also owns Holland America and Windstar.

The growth at Carnival, like the industry as a whole, directly translates into jobs. When Carnival Cruise Lines only had the *Festivale,* it employed 17 people in sales. Seven years later, with five ships in the fleet, it had 39 salespeople in the United States and 12 in Canada. Having again nearly doubled in size, the number of salespeople has nearly doubled as well.

Carnival has 1,100 "shoreside" staff at its Miami headquarters. The basic categories of jobs are sales and marketing; a passenger service department (works with passengers after they have sailed); group sales; group reservations; individual reservations; an air/sea department (works with the airlines); a travel department (issues the air tickets); and a marketing department (develops pricing). An in-house sales service department works with travel agents (since travel agents book 95 percent of all cruises). There is an accounting department, as well as computer/data processing programmers and system analysts. Quality assurance specialists fine-tune reservations procedures.

Carnival employs more than 6,070 operations people who work on ships. From 35 to 40 different countries including the United States, there are pursers, entertainers, casino dealers, shopkeepers, waiters, busboys, chefs, cruise directors, and crew (the *Ecstasy* has a crew of 920 including captain, chief engineer, staff captain, staff chief engineer, chief purser, chief steward and ship's doctor).

Sales representatives work in the field all over the United States and Canada; others are responsible for international sales. They earn salary plus travel expense and have a company-owned car, and two bonus plans which can more than double their salary. "They can earn six figures."

Dickinson noted that Carnival is different in terms of its

human resources. "We are one of the few cruise companies that is American-owned. We don't have the international, cultural problems of other lines. It makes a big difference – the mores of different cultures are sometimes difficult to reconcile. European owners have a hard time understanding the marketing techniques that are successful here, or those successful in Europe don't necessarily work here. The tendency in a foreign-owned cruise company is that the American marketing company is just a marketing company."

At Carnival, all the cruise ships and everything on the ships, even the casinos, are owned and controlled by Carnival. Other lines farm out catering, casinos, photography, and concessions. Thus, overall, there are more jobs for Americans in this line. (Carnival also has moved into the resort/casino business.)

Most American cruise companies tend to be inland-waterway lines. To operate an ocean-going ship under the U.S. flag, the ships have to be built in the United States. Carnival's ships are built in Scotland and England, and though they are American-owned, they fly a foreign flag.

There is a mystique about the ships, Dickinson reflected, "a magic which comes over me whenever I see one of the babies come in and out of port. I didn't have it at the start, but I have developed a love affair with the ships. . . . You position yourself in the vacation business, make a lot of people happy. This is a people business, and it is creative."

Opportunities in the cruise industry had been somewhat restricted for women, but this is slowly changing. There are now a few women who are vice presidents, at least one who is a ship's captain, and many who are social directors. One line had a woman president.

As it happens, most of the managers at Carnival are women. "They are very dedicated, motivated, and smart. I don't think any company in the entire travel industry employs as many women as we do in middle and upper management," said Dickinson.

Another Example: Cunard

Cunard Line, whose *Queen Elizabeth II* is probably one of the best-known ships in the world, dates back to the 1840s, when Samuel Cunard launched the first regularly scheduled trans-atlantic steamship crossings. The company continues to respond to the changes in the marketplace and is repositioning its product from a transportation service to a floating resort.

As a foreign flag carrier, based in England, the line hires most of the crew – waiters and waitresses, bartenders, deck staff – overseas. But cruise directors, lecturers, health spa staff, and entertainers are also hired in the United States. Americans may be hired as tour staff if they are familiar with a particular port of call.

The 350 employees based in the United States are mainly responsible for sales, marketing, and administration (including data processing and accounting). Telephone sales positions might start at $16,000 with a potential for incentive pay.

Most of the hiring activity is at entry level, in reservations and administration. Many of the more senior management positions are filled from among those that started in entry-level jobs.

In hiring for administrative positions, Cunard looks for knowledge about cruise practices and procedures. In candidates for sales, the company looks for people who are committed to cruising (though they do not necessarily have to have a cruise background), or as Fred Schenck, vice president of personnel for Cunard, described, "people who are pleasant, eager, ambitious, who take pleasure in servicing the public and have pride in the product. . . . We want those with ambitions of growing with Cunard because we see the need to maintain high standards of quality and service."

Operations positions deal with the movement and management of the ships in terms of scheduling and purchasing. Purchasing people are hired locally at ports of call.

There is tough competition for positions. There are probably 15 to 20 applications for every entry-level position. Cunard is often deluged by people who want to work their way across the ocean, but the line only takes on people who are looking for a permanent position. Mobility depends on the openings available and a demonstration of personal competence.

Cunard has seven ships including those acquired with Norwegian American Lines and Sea Goddess Cruises. The line has been successful in widening its customer base through diversified itineraries and varied pricing and has been aggressive in cultivating families, singles (with special rates), and travel-award winners as cruise passengers.

Said one veteran, "I find the business dynamic. We are dealing with a luxury leisure product. There is tremendous challenge to have cruises take a rightful place in the leisure market. People are just awakening to the pleasure and value of cruising, and Cunard is poised to take advantage."

Alternative Career Paths

Apart from the more traditional cruiselines, there are many alternative career paths for those who want to make a career on the water. Consider the following examples:

- Yachting companies, particularly those in the Caribbean (Windjammer Barefoot Cruises, Miami Beach, FL)
- Private yachts that operate out of most port cities (World Yacht Enterprises, New York, NY, which specializes in entertainment and dining on short sails from New York harbor)
- Specially designed exploration ships, such as those operating in Alaska and the Galapagos Islands (Salen-Lindblad, New York; World Explorer Cruises, San Francisco)
- Barge trips up the Thames, Rhine, Nile, and other waterways (Floating Through Europe, New York, NY)
- Riverboat companies (Delta Queen Steamboat Co., Cincinnati, OH)
- Sightseeing boat companies (Maid of the Mist Boat Tours, Niagara Falls, NY; The Circle Line, New York, NY)

There is even a vacation market among the freighter lines (American President Lines, Oakland, CA), which rent out a few cabins for cruises of unspecified length and destination. These cruises are suited for the really adventurous and for people with lots of extra time to spend. Finally, there are companies that specialize in booking cruises (International Cruise Center, Mineola, NY; Victory Tours & Cruises, New York, NY; Landry and Kling, Coral Gables, FL).

Cruise-Only Agencies

Cruising is the fastest-growing segment of the travel industry for travel agencies. Travel agents book about 95 percent of the cruise product. The CLIA's report that the cruise industry is potentially worth $30 billion to $80 billion means that it is potentially worth $3 billion to $8 billion in commissions, compared with $6.6 billion earned on airline sales in 1990. The success that agents have had in tapping into the cruise market has spurred many agencies to set up cruise-only divisions and some people to open cruise-only agencies.

Several franchisors specialize in setting up cruise-only offices, but caveat emptor (buyer beware) should be your rule of thumb (check track records and references very carefully). Cruise-only agencies are not subject to the same oversight as agencies that sell airline tickets.

Contacts and Sources

Cruise Lines International Association (CLIA), 500 Fifth Ave., Ste. 1407, New York, NY 10110, tel. 212-921-0066; provides directory of members.

National Association of Cruise-Only Agencies, 113 W. Sunrise Highway, Freeport, NY 11520, tel. 516-378-8006; is an educational association with more than 1,000 members; conducts seminars and conferences.

Trade publications include:

Tour & Travel News

Travel Weekly

Travel Agent

Ford's Freighter Guide has complete listings of freighter lines.

14

Rail Travel

U.S. Passenger Rail Service

Railroads opened up America, transforming the frontiers into commercial centers. They played a critical part in the industrialization process and made it possible for the nation to grow as big as it did and still remain united. Whole communities depended upon the railroad; in the age of the horse and buggy, the train was like the jumbo jet of today. Tiny stations developed into terminals; terminals, into commercial hubs.

However, it is not nostalgia that keeps what is left of the passenger rail service operating. Passenger rail service, now embodied in the form of Amtrak, a quasi-governmental entity, remains a vital, if often overlooked, element in the nation's transportation system. Though waging a constant struggle for survival against the budget-slashing of the administration, Amtrak has in many ways been reborn as it rekindles an interest in rail travel.

Many of the 24,000 people who work for Amtrak come to the line for the same reasons that many of the 22.2 million passengers who ride it do—the sheer love and fascination for trains and rail travel.

In 1929, during the heyday of rail travel when the great and legendary lines were still running, the nation's railroads operated 20,000 passenger trains and carried 77 percent of intercity passenger traffic by common carrier. By 1950, more than half the passenger trains had disappeared as the railroads' share of intercity passenger traffic declined to 46 percent. By 1970, rail passenger traffic had dwindled to a mere 7 percent, and the trains still operating numbered fewer than 450. Of these, 100 were in the process of being discontinued, and many were operating with only one or two passenger cars. The private automobile, which burgeoned to account for about 82 percent of all intercity traffic, was a key factor in the decline of the railroads, while the airlines had come to dominate the common carrier market.

By this time, many policy-makers began to feel that the excessive reliance on private automobiles and airplanes during the previous four decades had left the nation with a serious imbalance in its transportation system. Many feared that unbridled expansion of highways and airports would strangle the nation's central cities, produce environmental problems such as air and noise pollution, take up excessive amounts of land, and result in the dislocation of people. The gas crisis of 1973–1974 presented a clear demonstration of the danger of being overly dependent on petroleum-driven modes of travel.

The creation of a national rail passenger system was viewed as a means of saving an alternate form of transportation that possessed a priceless asset – existing tracks and rights of way into the major population centers of the nation. These rail facilities could be upgraded economically when compared with the costs of construction for new highways and airports.

Amtrak

Amtrak was created by the Rail Passenger Service Act, enacted October 30, 1970 (service began May 1, 1971), but from the beginning, the line seemed to be struggling uphill. It inherited an antiquated business, for, with passenger losses steadily increasing, the railroad operators had no incentive to maintain or modernize equipment or facilities.

For the first two years, Amtrak was almost totally dependent upon the private railroads, leasing equipment and using their facilities. An Amtrak customer could make a reservation, buy a ticket, and take a trip without ever coming into contact with an Amtrak employee. What is more, Congress had allocated only a two-year experimental term, which made planning future improvements impossible.

With echoes of *The Little Engine That Could,* Amtrak has made extraordinary strides considering the obstacles and has become one of the largest public carriers in numbers of passengers carried. Amtrak now operates an average of 252 trains a day over a 24,000-mile route system and serves 574 station locations nationwide. In fiscal 1990, Amtrak earned $1.3 billion in passenger revenue (but was still dependent upon the federal government to make up a $700-million gap). In summer, especially, it would have to be triple the size to handle all the demand for bookings.

The railroad has dramatically improved the equipment and facilities, bringing on the Metroliners, superliners, luxurious bilevel cars, sleepers, Amfleet cars, Heritage cars (refurbished and reconfigured cars), turboliners (which operate at 125 mph), Vista Dome coaches (with an elevated dome permitting 360-degree viewing), and self-propelled cars. Engineers are developing prototypes for new kinds of locomotives and passenger cars, and Amtrak is testing the first three-phase alternating current traction-drive system for a diesel locomotive in this country.

With the Northeast Corridor accounting for about half of all passengers, Amtrak has spent about $3 billion in capital improvements in this section alone. Also, the line has devoted about as much of its resources to improving the marketing and distribution of its services as to the fleet and track.

Amtrak has installed a highly sophisticated computerized reservations system that is now linked to travel agents through several airline reservations systems. It has also created a "Teletrak" telemarketing program, whereby Amtrak sales agents service smaller travel agency accounts by telephone.

Amtrak has also become innovative in attracting more long-haul (that is, vacation) travelers by introducing an air/rail program with United Airlines and a rail/sail program (take the train to a port, cruise, and then return by rail) out of Miami, Montreal, New Orleans, San Diego, and Vancouver, as well as a cooperative program with VIA, Canada's passenger railroad. Such programs are devised by the marketing and tour departments.

The line has been under constant pressure to reduce deficits and eventually become profitable. Toward this objective, Amtrak has expanded into contract work–doing track renewal for Southeastern Pennsylvania Transportation Authority; assembling subway cars for the Washington, D.C., Metrorail system; developing the first cogeneration plant (designed to produce steam and electrical power for both Amtrak and others); and hauling mail and packages for the U.S. Postal Service.

The line now is looking to introduce some new routes. One that is high on the list is a Chicago-to-Florida route, which would cost $200 million to $300 million just in new equipment.

Improvements like these will help bolster the feelings of employees who are frequently frustrated by the constraints of working for a private company that is publicly subsidized.

Amtrak's goal is to become self-sufficient by the year 2000 by bringing on more passengers and decreasing costs. With improvements in services, innovative products, and growing disenchantment with traffic on roads and in the skies, this goal may be attainable. Indeed, ridership has steadily increased, and the gap between revenues and subsidies has steadily declined.

Job Opportunities

Amtrak is a quasi-governmental entity, an operating railroad corporation with the federal government, through the Department of Transportation, as the sole stockholder. Consequently, it has many of the political hassles of a government agency, which are felt most intensely every two years when Congress must approve a new allocation. However, it is operated as a private corporation. While workers are not civil servants, about 90 percent of the more than 24,000 employees are union members. The remaining 10 percent (about 2,400 people) are management employees.

Many of the jobs at Amtrak are common to most major businesses (particularly transportation companies), such as those in sales and marketing, finance and administration, and personnel. But there are many jobs, such as those in engineering, passenger and operating services, and operations, that are unique to railroading.

Among the 24,000 employees, there are on-board service personnel (such as porters, dining-car employees, and chiefs who supervise long-distance trains); station personnel; about 500 reservations and information agents at five central reservations offices who handle requests from the general public and travel agents; city ticket and station ticket agents; and workers at maintenance facilities and yards. A new emphasis on training and development including management training and development and an employee safety education program has produced new jobs in these areas. Sales representatives call upon travel agents and other major clients (such as tour operators).

Train operating crews (such as engineers, conductors, trainmen, and brakemen) are employed by Amtrak as well. They have to be qualified by and generally come from the freight railroads that operate on the routes. There is considerable movement from and to freight railroads.

Perhaps due to the special qualities–the romance and excitement of railroading–and perhaps due to the feeling of being under constant siege, many people at Amtrak speak of a "familylike" atmosphere. "There is a common goal, a dedication. You get the idea that the number one priority for everyone is to move trains through a territory," an Amtrak veteran related. Many who apply for jobs had parents who had worked for a railroad. "It gets into the blood," another veteran said.

The headquarters personnel office in Washington, D.C., is responsible for hiring upper-management and administrative positions. Field offices recruit for all of the union positions, track, maintenance, and commissary. After a 30-day probation period, a worker usually joins a union. Railroad jobs are known for their excellent security.

Amtrak posts all openings for entry-level management, with summaries of duties and minimum qualifications. There is a policy of promotion from within that is enforced by the technical nature of most jobs. Most management positions require experience that can be acquired only from a union position. About the only entry-level management position that Amtrak has to go outside the company for is that of computer programmers.

As in so many travel businesses, rising up through the ranks frequently means being moved around to where job opportunities are. Amtrak has a career development program, but mobility is hampered by the fact that "there is so much talent and only 10 percent of the positions are in management," a spokesman related.

The marketing area is getting as much emphasis today as is

operations. Within the marketing department are tour planners who help create about 400 national tours (another 400 tours are created locally).

Salaries are "very competitive with the travel industry," he said. Union positions have a salary scale that pays 80 percent of full salary in the first year, 90 percent in the second, and 100 percent in the third. Benefits are "outstanding," but the packages differ for union and management; all packages, however, generally include health and life insurance and rail travel privileges.

In short, though rail travel is increasing, the number of job opportunities at Amtrak is not increasing as much because the carrier is under constant pressure to reduce costs by increasing productivity.

International Passenger Rail Services

Outside the United States, the passenger rail systems are considered national treasures. Indeed, the spirit of the Orient Express, with its aura of romance and adventure, survives in a re-creation of that famed line using some restored cars.

Thousands of people travel the world just to ride renowned trains such as the Orient Express in Europe, the Siberian Express through Russia, and the Blue Train in South Africa. In India, there is a train where each car is like a maharaja's palace. In China, one of the world's last steam-powered trains plies the Gobi desert to Mongolia.

Many of the foreign rail systems have an active presence in the United States for marketing their services. France, Germany, Italy, Switzerland, Great Britain, Austria, Belgium, Mexico, and the Netherlands all have offices here.

Eurailpass, a marketing association of 16 European nations' rail systems, offers a single unlimited travel pass for sale in the United States through the French, German, Italian, and Swiss railway sales offices. BritRail does not participate in the Eurailpass but has an active organization here that markets tours and an unlimited travel ticket.

Then there are many companies which specialize in selling rail travel and tours such as Rail Travel Center, St. Albans, Vt.

Contacts and Sources

Amtrak, National Railroad Passenger Corporation, 60 Massachusetts Ave., NE, Washington, D.C. 20002.

BritRail Travel International, 1500 Broadway, New York, NY 10036, tel. 212-382-3737.

Publications include:

Official Tour Directory

Specialty Travel Index

Public Sector and Nonprofit Entities

15

Destination Travel Promotion

Travel is not only big business; it is also the principal business of countless counties and countries. Travel and tourism is a gigantic generator of tax revenues for federal, state, and local governments and a major employer, particularly of women, minorities, and youth. Even during periods of recession, the travel industry has had an uncanny ability to generate new jobs. In areas where heavy industries are becoming outmoded or obsolete, travel and tourism has frequently been a salvation. Moreover, travel and tourism is a "clean" industry – it does not pollute or destroy the countryside – and is generally as politically popular and noncontroversial as "motherhood, apple pie, and the flag."

Only recently, however, have political entities come to realize just how important travel and tourism are in their areas and begun to allocate sufficient funds to develop and promote tourism. The budgets have become substantial – $340 million at the state level alone in 1989, according to the U.S. Travel Data Center (USTDC). As a result, what used to be a popular dumping ground for political patronage is becoming a professional career – public sector tourism promotion.

The $350 billion spent by U.S. and foreign travelers during 1989 translated into 6 million jobs, $74 billion in wages and salaries, and $43 billion in taxes to federal ($21.2 billion), state ($13.0 billion), and local ($4.5 billion) governments, according to the USTDC. Travel is now the first, second, or third leading industry in 37 of the 50 states.

Politics and Private Enterprise

Public sector travel promotion is a spicy combination of politics and private enterprise. There is an exhilarating sense of being in on almost everything that happens in a community because virtually everything impacts on a destination's ability to draw travelers for business, pleasure, or convention purposes.

You can see how tourism is used to breathe life back into city centers and ports where the commercial base has shifted. In Providence, RI, Philadelphia, Boston, Memphis, Cincinnati, St. Louis, and New York, abandoned factories, warehouses, shipping ports, and railroad terminals have been converted to chic complexes of boutiques and cafes as magnets for visitors and their dollars. The decisions to make the conversions were political ones, and they intimately involved the tourism officials in the community.

Tourism affects every business in a community. It is estimated that each dollar spent by a traveler ripples through the economy four times because of all the goods and services provided to meet the needs of the traveler either directly or indirectly.

In a nutshell, public sector travel promotion is sales and service. It means selling meeting and convention planners, tour operators, and wholesalers on the idea of choosing your destination for their program; it means servicing individual travelers (and their travel agents) with information and products that will make their business or pleasure trip more satisfying. Destination marketers have to be as expert at beating out the competition as any private company, but they work on behalf of their constituency. Unlike the private enterprises on whose behalf they sell, they never complete the sale, but "just whet appetites," passing over the leads to the companies that will then turn the profit.

The field is becoming more competitive as more and more cities and towns open up convention centers (nearly half of all convention bureaus in the United States were established after 1980). And, the competition is becoming more global in nature because the marketplace for travel and meetings is becoming more international in scope. Also, there is increased concentration on social, military, educational, religious, and fraternal meetings, as well as greater emphasis on corporate sales.

The rewards can be significant. A great deal of satisfaction in destination promotion derives from having a "tangible impact on the economic well-being of an entire community," said George Kirkland, president of the Los Angeles Convention and Visitors Bureau. Doing a good job means more jobs for the community. Destination marketers are in the center of the action. The work is constantly stimulating because instead of selling only one product or working in only one industry marketers become involved with countless products and business entities. An emerging profession, destination promotion is becoming a fairly well-paying field as well.

Moving Up May Mean Moving Down

Interestingly, destination promotion is a field where moving up may mean moving down the hierarchy. When Jeanne Westphal left her post as Undersecretary of Commerce for Tourism, this nation's highest tourism post, she became director of the Metro-Dade Department of Tourism in Miami. Marshall Murdaugh stepped down as commissioner of the state of Virginia's Division of Tourism to become president of the Memphis Convention and Visitors Bureau.

Indeed, though there may be more prestige in presiding over a state's tourism department, local convention and visitors bureaus tend to be more sophisticated about tourism promotion than the states, which have come to the activity much more recently, and tend to be higher paying than the states. Jobs are much more plentiful, particularly since new convention and visitors bureaus and tourism offices are opening everywhere, and they are generally longer lasting than at the state level, where politics still comes into play.

The typical career path is to start at a hotel sales office or in marketing or public relations, move into a convention and visitors bureau, move from there into a state travel office, and then perhaps step back down again to a convention and visitors bureau but at a level of greater responsibility and authority.

Marshall Murdaugh has had an opportunity to compare work at a state travel office with work at a convention and visitors bureau. After 13 years as the state travel director of Virginia, he accepted a position as president of the Memphis Convention and Visitors Bureau, a post that paid better and offered some new challenges. In the three years he spent in Memphis, he put into place a new marketing program and helped develop a new funding initiative that provided a 500-percent increase in budget and expanded the staff from 6 to 23 employees. Tourism revenues grew from $600 million to $1 billion.

Murdaugh next moved on to become president of the New York City Convention and Visitors Bureau, a plum position in the field. But just as he had accepted the post, the city government eliminated its budget commitment to the bureau, forcing massive layoffs, the closing of the visitors center, and the elimination of many marketing programs. In response, Murdaugh developed a legislatively dedicated tax plan that more than doubled the bureau's budget and provided for 20 more key marketing and sales personnel and the establishment of sales offices throughout Europe and Asia.

Working at the state level and working at the local level are essentially the same; both are umbrella marketing programs under which attractions, hotels, restaurants, travel and transportation companies, and other industry components rally to market their services. However, while the people you serve are basically the same, "you are closer to the results in a convention and visitors bureau than a state travel office," Murdaugh observed. Also, a convention and visitors bureau is somewhat less political because it is not part of government.

Prior to getting into destination promotion, Murdaugh's background was in marketing and communications. He had been a public affairs officer in the Navy, worked in local government as a research and public information officer, and was working as the public relations manager for Reynolds Metals when a friend who worked in the Virginia governor's office informed him that the director of tourism for Virginia was retiring. He encouraged Murdaugh to pursue the job, which essentially involved marketing communications. "But instead of a product, I was selling a service."

Like many people at the state level, Murdaugh learned the travel industry on the job and while teaching part-time at a local college. "Selling travel is not unlike selling a commodity, but the difference is the specialness of the experience and people's expectations. Travel is an emotional kind of thing." (Murdaugh was responsible for the "Virginia Is for Lovers" campaign.)

For Murdaugh, promoting tourism to Virginia was a chance to "make a mark." He believed firmly in the role of travel and tourism in promoting global understanding and peace. "Tourism is the social, political, economic fabric of society and a heck of a lot of fun," he said. "The products are so diverse in travel – there are so many components and so many businesses. The number one task anyone faces is to significantly increase business through tourism expenditures and ultimately increase jobs in the community."

Murdaugh advised people who aspire to destination promotion to take college programs in tourism development, hotel management, commercial recreation, or liberal arts and study marketing, public relations, or advertising. "Tourism is the business of providing goods and service to travelers. Motivation of the traveler is paramount, and the answer is found in marketing."

Convention and Visitors Bureaus

The greatest opportunities in destination promotion are at convention and visitors bureaus (C&VBs). Bureaus are opening all over the country, in virtually every town and hamlet. Even Harlem now has a tourism promotion association (formed with a grant from Citicorp to the Uptown Chamber of Commerce). In Illinois, bureaus have opened in Champaign-Urbana, Collinsville, and Danville, and one called the "Illinois–Quad Cities" bureau has opened in Rock Island. Even areas that do not have full-fledged bureaus usually have some kind of tourism information or promotion office, perhaps as part of local government or the chamber of commerce.

Some bureaus are attached to local government, but most are nonprofit organizations backed by the private sector and funded in part by local government. Thus, while the executive director or chief executive officer of the bureau might not actually be a political appointee, politics is very much a part of the process because the bureau must be responsive to a broad constituency.

Working for a bureau usually entails being on the inside of the political process, mixing and mingling with the movers and shakers in a community. It combines some of the power of politics with the dynamism of private enterprise.

In convention and visitors bureaus, it is not uncommon to find people who have spent their entire working lives at bureaus, rising up through the ranks generally by accepting higher posts in other cities.

George Kirkland, for example, president and chief executive officer of the Los Angeles Convention and Visitors Bureau and former president of the International Association of Convention and Visitor Bureaus (IACVB), has spent more than 20 years working in bureaus. He started in Oakland, CA, as sales manager in a chamber of commerce with a small convention and tourism department, went to Anaheim for five years as a convention sales manager, moved to the Hawaii Visitors Bureau as vice president of sales for three and a half years, and went to the Kansas City, MO, C&VB as president and chief executive officer for two and half years before spending six years as executive director of the San Francisco C&VB. He next served as president and chief executive officer of the Miami C&VB before moving back to California.

One of the principal advantages of pursuing a career in convention and visitors bureaus, Kirkland pointed out, is the advancement potential due to the growing professionalism. Other advantages include the increased sophistication of tourism marketing and promotion efforts, the greater appreciation of the economic importance of tourism at the local level, the increased funds being allocated, the expansion of bureau staffs with specialization of functions, and the opening of new bureaus all over the world. The growth in destination promotion, he said, "is part and parcel of the emerging trend that travel will be the number one economic activity in the world by the year 2000."

There are 386 member bureaus of IACVB (an association that helps members target leads for convention business) in 25 countries, up from 241 in 1984. (There are about 900 bureaus in the United States, of which 334 are members of IACVB.) The members collectively represent 55,000 businesses and employ 11,500 people. Their efforts help generate $54.6 billion in meetings and conventions business for their communities. The bureaus vary considerably in size and scope of activities. Some function with as little as $100,000 and three to four staff members; the largest has a budget of about $20 million and a staff of 100.

Essentially, all convention and visitors bureaus have three or four main activities: (1) convention sales (which could be a whole division, a department, or a single individual's responsibility and is usually the largest component); (2) pleasure travel promotion (which involves tourism marketing to the trade, such as tour operators, motorcoach companies, and travel agents, as well as the public); (3) administration (financial management and possibly membership services and fund-raising); and (4) public affairs (an area growing in importance among bureaus).

Working at a bureau is more of a career today, and the pay (beyond entry level) reflects this change. While salaries at the lower level are more typical of nonprofit organizations and are generally comparable to the hotel industry, salaries for chief executive officers of the largest bureaus run into six figures. "Remuneration for chief executive officers of a destination marketing organization has become quite good," stated Kirkland, due to the need to attract highly qualified individuals who can handle the increased responsibility of managing a bureau. "The biggest demand is for managing an organization in such a way as to show a solid return on investment."

People skills become vitally important since, among government sponsors in city agencies, private membership, and the public, "there are multitudes of people to service and satisfy." This can also be a source of frustration and a challenge. "Bureau staff are on a public stage more than in private enterprise," Kirkland noted. "While not necessarily a government agency, bureaus work in concert with local government and use public money."

Unlike the state travel offices, which have until recently gone outside the field to private industry to recruit professionals for upper management, large bureaus look for a successful track record with a public sector promotional organization. "Native sons may get some preference in small communities," commented Kirkland.

Getting In

Though there are vast opportunities in convention and visitors bureaus, you must be tenacious in pursuing a job because there are far more applicants than jobs, particularly at the large bureaus in the more desirable cities. Since the field is becoming more and more professional, fewer and fewer jobs are open to those lacking experience, except at the clerical level. You can increase your chances of getting a job by taking college courses in business management, marketing, and communications; getting an internship with a bureau; working in hotel or convention sales offices or for a convention center; and cultivating contacts in travel and other industries.

Small bureaus tend to have only a few very experienced people, but there may be openings at the clerical level that can afford you an opportunity to learn the business and work into an important position, particularly as the bureau expands. Larger bureaus may have more entry-level positions, but these jobs are harder to get because of greater competition, and they may not offer the same opportunity to learn since the jobs are more specialized.

While entry-level positions are usually filled with people who come from hotel convention and sales offices, frequently the way to get in is to create your own position. Moreover, getting in at entry level may entail some financial sacrifice since these positions are low paying (comparable to hotel positions). There are, however, greater growth possibilities.

Destination marketing requires an extraordinary commitment of time and energy. Many positions entail considerable travel for sales calls, conventions and meetings, trade shows, and promotions—and not necessarily to glamorous destinations. The thrill of travel can wear thin when you are on the road one week out of every month.

Still, for those who love hard work and can tolerate the detail involved, working for a convention and visitors bureau can be very gratifying. "Within a hotel, the product is reasonably narrow, well defined," said Kirkland. "At a convention bureau, you are selling the entire community."

"It is exciting because of the diversity. You represent the entire city," added Charles Gillett, who served as president of the New York City Convention and Visitors Bureau for 25 years. "Each day is different, and though there are many things that have to be done, it is never boring."

Rising to the top position is a bureau requires "a willingness to take risk and extreme patience. You must be possessed with a kind of dedication and must believe in your product. You have to tell the facts," commented Gillett, who had to ride out a period of time when New York City suffered under an image of being crime-ridden and near bankruptcy. It was then that Gillett's bureau launched its hugely successful "Big Apple" campaign, which boosted the city's image as the pinnacle of achievement and vitality.

The chief executive officer of a bureau, in particular, has to be able to get along with people. "You have to be sensitive, have to have a strong back to take the 'slings and arrows' and withstand the pressure," noted Gillett. A sense of humor and conviction are other important requisites. "It's an interesting job, but not an easy one. It is frequently frustrating, particularly fund-raising, which goes with the territory of a nonprofit association. You work for thousands of people."

An Example: New York City Convention and Visitors Bureau

"We don't sell anything, in one way. In another, we sell everything," said the vice president of tourism development at the New York City Convention and Visitors Bureau. The bureau represents some 1,500 to 2,000 separate entities ranging from the Empire State Building to Saks Fifth Avenue. It is largely through the bureau's efforts that the city draws 25 million visitors a year who spend some $2 billion in the city, which makes tourism the city's second largest industry.

For years, the bureau functioned with a modest stipend ($1 million) from the city and had to raise an additional $2 million through private membership. Then, when the city government abruptly eliminated its budget commitment, the bureau developed a legislatively dedicated tax plan (based on a percentage of the hotel occupancy tax) that more than doubled the budget.

The bureau now employs 50 to 60 people, depending on the amount of business. It is divided into the four main areas of administration, tourism development, convention sales, and membership and communications.

Convention sales is the key area. A staff of five tries to persuade about 5,000 possible conventions to commit to coming to the city. This is a critical enterprise because convention business usually is booked five to eight years in advance and gives the destination an economic cushion for its tourism enterprises.

Each convention has to be solicited in a different way – even to the point of knowing whether or not the spouse of the association's decision maker likes New York City. The convention sales manager has to know everything about the association or industry, its heads, and the time of year it holds its meeting. "You have to know the peccadillos of the convention manager," the executive said.

Tourism development involves working with travel agents, tour operators, hotels, tour and agency sales managers, and airlines on promotional activities. It is easier, in some respects, to sell the travel trade on the idea of bringing their groups into New York. Thus, the bureau's marketing goals include leveling out the peaks and valleys in visitor flows, getting more people to visit the boroughs outside Manhattan, and motivating more foreign visitors coming into the United States and Americans on their way out to stop over in New York before going on to other places. "Once you know the program and the tour operators personally, you have to be at the right place at the right time, such as sitting face to face with them at a trade meeting," she said.

The tourism development manager spends a great deal of time in face-to-face meetings with customers, going to trade shows and conventions, and conducting seminars and promotions and travels about one-third of the year to cultivate business during the off-periods. "It is both wonderful and tedious. We identify some important markets, arrange radio and television appearances, rack up free exposure, talking about New York, inviting people to send for the catalog and brochures," she said. In fall, she pushes winter; in spring, she pushes summer.

"[The job is] wonderful and rewarding," she declared, "because some people promote and sell stuff they can't get excited about – widgets. But if you are selling and promoting something you can identify with – a city you live in and love – it's an ideal job. If you like to deal with people and not numbers or papers or computers all day, if you like to get out, this is great. This is a people-oriented business."

There are advantages, too, over working in a hotel or at an airline or at some other travel company. "Then you are selling that hotel, airline, or sightseeing attraction," she said. "But 'selling' the city, you are dealing with all levels of the industry – Saks, the Museum of Modern Art. You are meeting with big tour operators on one day, going around with the deputy commissioner of traffic and parking on another, trying to identify where tour buses might encounter problems. One week I was abroad with the 'I Love New York' promotion, the next, welcoming three different familiarization trips. The job is not Monday to Friday, 9 to 5. The hours are long. But then, no key job in the travel industry is 9 to 5."

State Travel Offices

The activity of state travel offices may come under many different titles – state tourism division, department of economic development, department of commerce, recreation department, parks recreation and tourism, department of local affairs, department of industry and trade, or commerce and community affairs. All state travel and tourism offices, however, are in business for the same reason – to promote visitor business within the destination, whether for pleasure, business, or convention purposes, and from within or from without the state.

Some state travel offices hold cabinet status; some are commissions or agencies or divisions within other departments. Thus, the titles of the chief tourism officer are equally diverse – state travel director, commissioner of tourism, deputy commissioner of tourism development, or director of marketing services division.

Invariably, though, the state travel office is very much a political entity within the government structure. The director's position may last only as long as the governor's administration.

Those who work for a state travel office also have to contend with the frustration of the budgetary process and the bureaucratic rules and regulations governing purchasing services for the department. New York State's promotion budget, for example, went from a peak of $17 million to $6.6 million. "It is part of reality; we are a government entity," said Nan Eliot, NYS' tourism marketing director. "Politics always applies."

Nonetheless, working in a state travel office is becoming more of a profession, more of a career, and less caught up in political tides. The trend is toward mounting recruitment programs to tap talent nationwide rather than hiring native sons or political hacks. This trend contrasts with the recent past when "governors believed if you could promote the candidate, you can promote the state," as one state travel director put it.

As states gain more of an appreciation and healthy respect for the social and economic importance of tourism and begin to allocate huge sums toward tourism development and promotion, they are seeking out professionals to manage elaborate, targeted marketing campaigns. Many state travel promotion budgets have been rising at double-digit rates, and many states have budgets exceeding $8 million. "When you get to that level," asserted one state travel director, "they are not just putting in political hacks anymore. They are hiring people who may have some loyalty or allegiance to the administration but who are marketing professionals, and they are hiring people from other states."

While it is possible to make a career in state travel offices, particularly as assistants to the director, the top spot itself still has no guarantee of longevity. However, even those who do not see the director's position as the cap to their career are willing to undertake the challenge and tolerate the inevitable frustrations and modest pay. They see the high-visibility job as an invaluable springboard toward other opportunities in the private sector and other destination marketing positions in other states, local convention and visitors bureaus, or even other government offices.

"I find myself learning the travel industry," said one travel director, a former teacher who was brought into the department to create recreational and naturalist programs at state resorts and parks and who then moved into the marketing slot. At the state level, "you get a much larger perspective here that you can't get in a more narrow job in the private sector. Contacts, knowledge of the industry, involvement at the national and international level. Most regard the position as a springboard to something bigger and better. Though the state travel offices will become more career oriented, it is still looked at as a springboard now."

This director had 66 people on his staff, but for him the job was not about power—it was about influence. "You are a top executive in the state as it relates to travel and tourism. You carry the prestige. The position makes heavy demands on your time—you are the spokesman for the state's tourism. There is considerable responsibility—I won't say power. You have influence."

While marketing, promotion, and advertising skills necessary in private enterprise are needed to promote a state, there is a difference between the two that frequently make the jobs incompatible. "The private sector is freer; there is more flexibility and latitude to advertise and promote. The state travel office has to contend with strict purchasing laws, follow strict procedures, and promote the area in a businesslike way. There is strict accountability. Frequently, the person from the private sector [coming over to the state] gets frustrated," he explained.

Politics and Poker

Stephen Richer had always been interested in politics but also became active in travel very early on; while in college, he escorted tours overseas. After college, he worked briefly for a company, decided he was "too issue oriented," and preferred a less-corporate atmosphere, and went back to escorting tours to Europe for three years. Meanwhile, he became active in politics–specifically, in Brendan Byrne's campaign for governor of New Jersey. When Byrne was elected governor, he asked Richer to take on the bicentennial celebration effort.

That was in 1975. In 1977, Richer moved over to the governor's office; in 1979, at age 32, he became the state's first director of tourism after the state created a full-fledged separate tourism commission. (The state had previously had only a small office within the Department of Labor headed by a former union official.) Atlantic City had just won its controversial campaign for casino gambling, and Richer became involved in promoting the reborn destination.

As the new head of tourism for the state, Richer also undertook a research project and decided to target the drive-in market. He created an advertising campaign; developed a vacation guide, calendar of events, and other literature; and created the first tourism regions in New Jersey that interfaced with private businesses.

His staff ranged in size from 10 to 20, depending upon the budget. Some were newly hired, "referrals from the governor's office. . . . It was fairly political," he related. "Things can change pretty much as the administration and the legislature's budget change."

In contrast with New Jersey's methods, Richer subsequently won a job as Nevada's state travel commissioner over 100 other applicants in an open-interview process. Richer knew gaming and, from his involvement in national travel trade organizations, knew some of the people, such as then Nevada Congressman James Santini, and he impressed Governor Bryan.

In Nevada, where tourism is the state's largest industry (one-third of the population is employed in tourism), the state was "more business oriented" when it came to hiring. All 10 staff people in the office were selected for their talent; there were no referrals from the governor's office. "In New Jersey, I was expected to be involved in politics," said Richer. "In Nevada, I was expected not to be in politics."

Richer, who has since moved on to head up the Atlantic City Convention and Visitors Bureau, advised someone who aspires to a government travel office position to "get other jobs first. Find a niche in the government travel bureaucracy. But if you aim for the director's job, realize that though the field is more professional, politics will always be there." Essential qualities for the job include "a high level of adaptability to the political system, willingness to take risk, willingness to take a job knowing it will not last forever, and planning skills," noted Richer.

"You have a chance of getting things done," said Richer, "but there is a lot of bureaucracy. It is a good field. You get to do something really fun, and, for a short period of time, you can be in the middle of things."

Where the Jobs Are

State travel office jobs are relatively low paying compared with those in the private sector and even compared with those in convention and visitors bureaus, but salaries are getting better at the top. The salary for state travel directors can reach six figures, but the average is $40,000.

According to a survey of state travel offices by the U.S. Travel Data Center, 49 states and 5 U.S. territories have an official government agency responsible for travel development and promotion. In the fiftieth state, Hawaii, travel development is handled by a privately run, nonprofit organization, the Hawaii Visitors Bureau, under a state contract.

In 10 of the states, the head of the state travel office (the state travel director) is under the state equivalent of the civil service system. The chief assistants to a director generally stay in their position longer than the state travel directors (who average three and a half years), particularly if the post comes under civil service.

State travel offices vary widely in the size of their staffs. The staffs range from 5 to 129 full-time employees, with an average of 32 per office. Many offices also employ part-timers.

The size of the office, particularly of the management, marketing, and sales professionals, usually is tied to the size of the budget, which in turn reflects the economic importance of tourism to the state. In Florida, where tourism is the state's biggest industry, there are 23 management and 23 sales professionals out of a total staff of 115; Hawaii has 30 management and sales professionals.

A key activity for a state travel office is advertising, and almost every state has at least one person on staff who is responsible for the development of a travel advertising program. Almost half of the states employ someone to take charge of art, design, and layout of advertising materials. A sizable majority of states also have a matching funds program for cooperative advertising that is managed by a staffer.

Another key activity for a state travel office is promotion. More than half the states also operate in-state welcome centers, designed to extend visitors' stay by informing them of attractions, activities, and events. Most states also mount annual travel conferences to bring together travel sellers with buyers.

A third important activity involves press and public relations. Most states employ their own officer, and the rest hire an outside agency.

Moreover, many states have at least one staff person handling travel research. And, finally, most states have programs devoted to package tour development, many involving allocating a staff member responsible for tour packaging. In order to promote more state tours, the states also host familiarization tours for tour operators and travel agents.

National Tourism Promotion

The U.S. Travel and Tourism Administration (USTTA) is the nation's highest agency charged with promoting travel into the United States. Though working for USTTA may be the pinnacle of a career for someone in public sector travel promotion, few jobs are available. Unlike most governments, which have very aggressive national tourism offices, the U.S. government has never fully accepted its responsibility in promoting travel (leaving this activity to states, localities, and private enterprises), even though the government actively helps the private sector promote trade and even though tourism has become the nation's leading export.

In fact, in 1990, 38.8 million international visitors spent $51.1 billion in the United States, $3.2 billion more than Americans spent traveling abroad. The resulting trade surplus means that tourism has become a greater export revenue producer than even agricultural goods and chemicals. Moreover, the money spent by foreign travelers visiting the United States in 1990 directly supported over 700,000 U.S. jobs and generated $6 billion in federal, state, and local tax revenue, according to the U.S. Travel Data Center.

Despite the vital role that tourism plays, the fate of USTTA has continually hung in the balance as the administration from time to time has sought to cut funding entirely. As it is, the $19.5-million appropriation (for 1991) is meager compared with what other countries spend. Mexico, for example, spends about $182 million. Even Costa Rica, Malaysia, the Philippines, and scores of other countries spend more than the United States.

"There are those in Washington who wonder why we need to promote when we're already [the world's most popular international visitor destination]," declared Rockwell Schnabel, shortly before leaving office as Undersecretary of Commerce for Tourism. "The answer is very simple: If you don't you lose by default. This is still the promised land as far as people in most countries are concerned, but we can't afford to assume that they will come without encouragement from us."

Despite the underrated status of travel and tourism within the federal government, for those who are lucky enough to land a job in USTTA, the work is fascinating and important and the people who work at USTTA are dedicated to their task. At this level, it is possible to feel in a material way that you are contributing to the promotion of peace and better understanding through the personal contact brought about by tourism. You are also in a good position to see how you contribute to a better way of life for the thousands of people whose jobs have been created by tourism dollars.

"There is a unique benefit of working for USTTA," said Don Wynegar, who joined the agency in 1975 upon graduating with an M.B.A. and who spent 15 years in research before being promoted to deputy assistant secretary for tourism marketing. "There is a high level of interaction with the constituency–people in private sector travel companies who tend to be dynamic, gregarious, outgoing. There are always exciting developments, changes going on."

Wynegar literally fell into tourism. Upon graduating, he took the civil service exam to be placed on the Federal Register and was offered a chance to interview with USTTA (then called the U.S. Travel Service). He landed the job and has been there ever since.

Only about 85 people work for USTTA, of which 55 are abroad in one of 10 different overseas offices (United Kingdom, Germany, the Netherlands, Italy, Canada, Mexico, Japan, Australia, France, and South America). Their purpose is to promote travel into the United States by cultivating favorable press coverage and facilitating the efforts of foreign travel agents, tour operators, and other travel entities. Their challenge is to convince foreigners to choose to visit the United States over every other destination.

Generally, the overseas offices have only two Americans out of about five on staff–the director and the deputy director, who are responsible for marketing, research, and public relations efforts. A recent ad in a trade publication sought candidates with extensive managerial background in the tourism industry for overseas posts at salaries of $31,505 to $76,982.

About 35 people work at the Washington, D.C., headquarters. Included in this group is a small research staff that develops projections for inbound and outbound travel.

The head of USTTA, the Undersecretary of Commerce for Tourism, is a political appointee whose position lasts for the duration (if that long) of the administration and who is subject to the president's wishes. The rest are career civil servants who earn a civil service rating based on background and experience and who can stay in their posts for a very long time (the director in Japan has served there for 25 years). The jobs pay well. Openings are limited, but when they occur, are posted in the Federal Register and filled through the Department of Commerce.

To obtain a foreign post, it is necessary to take an exam (administered at the Washington headquarters) for USTTA's foreign service to be placed on the list of eligible candidates. Eligibility is for two years, after which time you must take another test. "You have to be realistic," said Wynegar. "It may take awhile." (Actually, the next 5 to 10 years will see a tremendous turnover of USTTA officials abroad because many are due to retire.)

Positions at headquarters do not require the test, but you have to take the government civil service exam. Salaries depend on civil service grade and technical skills and range from a GS-2 to an SES5 (senior executive service).

Among the advantages of working at USTTA are the high visibility, the wide range of contacts with the private sector, and the opportunity to gain a thorough and complete knowledge of the travel and tourism industry at a national and an international level. This experience is readily transferred to a private sector job. Apart from jobs in USTTA, officers in the foreign commercial service, another Department of Commerce entity, promote tourism to the United States in areas where USTTA does not have its own office.

Foreign National Tourist Offices

Most foreign national tourist offices hire Americans for specific positions, particularly in marketing, sales, public relations, and clerical support. In rare instances, Americans actually rise to the top ranks. The head of the Hong Kong Tourist Association (HKTA) in North America, for example, is an American, Torre Ossmo, and the head of the New York office is also a naturalized American, Terence Fu. The HKTA also hires Americans for secretarial and information positions.

Americans know the U.S. travel industry and the market and provide longevity (foreign nationals usually have to rotate every several years). "An American has a better knowledge of the way the travel industry works, and a better understanding of how the American press works, how newspaper travel sections are put together, the individual travel editors' likes and dislikes," said Bedford Pace, who has been the promotion department manager for the British Tourist Authority (BTA) for more than a decade. "My job isn't to know Britain, but to be a contact for a press person."

Pace had worked with a major public relations company and handled a tourism destination among his other accounts when he decided he liked tourism the best and would prefer to work for a single destination. He landed the position when his predecessor at BTA retired.

Pace arranges press trips, supervises a department that puts out its own news and features items to hundreds of newspapers around the country, fields inquiries from journalists, works with television stations that are doing a tourism segment, arranges for major British personalities to tour the United States, and promotes travel to Britain.

Contacts and Sources

While the best leads for jobs in destination travel promotion are through local convention and visitors bureaus, tourism promotion offices, and chambers of commerce, you should also contact the following organizations:

International Association of Convention and Visitor Bureaus (IACVB), 702 Bloomington Rd., P.O. Box 758, Champaign, IL 61820, tel. 217-359-8881; does not offer assistance to entry-level people, but circulates position-available information to IACVB present and former members (presidents and chief executive officers of bureaus).

National Council of Urban Tourism Organizations of the Travel Industry Association of America, 1133 21st St., NW, Two Lafayette Centre, Washington, D.C. 20036, tel. 202-293-1433.

States occasionally advertise travel promotion positions in the trade press (*Tour & Travel News, Travel Weekly*). Another source of job leads, short of contacting your own state travel office, is:

National Council of State Travel Directors of the Travel Industry Association of America, 1133 21st St., NW, Two Lafayette Centre, Washington, D.C. 20036, tel. 202-293-1433.

For job leads in national tourism promotion, the best source is:

U.S. Travel and Tourism Administration (USTTA), U.S. Dept. of Commerce, 14th and Constitution Ave., NW, Washington, D.C. 20230; contact Director of Administration.

Consult the telephone directory or national consulate for locations of foreign national tourist offices in your locality. Major centers are in New York, Washington, D.C., Chicago, and Los Angeles.

16

Airport/Aviation and Port Management

Airport/Aviation Management

In aviation, most of the attention is focused on the airlines and not on the gigantic, complex system of airports, air traffic control facilities, and regulatory bodies that make commercial and private aviation possible. Airports are literally the foundation of the system, and the challenging task of managing them falls to a small but elite group of professionals.

There are some 17,490 airports in the United States, of which 5,089 are publicly owned. Out of all these, only 680 are certified by the Federal Aviation Administration (FAA), and only 403 have enough volume of flight operations to warrant a control tower. A mere 50 airports account for 82 percent of all air traffic. The American Association of Airport Executives (AAAE) estimates that only about 500 airports employ a full-time manager.

Airport management is a small area—it employs only about 10,000 people. Until recently, it was also a fairly closed club, and the vast majority were men who more often than not were World War II pilots. Now, a new breed of airport manager is appearing on the scene, one who is much better equipped to deal with an extremely complicated environment.

Airport managers must balance conflicting interests: local political entities, which are usually their employers; private companies, which are their tenants; airlines, which are both an airport's client as well as its product; the community, which benefits materially from an airport's services, but pays a price in noise and air pollution; and the airport's customers, the air travelers, who may or may not be from the community.

There is an intense love/hate relationship with their airports, which airport managers feel deeply. Airport management comes into direct conflict with communities when they seek to expand, yet many communities would undergo economic hardship were it not for the commercial vitality brought by the airports.

An airport is a fascinating mixture of a political entity, a commercial venture, a public utility, and a service utility. Managing an airport is akin to managing an entire city, with shops, restaurants, hotels, transportation systems, parking lots, fire and police protection, and tens of thousands of people.

The primary responsibility of an airport manager is to operate a safe facility; the primary task is raising funds to keep it safe. Maximizing safety can pit manager against community on issues such as noise abatement (the safest takeoff or landing may exceed accepted noise levels) and runway obstructions. It can also prove costly, especially in terms of maintaining expensive crash–fire–rescue (CFR) equipment and manpower when statistics say they are not needed.

"Airports are like any other municipal entity," said one airport manager. "We all compete for dollars. . . . Everything is a compromise. Grooving costs $1.10 a square foot, and you have a runway 7,000 feet by 150 feet. Do you do that or buy a fire truck? Or do you make sure there is adequate drainage? And on and on and on. You put your dollars where they do most good. That's management."

"Airport management always had two basic goals," said another manager, "to be a safe airport facility for the public to use and to be a business and make ends meet. I have always seen a conscientious effort for safety projects—nothing is ever done that would compromise safety. But the definition of safety is elusive. The airport manager knows what is safe."

Deregulation, which gave airlines freedom to enter and exit markets, has added a new dimension to airport management.

Airports are now faced with the problem of competing for passengers as well as for airlines. In this new environment, airports are caught in a catch-22 that forces them to concentrate more on passenger conveniences, such as terminal facilities and parking lots, that make their airports more attractive to passengers because, without passenger numbers, they will not have the airlines to draw the passengers in the first place.

Under deregulation, airlines also can change their capacity and equipment, which can also present a problem if an airport is not prepared for the change in the makeup of aircraft that are coming in.

As a result, some airports, such as Washington National, are getting more traffic than they were designed for, while others, like Raleigh/Durham, are underutilized.

Then, there are the airport tenants–the shops, restaurants, car rentals, and other services–that can generate as much as 75 percent of airport funds. These funds are critical. If airlines had to bear the brunt of the airport costs and if fees were too high, they would move to another airport.

Landing fees are dramatically affected by the number of landings; the more landings, the lower the cost for each one. An airport that is losing traffic becomes even more uneconomical to the remaining carriers.

A portion of airport operating funds is raised from tax revenues, but a large part comes from the bond markets. Even here airport managers are being frustrated by the competitive marketplace. Bond ratings, which determine how high an interest rate the airport must pay, depend largely on projections of future traffic, how dependent the airport is on any one carrier, whether there is a competitive airport offering cheaper fees or better service, and whether there are expectations of large financing needs.

An Example: Atlanta Hartsfield International Airport

Out of some 35,000 people who work at Atlanta Hartsfield International Airport, only about 20 are responsible for administration (the rest work for airlines and concessionaires). The entire department consists of 160 people (not including fire fighters and police), of which 100 are in maintenance, most of the rest are in clerical positions, and a few others "could as easily be in the insurance business," said John R. Braden, director of marketing in the airport commissioner's office.

"You get very specialized in what you do," said Braden. "Not much of what I do is transferable to another field."

Airport authorities tend to have more staff and more independence from the local political organization than airports that are operated as a city department. In Atlanta, the airport is operated as a city department, and the commissioner of aviation, who theoretically has airport experience, is appointed by the mayor. Under the commissioner is a deputy and a group of directors of accounting, properties management, marketing and public relations, maintenance, operations, planning, noise mitigation, and community relations. There are a few other staff positions, such as a technical person who acts as a liaison with the Westinghouse Company, which operates the airport's "People Mover" system.

Since the airport is operated as a city department, requests for new staff are filled through the city's personnel department. The department sends over candidates, and the commissioner of aviation makes the final choice.

"At a smaller airport, the biggest function of the manager is to keep enough money in the till to repair potholes. At a big airport, you become a landlord. You build huge facilities and lease them," explained Braden.

But, Atlanta had a tougher challenge. A short time ago, Atlanta was only a regional airport. Largely because of its excellent marketing, the airport has become a major hub for domestic and international traffic and a catalyst to the commercial boom in the Southeast.

Despite the fact that the airport collects $3 billion in income (which translates into an economic impact of $7 billion) and is the largest single employment center in the city, there is an intense relationship with the community. "It is more of a hate relationship," declared Braden. "The community thinks more about the noise than the $3-billion-a-year income. We spend a lot of time and money to cultivate good relations in the community. Atlanta would dry up and blow away without the airport."

Braden's advice for getting into the business: "People generally get into the airport system at a smaller airport and then move up by getting a lesser job at a bigger airport and moving up slowly.

There are a lot of peripheral jobs at airports with fixed-base operators, such as refueling aircraft, pumping air into tires. You learn a little and move up a bit until you can find an assistant-operator or clerk's job at an airport. You have to stay abreast of new developments. You join AAAE, which does a lot of work helping airports find qualified applicants, but also keeps the circle closed."

A Special Breed of Managers

Airport management is truly a distinctly different business–challenging, frustrating, but immensely satisfying–as evidenced by the fact that few people leave the field. "Being an airport manager is like being the chief executive officer of a multimillion dollar corporation," said Spencer Dickerson, deputy executive vice president of AAAE. But, "you don't go in to travel," he said. "You go in because of a love for aviation and the skills that go with it."

Much technical expertise is involved, as well as problem solving and business management. An airport manager has to know as much about concrete, deicers, fire trucks, friction testers, and lighting equipment as about how to work with local, regional, and federal governments, the community, the press, banks, and bond markets. Negotiating contracts and leases and developing new business opportunities are also part of the job. Then, there is the excitement of the airport itself–constant activity, constant challenge.

If these challenges are the sort that interest you, the greater challenge is breaking into the field. Very few entry-level jobs are available; most of the jobs are in highly responsible areas. Also, most people already in the field have spent their careers in it and consider airport management a "brotherhood." While there is mobility among professionals (moving up mostly by moving on), there has been little turnover and little expansion of new jobs. Because most of the airport authorities are agencies of the local government, salaries are relatively modest compared to the responsibilities involved. At some airports, top positions change with the political administration; at others, positions are more secure.

Due to the environmental restrictions on the expansion of the major airports (like Chicago, New York, Los Angeles) and the obstacles to building new airports of any size, growth in the field will have to come from among the so-called reliever airports–

smaller secondary facilities that mainly handle general aviation. Many of these smaller airports are thriving with the trend toward hub-and-spoke airline route structures.

Few people in the industry are confident of any significant expansion of positions. The largest airports are actually run by very few people. Atlanta Hartsfield International, for example, is the second largest airport in the world, handling 48 million passengers a year at a facility where 38,000 people work, yet only 20 people are actually involved in airport management. At small airports, a single person may handle the major functions of preparing budgets, controlling operations, and overseeing maintenance.

Part of the difficulty in getting into the field stems "from the local government ownership of airports," said Dickerson. "Very often, the lower-management positions, where someone might enter the profession, are only advertised locally because of civil service restrictions or local policy. And even when a position is advertised nationally, the competition is often so fierce that the position is filled by someone with expertise in airport management."

The AAAE is often called upon to circulate position-open notices. However, most of the notices published by this association are for the more responsible positions, which require at least three to five years' experience in airport management at a busy airport. "Many individuals have run into the frustrating dilemma that it takes experience to get a job, and a job to get experience," Dickerson said. "Another problem many people find in breaking into airport management is the financial sacrifice necessary. Although salaries at the higher positions have become more competitive in recent years, the remuneration at lower positions can often be below comparable levels in industry. It is certainly not impossible to break into airport management. However, it does require initiative, patience, and initial sacrifice in most cases."

Indeed, someone running a $400-million enterprise with more than $1 billion in capital programs in the private sector can make four to five times as much as an airport manager.

But, as airplane travel becomes more commonplace and airport management more complex and as financial costs and rewards grow, it would seem inevitable that there will be substantial increases in airport facilities and staffs. Also, currently, half of the executives are approaching retirement age, while another half are in their twenties to forties.

While in the past airport managers tended to come from the ranks of military and commercial fliers, the new breed of manager is coming in with a business, law, or accounting background or with local or county government experience since business expertise and political savvy have become essential skills. Many managers are also coming out of an increasing number of aviation management programs at colleges, such as those at Embry-Riddle Aeronautical University and Auburn University.

A Wide Range of Job Titles and Salaries

Job titles, responsibilities, requirements, and salaries vary widely due to the broad range in airport size and facilities. A sampling of positions follows.

Airports Director. Responsible for international airport and secondary airport; required five years of experience and B.S. in aviation management or public or business administration; salary $50,000 to $65,000.

Director of Aviation. Responsible for small airport, for planning and directing all operations, for administration and improvement projects; required five years of experience; salary $46,800 to $54,200.

Managing Director of Operations. Responsible for metropolitan airport; salary $45,900.

Director of Operations. Responsible for metropolitan airport, to supervise, direct, administer, and coordinate crash–fire–rescue, police, maintenance, and custodial departments, to handle construction, design, planning, public affairs, and airport operations matters; required four-year college degree in aviation management, engineering, or business administration and three years of experience; salary $42,000 to $56,000.

Airport Manager. Responsible for regional airport, for administration, supervision, and direction of maintenance, security, operations activities, and personnel; required B.A. in aviation/airport management, business, or related field and five years of senior airport management experience; salary $37,000 to $56,000.

Property Manager. Responsible for large international airport; required two to four years of property management experience at an airport, airline, or aviation concern and degree with course work in real estate, economics, or business administration (law degree could substitute for some experience); salary $46,000.

Finance Director. Responsible for mid-sized airport; required five years of financial administration experience and supervisory/direct computer systems administration; salary $45,000.

Business Development Manager. Responsible for international airport, to administer accounting systems, contract and leasing activities, and automation of all functions; required degree in accounting and five years of experience; salary $45,000.

Airport Facilities Supervisor. Responsible for small-sized airport; required four-year degree in business administration, building construction, engineering, aviation management, or related field and three years of experience in operation and maintenance of a major facility (airport, hospital); salary $41,000.

Airport Manager. Responsible for county airport; required two years of post–high–school education in airport management, business administration, public administration, or closely related field and three years of experience in managing or operating an airport; salary $36,800.

Manager of Marketing and Communications. Salary $30,500 to $45,700.

Noise Abatement Officer. Responsible to a major aviation authority for overseeing noise control for two airports; required degree in aeronautical engineering, airport administration, public administration, public relations, or related field and four years of experience (one in noise control related field); salary $30,000.

Airport Marketing Manager. Responsible for implementing aggressive marketing/public relations program to inform public about various services and facilities available at two municipal airports; salary $40,000.

Assistant Manager of Administration. Responsible for regional airport; salary $33,000.

Maintenance Supervisor. Responsible for regional airport; salary $30,000.

Airport Operations Supervisor. Responsible for small airport, to oversee construction, maintenance, and operations activities; required high school degree and seven years of experience in airport operations (two in supervisory capacity) or B.S. and three years of experience; salary $23,000.

AAAE offers an airport management accreditation program for people who are actively working in airport management. The association's conferences provide valuable education and invaluable contacts, and its newsletter posts some job openings. AAAE also publishes a directory of its 1,500 members, as well as a bimonthly magazine, *Airport.* It also has student chapters. Many airports offer internships, as well.

Fixed-Base Operations

Another way of moving into aviation management is through a fixed-base operator (FBO). Indeed, FBOs were the forerunners of today's airports.

Before there were FBOs, there were only barnstorming, field-hopping, post–World War I pilots with no fixed base of operations. The founder of the first FBOs were pilots, but they were also businesspeople who recognized the need for stable, professional flight and ground services for air customers from a permanent base of operations.

Today, FBOs provide the ground services and support required by general aviation and, at many locations, for major airlines and military units, according to the National Air Transportation Association (NATA), the trade group for FBOs, commuter airlines, and air taxis. While there may not be an aviation manager, there is most certainly an FBO at virtually all airports accepting transient aircraft. The FBO provides products and services such as aviation fuels and oils, aircraft repair and maintenance, aircraft sales and rental, flight instruction, air taxi or commuter airline service, hangars and tie-downs for aircraft, pilot and passenger lounges, avionics service, aircraft parts, and pilot supplies. Because FBOs are directly responsible for maintaining, servicing, and fueling aircraft and, in some instances, maintaining runways and taxiways, they have a critical responsibility for aviation safety.

Sometimes, a single full-service FBO will provide all of these services. Some 80 percent of all FBOs maintain an air taxi service, making this type of company an integral part of the air transportation system.

Most FBOs are relatively small companies. A medium-sized operator might have 50 people and annual sales of $5 million from all sources; they might support 40 based aircraft.

NATA estimates that there are about 4,000 FBOs, employing 45,000 people. Mean salaries, nationwide, for managers/ supervisors, according to NATA are:

Avionics Manager, $34,800
Building Maintenance Manager, $24,000
Chief Flight Instructor, $25,200
Chief Pilot, $33,600
Comptroller, $42,000
General Manager, $45,600
Flight Operations Manager, $40,200
Line Service Manager, $26,400
Line Service Supervisor, $22,800
Maintenance Manager, $38,400
Maintenance Supervisor, $32,400
Marketing Manager, $37,200
Parts Manager, $27,600
Parts Supervisor, $27,600

Hourly wage earners include:

Avionics Specialist, $12.67
Dispatcher, $8.50
Inspector, $15.00

Line Personnel (who fuel/direct planes), $7.00
Mechanic with A&P, $11.25
Mechanic without A&P, $8.60

Deregulation has vastly increased business for FBOs, particularly among the new carriers, which cannot afford to have their own service and maintenance facilities. Most airlines today, however, are also interested in contracting out services, particularly when they go into a new location. Even at large facilities, aircraft refueling and deicing are done on a contractual basis by the airline and the FBO. "They [the airlines] save the capital investment in equipment and personnel and if they decide to leave, they can pull out without transferring investment," said Alan J. Stearn, president of Hudson General, a $35-million FBO based in Great Neck, NY.

A few FBOs actually operate the airport. Lockheed operates three airports (Columbus, OH, Hollywood-Burbank, and Republic Airport, NY).

Among the largest FBO companies are Page Avjet, Rochester, NY; Butler Aviation, Montvale, NJ; AMR Combs, Denver; Van Dusen Airport Services, Minneapolis; and Hudson General.

Butler Aviation International, a subsidiary of Butler Aviation, for example, employs 3,000 people at 31 airports spanning North America, plus Bermuda and Hawaii. In addition to providing fueling, ground support and maintenance services, Butler Aviation also supplies security, warehousing, disabled passenger transportation, and baggage system maintenance. It even publishes its own corporate in-flight magazine.

NATA, with about 1,900 members, has taken a more active role in government affairs by representing industry positions with the FAA, Environmental Protection Agency, and IRS, among others. One benefit of working at a NATA member business is the association's interline program, which provides reduced-rate travel through agreements with various airlines, Caesar Hotels, Pacific Interline Tours, and others. Another benefit is its 401K program for member employees.

Role of the Federal Government

Another active partner in the aviation system is the federal government. It acts as both the manager of the airspace and the monitor of the control system to ensure the public's safety.

Some 45,000 people are employed by the Federal Aviation Administration within the Department of Transportation; almost half are engaged in air traffic control. They staff some 430 airport control towers, 23 air route traffic control centers, and about 200 flight service stations.

About 9,000 technicians and engineers install and maintain the various components of the system, such as radar, communications sites, and ground navigation aids. For example, the system includes more than 275 long-range and terminal radar systems, more than 800 instrument landing systems, and about 950 very-high-frequency omnidirectional radio ranges. The FAA also operates its own fleet of specially equipped aircraft to check the accuracy of this equipment from the air.

The FAA is in the midst of a capital investment program to continuously overhaul the National Airspace System by installing state-of-the-art technology that will keep a cap on additional employment while enabling the system to double in capacity. Much of the research and development (R&D) for the National Airspace System Plan came from the FAA's own Systems Research and Development Service and the FAA's Technical Center in Atlantic City, NJ. Many engineering and development (E&D) projects are also done in-house at the Technical Center at Atlantic City, as well as at the Transportation Systems Center at Cambridge, MA. At the Technical Center in Atlantic City, for example, engineers are looking into safety issues by studying ways to improve the crashworthiness and fire safety of aircraft. Aeromedical research is done at the FAA's Civil Aeromedical Institute at Oklahoma City.

A key responsibility for the FAA is aircraft and pilot/technician certification. There are more than 200,000 civil aircraft in the United States, and the FAA requires that each be certified airworthy. FAA aeronautical safety inspectors work along with factory engineers. The FAA has a team of specialists to approve airline maintenance programs. It also licenses repair stations and conducts regular inspections.

The FAA employs 3,400 flight standards (safety) inspectors. Starting salaries are $22,894, $27,700, and $33,200, depending on civil service grade.

Air carrier airworthiness, general aviation airworthiness, and avionics airworthiness inspectors have several functions. They evaluate mechanics and repair facilities for initial and continuing certification, evaluate mechanic training programs, inspect aircraft and related equipment for airworthiness, and evaluate the maintenance programs of air carriers and similar commercial operators.

Manufacturing inspectors inspect prototypes of modified aircraft, aircraft parts, and avionics equipment for conformity with design specifications and safety standards. They assume FAA certificate responsibility for manufacturing facilities, determine the airworthiness of newly produced aircraft, and issue certificates for all civil aircraft including modified, import, export, military surplus, and amateur-built aircraft.

Applicants for inspectors' jobs must have three years of general experience in aviation that has provided familiarity with aircraft operation or in the aviation industry related to the specialization (advanced education in related fields such as aeronautical engineering or air transportation can be substituted for general experience). In addition, two or three years of specialized experience that has provided a broad knowledge of the aviation industry, aviation safety, and the federal laws, regulations, and policies regulating aviation are also required.

The FAA employs more than 17,000 air traffic controllers and is continually hiring new controllers. The FAA normally recruits controllers twice a year, in April and in October. Controllers work at any one of three categories of air traffic control facilities: (1) en route traffic control centers (which control aircraft operating under instrument flight rules between airport terminal areas) (2) airport control towers (which handle flights in the terminal areas) and (3) flight service stations (which provide pilots with a range of weather and flight services).

Much attention has been focused on the high stress of the air traffic controller's job. In fact, most of the time the work is very tedious and routine. The problem is that at any moment you can be looking down on the screen at tiny blinking lights representing aircraft and see a catastrophe about to happen.

Applicants for controllers' jobs must pass a written examination and meet other job qualifications (generally, candidates must not be over 30 years old) in order to be added, according to individual rankings, to the list of eligible persons. Those chosen are sent to the FAA Academy at Oklahoma City for an initial training course of up to 15 weeks before they move on to a facility for additional on-the-job training. Starting salary is $21,000, but experienced controllers are well paid; in a large metropolitan facility such as New York, Chicago, or Los Angeles, experienced controllers can earn as much as $90,000.

The FAA is also responsible for rule making to ensure a safe system. Thus, it employs many attorneys on staff.

Job openings at the FAA are advertised in the Federal Register. They are also listed by the Office of Personnel Management, which has offices in Washington D.C. and most large cities.

Port Management

Besides the airports, the nation's leading ports for passenger shipping provide additional job opportunities. There are 180 ports in the United States. The largest ports, which handle millions of passengers a year, like the Port of Seattle, may have thousands of employees; the smallest ones may have only two or three (director, secretary, and an assistant). The busiest ports for passenger shipping are Miami, Port Everglades (Ft. Lauderdale), Port Canaveral, Los Angeles, Vancouver, New York, St. Petersburg, Palm Beach, San Juan, and San Diego. The average number of employees is 279.

Many ports are part of a port authority that may also manage the airport and may be a public entity. Governmental port authorities are usually headed by political appointees, which helps these authorities negotiate difficult political waters. Of the 28,000 people nationally who work in port management, about one-third work for the Port Authority of New York and New Jersey, which manages three airports and the World Trade Center in addition to the seaport.

According to the American Association of Port Authorities the average U.S. port director's salary is $79,518, with a range of $42,283 to $170,000. The average age of a port director is 50, and the average tenure is 5 years.

The major passenger shipping ports usually have a marketing department responsible for attracting cruiselines to the port. Other types of port positions and average salaries are:

Deputy Port Director, $65,448

Executive Assistant, $39,232

General Counsel, $49,795

Director of Administration, $55,693
Director of Finance, $50,000
Manager of Computer Services, $46,833
Port Engineer, $59,620
Director of Environmental Affairs, $51,716
Director of Government Relations, $53,693
Director of Personnel, $43,130
Risk Manager, $40,456
Director of Planning, $52,183
Director of Research, $50,543
Director of Operations, $53,863
Chief of Security, $41,912
Harbor Master, $39,928
Traffic Manager, $45,819
Trade Promotion Coordinator, $51,825
Director of Trade Development, $56,207
Manager of Intermodal Services, $51,769

The American Association of Port Authorities represents 125 port authorities in the United States, Canada, and Latin America. Professional opportunities are posted in its newsletter, and the association helps field inquiries.

Safety and Security

Safety-Minded Professionals

Every airline has a safety director, typically someone who has come up through engineering. A flight safety analyst reporting to the director of flight safety for one international carrier, for example, was responsible for identifying problems that could interfere with safe cockpit operations, analyzing flight accident/incident data and writing reports for management to use in preventing accidents/incidents, and investigating and reporting on serious incidents; this safety analyst earned $33,500.

Safety-minded professionals are also employed by the National Transportation Safety Board, a federal agency. It has 315 employees, most of whom are accident investigators, clericals, computer professionals, and management people. Civil service jobs are posted by the office of Personnel Management, Washington, D.C.

Increased Concern with Security

Since the 1970s, when airlines became a popular target for hijackers and terrorists, the FAA and the aviation industry, in particular, have become concerned with security issues. Every airline now has a security department. American Airlines, for example, has a department of 40 people who handle 500 to 600 investigations each month. They are involved with international terrorism, fraud (such as stolen tickets and credit card fraud), and drug trafficking.

Security departments are usually filled with retired law enforcement officers as well as attorneys because they are familiar with federal and local laws. Occasionally, airline ticket agents can shift over to security, due to their expertise in ticketing.

Homer Boynton, managing director of security for American Airlines, said he regards himself as a "businessman rather than a travel professional." Nonetheless, "the airline industry itself is fascinating." Indeed, the department is flooded with 10 to 15 résumés a week.

A host of consultancies also have emerged. Many, such as Security International, Herndon, VA, and Secure Flight International, Washington, D.C., have been set up by former FAA officials. Security firms employ a spectrum of professionals including engineers, accountants, and lawyers.

Security International is involved in developing security systems for airports that screen passengers and baggage and control access to preserve a "sterile environment" within the airport. Techniques involve badge readers, closed-circuit televisions, computer systems, and architectural design and planning. Some other consultancies are involved in the international arena, setting up systems for airports abroad.

Maritime security also presents many opportunities with shiplines and ports. These professionals focus on the smuggling of contraband and narcotics (multimillion dollar fines levied by the government when drugs are discovered have put some shipping companies out of business). They have become increasingly concerned with terrorism. Cruise ships, which are actually small floating cities, also present most of the problems that occur onshore, including burglaries, assaults, and rape.

Many cruiselines have small security departments and contract security companies at the ports of call. Every port has a security department, as well; the Port of Miami, for example, employs 55 people.

Part of the responsibility of a port's security department is to work with the many federal, state, and local agencies also concerned with law enforcement, including Customs, Immigration, border patrol, Agriculture, Health, FBI, Secret Service (since dignitaries and presidents regularly pass through ports), Coast Guard, and Marine patrol. Mock exercises are held to make sure that all the appropriate agencies work together as a team during a security crisis such as a terrorist attack.

Contacts and Sources

American Association of Airport Executives (AAAE), 4212 King St., Alexandria VA 22302, tel. 703-824-0500.

National Air Transportation Association (NATA), 4226 King St., Alexandria, VA 22302, tel. 703-845-9000; provides a membership directory (available to nonmembers for $45).

Federal Aviation Administration (FAA), Special Examining Division, AAC-80, P.O. Box 26650, Oklahoma City, OK 73126; provides applications for FAA inspectors and controllers jobs (as does the Office of Personnal Management).

Office of Personnel Management, 1900 E St., NW, Washington, D.C. 20415; posts civil service jobs relating to airport/aviation and port management.

American Association of Port Authorities, 1010 Duke St., Alexandria, VA 22314, tel. 703-684-5700.

National Transportation Safety Board, 800 Independence Ave., SW, Washington, D.C. 20594.

American Society for Industrial Security, 1655 North Ft. Myer Dr., Ste. 1200, Arlington, VA 22209, tel. 703-522-5800; represents 47,000 security professionals worldwide.

Ancillary Functions

17

Support Services

Support Services Overview

An industry as large and as complex as travel and tourism gives rise to a whole host of support services that indirectly make their activities possible. The list is endless but includes technology, research, marketing, advertising, graphic arts, law, and finance.

Though many of these services may actually be outside the industry, people who work for support services become integrated into the industry as they work with the same people, react to the same issues, develop the same product, and work toward the same goal of promoting travel and tourism. While many of these jobs also provide ample opportunity to travel, there is an added advantage of working on the periphery of the industry: The pay levels reflect the industry that you are actually in rather than the one that you are on the edge of and thus may be higher. Frequently, too, working in a support service can be a way into the travel industry from a nontravel work background since you learn the industry as well as any insider, go to many of the same conferences and meetings, and make the same contacts.

For so many who come into the travel industry, working in travel fulfills a dream of traveling. Many other kinds of interests and activities, however, are equally compelling—such as journalism or photography, for example. For people who have been frustrated to find conventional career paths in these fields closed, support service companies provide a suitable alternative for realizing a professional dream.

Countless activities provide the opportunity to practice a craft and yet enjoy the dynamism, vitality, and excitement of the travel industry and its people. This chapter deals with only a few support services, including:

- Travel technology
- Research and marketing
- Advertising
- Public relations
- Travel writing
- Travel photography
- Education and training
- Association work
- Travel industry law
- Off-tariff retailers, consolidators, and travel clubs
- Nontravel services

Travel Technology

The travel industry is evolving into an information business. Those who have access to and can deliver the best, most complete, and accurate information the fastest will be the most successful.

Travel is a completely perishable product—after all, airline seats or hotel rooms cannot be stored on the shelf for a markdown sale at some later date. Profitability often hinges on forecasting demand precisely and stimulating sales where necessary with prices. Pricing has become extremely complex, sensitive to seasons, months, days, and even the time of day. Pricing is so complex that the only way to keep track of inventory is via computer and the only way to communicate to travel agents and others who sell the product is by computer-based communications systems.

Being computer-literate has become almost a prerequisite for many positions, particularly for travel agents. Virtually every company of any size, whether it is a travel agency, a hotel company, or an airline or a tour operation, now has a management information systems (MIS) department. But, apart from the legions of computer and technical people at individual companies, an increasing number of technology companies are emerging to cater to travel. Indeed, travel technology is emerging as a separate, multibillion-dollar industry.

It is only natural that technology should continue to shape the travel industry since the industry has always been technology driven: The ocean steamer, the railroad, the airplane, the jet, the elevator, and air conditioning all revolutionized travel. The latest wave of technology, however, has impacted most directly the marketing and delivery of services rather than the product.

Technology is a tool of competitiveness, a way of managing product and price (yield management) and boosting productivity. Because new systems can cost millions of dollars to develop, technology has been a factor in changing the economics of the travel industry, pressuring small-scale companies to consolidate into bottom-line-driven big businesses.

The ability to forecast demand, modify prices for specific departures, and relay this information to retailers and consumers is especially critical to cruiselines, for example. Cruiselines only break even after 90 to 95 percent of the berths are sold. Being able to sell off the extra 5 to 10 percent of seats is the difference between profit and loss.

Computer-based information systems have become a multibillion-dollar industry within the travel industry, and this is only the beginning. Scores of systems and software are being developed for the trade—computerized listings of tours, cruises, and destination information; accounting systems; reservations systems; and ticket delivery; to name just a few.

Different Facets

There are many different facets of travel technology. Computer reservations systems (CRS) that serve the airlines is probably the largest and most encompassing area. These entities originated with American, United, Delta, TWA, and Eastern Airlines but are increasingly being spun off as independent companies (such as AMR's Sabre Travel Information Network, a $655-million company; Worldspan; Covia Corporation; and SystemOne). Now, even IBM and EDS are getting into the act, hoping to acquire one of the systems.

The increasing sophistication of the travel business has spawned a subindustry of back-office computer systems that link up with the front-end airline reservations systems. Estimates put this industry at $50 million a year. Perhaps 20 or 30 companies are producing software. The leaders in the field are the subsidiary companies of American (ADS) and Covia (ABS), but there are many smaller, independent companies.

Satellite ticket printers (STPs) represent the fastest-growing segment of retail travel. A more sophisticated concept of satellite ticket delivery networks is evolving from the concept of STPs—electronic ticket delivery networks (ETDNs). Moreover, self-ticketing devices, operating much like bank automated-teller machines (ATMs), are paving the way for new entrants into retail travel, including banks.

There is an explosion in videotext services, which yield "information on demand" and are being used by destinations to facilitate travel through their areas using computerized "welcome centers" at highways, resorts, and parks. There is also a whole new field of slick video travel brochures, which combine advertising, commercial television production, and marketing.

Videotext and various forms of information-on-demand technologies are being devised to integrate the computerized reservations systems with video images (such as PARS' IRIS, Sabrevision, and Jagua). These systems are intended as tools for travel agents. Consumer-oriented equivalents (videokiosks) are being developed by some entrepreneurial companies and will enable consumers to learn about travel products and book trips through a device at the place of purchase, such as a supermarket or department store.

Computer-based shop-at-home systems have sprung up that enable travel suppliers to reach consumers instantly and give them an ability to sell off unsold products at discounts as departure dates near. Examples are CompuServe, The Source, and Prodigy. Most of the airline reservations systems have introduced consumer versions accessible on personal computers using these networks.

Technology-based travel companies are also emerging. One such company, Faxnet, based in New Jersey, intends to link consumers in hundreds of retail outlets nationwide into one central agency via fax.

Great Demand

Travel technology companies have a great demand not only for computer and telecommunications specialists but also for marketers, salespeople, and graphic artists. Technology people are well paid. Some examples of positions and salaries include:

Group Vice President of Marketing of sales and services for a CRS company, $175,000

Director of Systems and Operations for a large travel management services company, $85,000

Director of MIS for an airline, $66,000

Manager of Field Operations for a hotel company, $55,000

Manager of Systems Assurance for a hotel company, $45,000

Manager of Computer Operations for a travel agency, $30,000

This field will see phenomenal growth during the decade. A source of job leads in this area is the Information Industry Association. Trade publications also regularly follow technology developments and companies.

Research and Marketing

Seemingly trivial matters such as whether to change the number of seats in first class on an airplane, convert a floor in a hotel to make it exclusively for women, or introduce a tiered price structure for ski lift tickets can have vast financial consequence. Such decisions are not made without extensive market research. Research guides decisions such as whether a business should open at all, whether there is a niche for a company, whether there is sufficient demand to move into another's market, whether a "package" for the product (the brochure, direct-mail piece, hotel interior design) is effective, or what level of discount will stimulate sales and yield a profit as well.

As the travel industry has grown and become more sophisticated and more professional, the financial stakes have been raised. Consequently, a whole industry of professional research companies has sprung up to service travel companies, destinations, governments, and developers.

Generally, only the large companies can afford to support their own research staff person or department or to commission a study. But increasingly, even smaller entities are committing resources to research. The Hilton New Orleans Riverside and Towers, for example, employed its own research analyst. Research professionals are employed by airlines and other transportation companies, hotel companies, tourist offices, trade associations, advertising agencies, the consumer and trade press, in addition to being employed by specialized research companies.

The number of research companies specializing in travel and tourism has exploded in recent years. Many general companies, such as Gallup and Louis Harris, have also become active in the field. Most of the research firms dedicated to travel and tourism are small, but there are giants such as Pannell Kerr Foster, a company specializing in hotel research, which has offices worldwide and thousands of employees.

"We deal so much with the vice presidents of marketing of airlines, cruiselines, and the like," stated Stanley Plog, president of Plog Research, a large research company in Reseda, CA, which handles travel research projects among others and employs several hundred people. "You are at the heart of the dynamics of the industry. Markets are changing all the time."

Even before deregulation, change was constant. But then, there was a certain predictability, even seasonality. Now, companies have to be able to respond sometimes the very same day to a competitor's initiative.

"Clients have to figure out how to position themselves," said Plog. "That's what research does. We help them develop a strategy. We help them think about the future in a different way. We help design new airplanes with the customer in mind. We work with cruiselines and destinations on how they should advertise themselves. We help developers design a resort, help transportation companies create an appropriate fare structure."

Companies also need to monitor themselves to make sure they are "delivering" what is promised. To measure how well companies are accomplishing this, a research company may survey travel agents. Research can also tell clients whether travel agents are "delivering" for them effectively.

Research companies usually look for people with a background in behavioral sciences and experimental methodology, statistics, or economics. Jobs include analysts, statisticians, interviewers, and computer specialists. The field also demands creativity. "You better be creative to survive," said Thomas Lea Davidson, principal of Davidson-Peterson Associates, Inc., New York. "Numbers are crunched by computer; people have to analyze them. We are not as concerned with statistics or research methods. We are concerned with personality—we look for a person who is brighter than average (this is a thinking business), willing to be involved in what we are doing, excited by the concept of research, inquisitive about why things work. They can have a tourism background."

Entry-level positions pay in the mid to high teens. Growth depends on ability. At senior levels, salaries are on par with a senior account executive in advertising agency.

One of the exciting aspects of working in research is that you develop proprietary information and deal with the client's top management. Consequently, the research organization can also be a steppingstone to other areas of travel. Project managers travel to the places being researched and, in fact, log many miles.

USTDC: The Pioneer in Travel Research

The U.S. Travel Data Center (USTDC), the pioneer of the field, is one of the premier travel research organizations. The nonprofit research company, now an affiliate of the Travel Industry Association of America (TIA), was founded in 1973 by Dr. Douglas C. Frechtling. He had been the chief of a team that designed and implemented the National Travel Expenditure Model for the federal government. He established USTDC with a mission to demonstrate the economic importance of travel and tourism to the nation.

At the time, the industry was faced with its most severe challenge. Federal legislators were calling travel "frivolous and nonessential" and were making the industry bear the brunt of measures to conserve energy. Mandatory gasoline station closings threatened to ruin thousands of hotels, motels, attractions, and tour companies. No one, least of all the legislators at the federal and state level, had any idea of the devastating impact such a law could have on the entire economy because they had no sense of the economic importance of the travel industry—how many jobs depended upon it, how much tax revenue was generated by it, and how whole communities could be bankrupted by such an assault on travel and tourism.

The data collected by USTDC was used as ammunition for a lobbying effort that led to legislation preventing any such discrimination against one industry ever again. It also was used to enhance the prestige, status, and even power of the travel industry.

"No one knew the length and breadth of the industry until we started measuring," said a spokeswoman. The data is now also used to support state efforts to obtain funding for tourism development and promotion.

The battle still goes on in current controversies over the government's moves to eliminate the tax deduction for business meals and overseas conventions. Its efforts to eliminate subsidies for Amtrak and funding for the U.S. Travel and Tourism Administration (USTTA) present further challenges.

Beginning in 1979, USTDC branched out from doing only economic research (measuring the economic impact of travel) into marketing research, allowing clients to add questions to its monthly national travel survey for a fee. USTDC now publishes 12 scheduled reports a year, a monthly newsletter, customized studies, and special subscriber surveys. It also conducts a summer vacation forecast, a travel outlook forum, and a travel review conference. This voluminous work is accomplished by only 13 people on staff, including 8 researchers, a media coordinator, a public relations assistant/secretary, a computer expert, and a marketing communications specialist.

USTDC staff personnel are responsible for refining the numbers and putting them in presentable form (the actual telephone interviews, data collection, and computer printouts are handled by another firm). They do not consider themselves "number-crunchers," however. "We consider ourselves part of the travel industry rather than part of the research industry," said the spokesperson. "We are exclusively dedicated to travel."

Mobility is limited in an organization like USTDC because it is so small. On the other hand, small organizations give people a lot of room to work. "You become what you become. You create your own position that fits your own characteristics and background."

USTDC receives from 5 to 10 résumés a month, many from students of travel and tourism (particularly from nearby George Washington University). "There's no shortage of people. We take people with a research background and give them a travel background." With the growth in travel research methods at universities, however, research companies like USTDC will be looking for the specialized background.

TTRA: The Association for Research/ Marketing Professionals

Most of the travel-oriented research companies and companies that have their own research staff are represented by the Travel and Tourism Research Association (TTRA), headquartered in Salt Lake City. TTRA at one time reflected a distinct orientation to the academic community, where most researchers resided, rather than to the industry. Now, though universities and colleges are very active in the organization, TTRA has shifted its emphasis to research and marketing professionals.

Like so many facets of the travel industry, there is an oversupply of people looking for entry-level jobs but an undersupply of experienced people. Salary levels reflect supply and demand. Research is just as much an art as a science, and people who have a talent are well paid.

There is no shortage of people to handle the peripheral jobs, those that require mainly rote and manual work. True researchers, who are able to create a study and interpret the results, are in short supply, however.

TTRA handles some job referrals, mostly in the academic arena. Its meetings and conferences bring together marketing and research people from all the companies and entities that employ them—airlines, hotel chains, car rental companies, universities and colleges, destinations, advertising agencies, consumer and trade publications; it does, therefore, provide a network for job-hopping. So far, only a few companies offer internships.

Preparation for this work should involve academic courses in economics, statistics, and research methods. Some of these courses are included in travel and tourism programs. It is much easier coming into travel research as a research professional rather than as a travel professional.

Advertising

Advertising agencies become intimately involved in the marketing strategy of a travel and tourism client (airline, hotel, tour operator, car rental company, cruiseline, or destination). They are very much at the heart of a debate over whether travel can be marketed like a soap, a dream, or a service. They must be sensitive to changing lifestyles, values, demographics, and whether "cheesecake," "beefcake," and sun-and-sand are the way to sell the Caribbean or whether culture, sports, or some other theme would be more persuasive. They decide how the client should be positioned in the marketplace—to upscale, sophisticated travelers, or to the mass market, or somewhere in between.

For account executives, there is considerable travel to client destinations or utilization of client products. On the other hand, their fortunes rise and fall with those of their clients; a bad season can put them out of work.

Some advertising agencies, particularly small ones, have a disproportionate share of their business in the travel field. The advertising executive can thus feel very much "in touch" with the travel industry. "I take the 'slings and arrows' more seriously even than my clients. I make myself as informed about the industry as I can," said Stuart Herman, vice president of Herman Associates of New York, who started with a single travel account in 1967, found that he adored the product, and slowly developed a specialty in the field.

An agency like Herman Associates, which handles mainly international destinations and travel companies, may have an added role of explaining the American market to a foreign tourism director, who may be at the start of a three- or four-year stint here. The advertising agency has to identify the market, choose a theme, develop a concept, determine positioning for ads, decide strategy for running the ads—in short, "get the best bang for the buck." While this is true for advertising any product, travel is different because, according to Herman, "so much of travel is illusion."

"Every type of business has its own eccentricities," Herman said, "its good times and bad. But travel advertising has almost a total absence of long-range planning. You have to be extremely fast on your feet to respond to the changing situation—for example, the client who says his objective is to increase sales from individual travelers, and then four months later turns to groups or incentives. It is so volatile."

Unpredictable events such as earthquakes, hurricanes, airplane crashes, political unrest, currency fluctuations, and strikes can render an ad campaign useless. "Your biggest client may be a hotel in a country that becomes a hotbed overnight. There are tinderboxes all around the world. You don't know what to expect one day to the next."

There are definite rewards, however. There is a fair amount of travel (but not all of it is subsidized). The biggest benefit, said Herman, is that "I have clients all over the world; I have friends all over the world." In Herman's case, he can also point with satisfaction at helping to put a new destination on the American tourist's map – Yugoslavia.

More than simply creating pretty displays for newspapers and magazines, an ad agency plays a key marketing role. Inasmuch as tourism is a major source of foreign exchange for a country, an ad agency also plays a key role in its economic vitality.

Herman Associates, which was founded by Herman's wife, Paula, in 1963 (after she was fired from a job for being pregnant), is small, employing only 25 people. "We are not an Ogilvy and Mather. Clients here don't get a second and third team," said Stuart Herman. "We have only one team." Being small has some advantages for the staff. "There is a sense of involvement here that you might not have at a bigger agency. At a bigger agency, there may be so many layers, there is little exposure to the client, work is far removed, frequently comes back unrecognizable, and there is no control. Here, there is far less to cut through to make your ideas known and listened to."

Also, the staff is more likely to work on several different campaigns at once rather than on just one. The art director may work with six to eight clients largely because the agency does not have the volume from a single client.

Salaries are modest at entry level but are excellent at senior levels.

Herman's advice for getting into an ad agency is: "I hire people with advertising experience, but not necessarily travel advertising experience. I look for someone who is bright, who is also widely traveled. You can be the greatest art director in the world, but if you have never been to Europe, you haven't experienced travel." The media planner also should have a "feeling" for matching up the product advertising with the correct media that will go to the right markets.

Many ad agencies like Herman Associates are also accommodating a trend of clients' wanting other services, such as public relations. "Today," explained Herman, "you are not just dealing with advertising, but communications. There used to be a war between public relations and advertising. But in the last decade, clients appreciate coordinated marketing effort between public relations and advertising."

The other side of advertising is space sales—that is, working for print and broadcast media in the travel category. Publications like the *New York Times, Texas Monthly, Food & Wine, Gourmet, Connoisseur* (the list goes on and on) all employ advertising space salespeople to specialize in the travel category.

Public Relations

Some public relations firms specialize in travel accounts, particularly some of the smaller, "boutique" agencies. Public relations plays a vital role in the marketing process but has a very different purpose from advertising. The object of public relations is to cultivate positive image and awareness of a client, to generally inform the public. The message usually has higher credibility than an advertisement since it is written by a third party, the reporter.

Public relations professionals handle press inquiries, write releases, use their contacts in the trade and consumer press to encourage reporters to follow up on stories, set up interviews and press conferences, and frequently arrange and conduct press trips. Even large companies that already have a public relations staff frequently go to outside agencies for additional support.

Generally, public relations agencies try to hire people who are already doing public relations for a travel entity. Sometimes, they try to hire from among the reporters for the trade press. "It is possible to be a public relations practitioner who happens to have travel accounts," said Lynne Rutan, "but I personally feel I am part of the travel industry." Rutan entered "travel" as an account executive with AC&R Public Relations, handling the Greek National Tourist Office account. She next became the public relations officer for the American Society of Travel Agents (ASTA), the leading trade association, which put her solidly in the throes of industry issues. She then went back to a public relations agency, and eventually found her way to a position in Paris.

There are some unique aspects to representing a travel entity. For example, a public relations executive is more likely to be involved with press trips and will probably travel in conjunction with these trips. When Rutan worked on the Greek account, she spent about three to five days a month traveling for two years. When she worked at ASTA, she did not expect to travel but had to travel to regional and national conferences. She also wound up producing a film and had to travel around the world for two months to handle the shooting.

Promoting travel is also unique because the markets—the audience—and consequently the potential media in which you can place stories are so much more varied than, for example, products such as computers, soap, or cereal. The same client can generate a story for trade, consumer travel, food and wine, lifestyle, news, or financial editors. Then, there are the broadcast media. It is challenging to a public relations person to think of the various story placements and how to "sell" the story to a skeptical editor who may not be in tune with travel.

Public relations requires writing and verbal communications skills, organization, capability to take a campaign from conceptualization to implementation, and also salesmanship (to sell the concept to an editor). People skills, particularly in handling clients and editors and reporters, are also important.

Public relations agencies are set up differently and specialize in specific aspects of the field. Some are more promotions oriented; some are more marketing oriented. In some agencies, "you are pigeon-holed into doing just one thing for one client; in others, you do everything. It depends on the size and organization of the agency," said Rutan.

Public relations can be frustrating, as well. "You may have what you think is a terrific story, but the timing may be off or the client may not be willing to present the product in such a way as to interest an editor. Also, it is frustrating to explain to the client that the presentation should be kept as objective as possible, that it is not a sales piece."

The publicist may have to tell the same story over 50 times to various editors and then start over with the reporters. "But that can be fun, too, tailoring the pitch to the audience, picking out what is new and exciting."

Getting into public relations is not cut and dried. For many, it is a matter of luck, or falling in. Many public relations people specializing in travel come from trade publications or travel companies such as hotels and simply move over to an agency. Some get in by doing clerical support or interning.

Public relations can be lucrative as you move up; it is certainly better paying than the trade publications. Not all areas pay the same; an account executive handling a bank's account is likely to be better paid than one handling a travel account because travel accounts tend to be smaller and not pay as well.

Travel Writing

Trade Press

One of the best ways to enjoy the excitement, dynamics, and glamour of the travel industry is to join one of the many trade publications. The trade press is generally easier to get into than the consumer press, which has greater visibility and prestige. Trade publications tend to be low paying but afford an opportunity to take on more responsibilities and to advance more rapidly. Trade reporting usually has more depth than the consumer press; readers rely on trade articles to keep them abreast of latest developments, and these articles directly influence decision making.

Since staffs tend to be small, there is considerable opportunity to do many different kinds of reporting and have many different "beats." Also, great satisfaction comes from being able to put "faces" on the readership—you meet some of your readers at industry meetings and conferences and may wind up interviewing them. Trade reporters frequently become well known in their field and are often invited to speak at functions. Indeed, trade writing can frequently lead to positions in the industry, in public relations, marketing, consulting, or advertising.

Trade reporting is intrinsically different from consumer reporting. There is little in the way of on-the-spot flowery descriptions of sunsets, swaying palm trees, and powdery sand. Although there is some coverage of destinations, most of the articles are hard news accounts of developments in the industry, reports about companies, or articles on legal and business issues. While most of the reporting is done via telephone or face-to-face interviews, there are frequent opportunities to travel. And, due to the importance of travel and tourism to the economic vitality of nations and states, it is not uncommon to be in the company of presidents, prime ministers, and monarchs at major industry conferences.

There are scores of travel trade publications for each specialty, including travel agents, aviation, hotels, incentive travel, corporate travel, meetings, and motorcoach travel. Among the major travel industry publications are the following: *Travel Agent, Travel Weekly, Travel Management Daily, ASTA Agency Management, Travellife, Travel Trade, Travel Age (East, West, MidAmerica), Tour & Travel News, Business Travel News, Corporate Travel, Jax Fax, Meeting News, Meetings & Conventions, Successful Meetings, Lodging,* and *Aviation Weekly.*

It is best to start in travel writing when you are right out of college, preferably with an internship. Trade associations can supply you with the names of leading publications. Publications regularly advertise for help in local newspaper classified sections.

Consumer Press

Breaking into writing for consumer publications is very difficult. Most major newspapers and journals already have a syndicated columnist or staff writer.

Many consumer-oriented travel magazines (*Travel/Holiday, Travel & Leisure, Conde Nast's Traveler*) rely on staff and freelance articles. *Vogue, Glamour, Seventeen,* and specialty publications such as *Gourmet, Town and Country,* and *Tennis* also have regular travel sections or features.

While travel writing is not easy to get into, you might try to enter the field by writing for a local paper. Once you establish credentials as a travel writer, then it is possible to be included on press trips (though many publications have strict policies against accepting free travel).

One of the problems with this field is that many people, including editors and amateur travel writers, assume travel writing is a joyride, a lark, an endless spree of first-class air travel, luxurious accommodations, and extravagant wining and dining. They fail to see the amount of work that goes into the writing, from the first hustle for assignments, to the pretrip research, to the sheer physical effort that a trip requires, to the arduous work of banging out a story by deadline. As a result, fees for travel stories are well below those for any other kind of article and sometimes do not cover the expense in time and effort.

The Life of a Freelancer

Eunice Juckett, a professional travel writer since 1948, had just turned 71 when her doctor diagnosed "fatigue syndrome" and advised her to cut down on her rigorous travel schedule.

"People don't think I work. They don't know how hard it is." She would rise at 4 A.M. to write for 4 or 5 hours before the phone started ringing. When traveling, she put in 16- to 18-hour days. "You try to do personal investigation, wander around the city, get a feel. You try to observe what's happening, the people, other tourists, where the popular places are. You ride the local transportation."

Even the writing is more difficult than it looks. "You have to go beyond the normal guidebook stuff–you must give insights about travel in relation to other destinations, not just the hours the museums are open and how much the hotels cost," she said.

As a freelancer, unattached to any single publication exclusively, Juckett maximized the value of her assignments by selling each story to as many publications or media as possible. She would do one story for about 15 different publications, changing the lead and the body to fit the audience. Types of audiences are limitless, ranging from the trade press to local newspapers, special-interest magazines (food and wine, travel, sports, inflight magazines) and senior citizens and religious publications.

Some assignments come from editors or are initiated by the public relations or promotional people for destinations and travel companies. The good travel writer, however, also creates ideas for stories and, simply by asking questions, can influence the development of new products, programs, or policies. For example, Juckett did a story on what cruiselines do to make all the procedures that come on the last day of the cruise easier for passengers. "Many didn't even think about the issue until I asked."

Breaking into travel writing is difficult for several reasons. Just as someone who snaps a picture may think he or she can be a photographer, a person who can type and takes a trip thinks that he or she can be a travel writer. Editors will generally never use an unpublished writer. "If your name isn't known, editors are skeptical about what you are saying." The best way to break in, advised Juckett, is to "write about what you know well, and get two or three stories under your belt before you approach an editor."

Another reason travel writing is difficult to get into is that there are only about 300 professional travel writers–individuals who make their living from travel writing (thousands more write occasional travel pieces)–and they are an exclusive group. These writers, who typically are members of the Society of American Travel Writers (SATW), are invited to take trips by tourist offices, travel companies, and airlines and have the credentials to get assignments from editors. Writers outside this group usually experience a "chicken-and-egg" syndrome–they will only be invited on a trip when they already have an assignment. Frequently, too, editors will not take a submission about a destination that they themselves hope to be invited to cover.

Juckett, a fiction writer since her childhood, started her travel writing by doing articles about Long Island, NY, where she lived. "I wrote a story about East Hampton celebrating its 300th anniversary and sent it to the *Herald Tribune*. It was printed in the Paris *Herald* before here. And I was off and running." The key is to cultivate an association with one publication and then expand.

Since 1948, Juckett has visited about 117 countries, including South Africa, Lebanon, and Northern Ireland. "As a travel journalist, my responsibility is to report what is there," she said about visiting controversial places. She traveled 75 to 80 percent of the year.

A considerable amount of a travel writer's time is spent setting up assignments with editors, getting invitations for trips, reading background material and preparing for trips, setting up interviews, handling correspondence, arranging an itinerary, and booking transportation and lodgings. Publications have their own special audiences and their own policies. Some do not allow the travel writer to take any "freebies." Others insist that the articles support the advertisers, who are likely to be the expensive tours and resorts rather then the cozy, inexpensive inns and do-it-yourself adventures.

Many travel writers have been in the field for decades and have literally locked up syndicated columns and relationships with publications. But, a new generation is coming up. "They are clever. They study the market–you have to. You have to decide what facet of travel writing you want to be in. You can't be a specialist in everything. Some are better writers than others; others are mediocre but have good ideas; some are better at gathering facts but can't put them together in a publishable story; others are good writers but poor at research.

"Also, some are great writers, but you also have to be able to market the story and yourself–analyze the market, what will sell, and when.

"You have to be able to sort out from all you see and experience, and write about what is important to the reader.

"You have to be able to keep up with 16- to 18-hour days, to keep going and do interviews even if you are suffering *turista* or some other ailment. You have to face hassles, like airline delays or cancellations or rerouted flights. You have to be an organized, detail-oriented person, and keep tremendous files, read everything about the topic you intend to write about. You have to be flexible, adventurous, curious, interested in people, able to absorb, assess what you have seen.

"The travel writer has to be many things–that's why I got into photography, because the photographer was earning more than me. You have to sell yourself, and to know whether a trip will be profitable–if it is worth spending six days in Arkansas, for example."

Travel writing can pay well, but only if you hustle. Many publications feel that travel is a perk and therefore pay less (even as much as one-third less) for travel stories as opposed to other features. Moreover, cash flow can be a problem. Travel writers have to spend sums of money and wait for publications to reimburse them for their expenses and to pay their fee, either after acceptance of a manuscript or after publication. Sometimes, publications will assign a story but then not print it, and the travel writer has to collect a kill fee (only a portion of the full amount). In short, travel writing, particularly freelancing, is an insecure field, one of feast and famine.

Travel writing, however, is more than newspapers and magazines. It is also radio, television, cable television, cassettes, walking tours, lectures, and books. There are vast new markets for travel writing, such as serving as a consultant to a large department store that may by tying a merchandise promotion to a foreign country. You must be creative to find new avenues and niches.

One of the difficulties in being a travel writer, Juckett reflected, is that "you lose contact with your hometown." On the other hand, a travel writer becomes part of a world community and forms friendships around the globe. "You are reminded of that when someone you met in India and haven't seen for years phones up out of the blue."

The Society of American Travel Writers does not offer much assistance to those trying to break into the field (in fact, membership is restricted to working professionals who meet certain criteria and are sponsored by members). However, SATW does offer members seminars and a base for networking.

Guidebook Writing

Twenty years ago, there were few travel books and they vied for attention on cramped bookstore shelves. The popularity of guidebooks skyrocketed during the "go-go" 1980s. Today, there are massive travel sections and even entire bookstores devoted to travel and a seemingly insatiable appetite for guidebooks on the part of consumers.

Some 6,000 travel books are in print today; about 1,500 new titles are published each year (about twice the number of cookbooks). Some of the biggest, best-selling, brand-name series titles, such as Frommer, Fodor's, Fielding, and Birnbaum, sell 50,000 to 100,000 copies a year, and industrywide sales amount to $100 million a year.

Guidebooks have an enormous impact on travelers and the travel industry. They can literally put a destination, or a hotel, or an attraction on the map. Many travelers regard their guidebooks as bibles and follow the suggested itineraries religiously.

The swelling demand for guidebooks is being met by an even greater outpouring of books; competition is intense. Moreover, since travel books are incredibly costly to research and produce, publishers are hesitant to take on new authors.

Nonetheless, there are opportunities. Some brand-name publishing companies hire writers to produce whole books or a few chapters or to research some special interest. "Our writers are usually professionals with some association with the destination," related Arthur Frommer, whose *Europe On $5 A Day* spawned a revolution in mass travel when it was first published in the 1950s. "We get letters from people everywhere. We ask them to audition: 'Imagine you are writing a guide; give us 10 sample pages of a hotel chapter.' Many times, people are hired that way. One of our writers had never written before, but she wanted to do Washington, D.C. For her audition, she compared the quality of government cafeterias. It was so colorful and fun to read, we hired her to do Ireland, New Zealand, and Washington, D.C.—she has made a career for herself."

It takes an author, or a battery of writers, an average of one to two years to research and write a guidebook. Frommer spent five years researching his newest, *The New World of Travel*, which is already expected to set off a second revolution in "intellectual, experiential" travel.

Margaret Zellers has authored *Fielding's Caribbean* guide since 1979, updating the book annually. Unlike most authors, she owns the book and holds the copyright. She is also scrupulous about paying her own way and not accepting any hospitality so that she can be free to set her own schedule and report her observations even if it means warning readers against overcharging or surly immigration officials. Her book sells 50,000 to 100,000 copies a year. "Readers write to me."

"When I first started in this business, it was wonderful," she related. "I wouldn't start today, though. The competition is vicious. Travel writers are running all over each other. It's a game of sharks. It's a lot of hard work—I travel three-fourths of the year [and pay my own way]. But it's been my life, and I love it."

Among the leading publishing houses are Prentice-Hall, which publishes 10 major travel imprints including Frommer, Insight, Real Guides and Mobil; Houghton Mifflin (Birnbaum); Fodor's; Moon Publications; Lonely Planet; Passport Press; John Muir Publications; and John Wiley & Sons.

Travel Photography

The professional travel photographer faces even greater frustrations than the travel writer. Low pay, intense competition from everyone with a 35-mm camera who thinks they can take a snapshot (including travel writers), and, as some have found out, lack of creative outlets are all part of the job.

Lisle Dennis has been a professional travel photographer for 20 years. "You don't get into it for the money," she said with exasperation. Getting in 20 years ago was relatively easy – there were lots of press trips and invitations even without confirmed assignments from publications. "It's the end of the flying carpet era on the public relations side," she said. "Things have really tightened up." Now, you need a letter confirming an assignment or an outlet for the photography before a sponsoring group will provide free travel. Then, as now, budding photographers would need to join the Society of American Travel Writers in order to network with magazine editors, but membership requires that a professional already be established in the field. Even getting a plum assignment from a top publication like *National Geographic* or *Travel & Leisure* is no guarantee of future assignments.

To understand the problem, it is important to examine the markets for travel photography. Scores of consumer magazines feature travel articles. The trouble is, the articles may use only a single shot for illustration, and they rarely make assignments; many prefer to obtain photographs free from the tourist offices or to buy them from the stock houses.

Other markets for travel photography include the airlines' own in-flight magazines, as well as newspapers, books, calendars, and even greeting cards. Other clients for travel photography include airlines, hotel companies, tour companies, and tourist offices.

Advertising is a major market, but Dennis was very critical of the quality and creativity there, which she attributed to the low budgets applied by travel companies. Per diem rates are meager compared with those for other types of photography – perhaps $1,000 versus $2,500 for nontravel assignments.

About the only way that a professional travel photographer can make a living is to shoot for stock houses (agencies that are libraries for millions of slides from hundreds of photographers), which sell the rights to use the photographs to magazines, textbooks, calendar companies, advertising agencies, and so forth, splitting the fee 50:50 with the photographer. Some stock houses are Gamma/Liaison, Black Star, Freelance Photographers Guild, and Photo Researchers, all of New York (consult the *Yellow Pages* for others).

It is difficult to make a living as a full-time travel photographer; yet you cannot be a part-timer, either. Hustling assignments and shooting stock that is current and in demand take a lot of time. "If you don't devote full time, you won't sell," said Dennis. "You may hit a local publication once or twice, or sell a few shots for postcards or calendars, but that's it."

A very different type of travel photography is shooting the "news" of the industry. Bill Concilliare has made a career out of being the "official" photographer at most industry functions, and he has traveled the world shooting.

Education and Training

The area of education and training had become a megabucks business within the travel industry. The intensifying pace of the industry, the growing sophistication, and the pervasiveness of computer systems have made on-the-job training virtually a thing of the past. Everyone wants to hire experienced people, and no one has time or money to hire trainees. It has become almost essential for anyone striving to enter the travel industry to get a foundation at a reputable travel school.

In addition to the education and training of neophytes, companies are increasingly introducing their own programs to raise productivity or advance workers. Trade associations also mount training and education programs, employing a staffer to oversee programs.

Apart from some 200 colleges, universities, and community colleges that have introduced travel and tourism programs, more than 600 vocational schools have been opened by educators as well as travel agents. With tuitions ranging from a few hundred to a few thousand dollars, travel training has become a significant profit center.

Most of the teaching positions at the better vocational schools are reserved for industry people (such as working travel agents and executives from the airlines and hotels). Certain kinds of courses, however, can be taught by professional educators.

The area of training and development is becoming increasingly important to many major travel companies. The hotel industry has always been particularly keen on training, but travel agency chains (such as Rosenbluth), car rental companies, and even Amtrak have programs, as well. In this area, a professional educator can create his or her own position by targeting a company with a need.

Most educators come out of the industry first, sometimes winding up a career in travel in the education side, like William Prigge, who had been a top executive with Hilton Hotels before joining the faculty of Cornell Hotel School and the New School for Social Research. Many move into education in the middle of their careers; some, at the start. Some professors collect their master's degrees and Ph.D.'s in recreation, hospitality, tourism, or some other related topic; teach; cultivate relationships in the industry; and move into the industry. The demand for tourism professors has burgeoned with the explosion in enrollments and mass openings of programs at schools, and some instructors have been tapped from other disciplines.

Perhaps more so than in other disciplines taught in school, instructors do become directly involved in the industry. The dynamics of the industry demands it, and there is pressure on the schools to offer more relevant presentations. Many professors become members of major trade associations. "That was one of the things that was wrong with some of the advanced-degree programs of the past–they were disassociated from the industry," said one veteran.

One of the advantages to being on the education side, versus the industry side, is the amount of free time; teachers generally work for nine months and have summers and holidays off to pursue their own tourism interests. There are also opportunities to author texts, conduct research, consult, and conduct study abroad programs.

The Society of Travel and Tourism Educators allows members (about 250) to exchange ideas and techniques. One of the aims of the society is to cultivate stronger ties with the industry in order to make programs more relevant.

Trade Associations

The travel industry is distinguished by its fragmentation and segmentation. Far from being a singular entity, it is composed of some 500,000 businesses in dozens of different categories. Consequently, dozens of associations represent their separate interests, and one massive umbrella organization, the Travel Industry Association of America (TIA), represents them all.

Association work is a very specialized career, but working

with travel-related associations presents yet another avenue for a career in travel. Associations may be formed primarily as a lobbying group, such as the Airport Operators Council, or as a marketing organization, such as Cruise Lines International Association. Associations may have a staff of one or a few, but some employ hundreds of people, with much the same organization as a large corporation.

Pat Duricka Kelly was director of communications for TIA for five and a half years before moving on to become public relations director for the International Association of Amusement Parks and Attractions (IAAPA), where she was responsible for overseeing media relations, developing industry promotional programs, and supervising the association's publications. "In some ways, association work is analogous to corporate jobs," she commented. "The experience gained could be used as a jumping-off point to private enterprise, and vice versa. But it is more common, at the higher level, to come from the private sector into the association – in the travel industry, especially."

People who work in associations usually stay within the associations field. They move up through the ranks by moving from organization to organization and rarely go from the association into private enterprise, expect perhaps as a consultant. Kelly, for example, had been with a professional education society and then went to an association representing the construction industry before going to TIA. "I'm in the association business. I prefer the association slot in order to promote generically. We don't have to be concerned about carving out market share. One's livelihood is based on satisfying needs of members."

Associations have basic functions such as professional development, annual meetings, information sharing, publications, government relations and lobbying, public relations, and membership development. Similar to marketing in the private sector, they may even have a marketing function and include fund-raising. Other functions include meeting planning, exhibit-booth sales, and corporate travel. The largest associations also have areas of legal counsel, research administration, and trade show planning.

To fulfill these functions, associations employ educators and trainers, meeting planners, public relations specialists, writers, marketers, lawyers, research analysts, and administrators, as well as artists, designers, librarians, journalists, and filmmakers.

"For women and minorities, particularly, associations may provide a proving ground of what you can do, far beyond what is required in the paycheck," noted Kelly. For example, working in associations provides an opportunity to head committees, speak at functions, and publish articles.

Working for a travel-related association has particular appeal. "The character of the industry is transcended into the character of the trade association," Kelly said. "The kind of members – people in travel – tend to be creative, lively, gregarious, sociable. There is comradery. There is a travel industry 'type,' even more so a 'hotel type,' etc. It permeates the trade association."

There is also generally more opportunity to travel (primarily to annual conventions, trade shows, seminars, and board meetings) than at other trade organizations. However, "just wanting to travel is not a reason to work for an association. You must be interested in the association business itself and the industry it represents in particular."

Deregulation has made for an especially exciting time, a period of challenge and flux, and has made the role of trade associations even more vital. Organizations like the Air Transport Association and the National Tour Association had to change their focus (NTA even changed its name from National Tour Brokers Association). "As the industry's needs change, so do the association's." This was the case for IAAPA, where Kelly helped introduce marketing research.

Kelly noted that association management work has also changed with the times. "There was a time when you could say association work was institutional in terms of stability and growth. There were few cutbacks, and jobs were dependable." There is less security today, but positions still tend to last longer than those in the private sector.

While the association field is becoming more professional, it is still relatively easy to get into, particularly through clerical positions, administration, or law. Advancement often comes by leaving one trade association for another. Salaries of association staff generally reflect those of the industry it represents.

Association work provides an opportunity to participate in an industry but at a certain objective distance. It also provides a complete view of the entire industry. "It makes you a great generalist."

The travel industry is particularly rich in associations. Some examples include:

Air Transport Association, Washington, D.C.
American Bus Association, Washington, D.C.
American Hotel & Motel Association, Washington, D.C.
American Recreation Coalition
American Ski Federation
American Society of Travel Agents, Washington, D.C.
Association of Retail Travel Agents, Arlington, VA
Cruise Lines International Association, New York
Highway Users Federation
Hotel Sales and Marketing Association International
International Association of Amusement Parks and Attractions
International Association of Convention and Visitor Bureaus
National Air Carrier Association, Washington, D.C.
National Campground Owners Association
National Caves Association
National Restaurant Association
National Ski Areas Association
National Tour Association, Lexington, KY
Recreation Vehicle Industry Association
U.S. Tour Operators Association, New York

Other examples are:

Association of Group Travel Executives
American Association of Airport Executives
Institute of Association Management Companies
International Association of Fairs and Expositions
National Air Transportation Association
National Business Travel Association
Regional Airline Association
Society of Incentive Travel Executives
Travel and Tourism Research Association

Travel Industry Law

An elite but growing group of lawyers, skilled in the nuances and workings of the travel industry, are very much in the center of the activity. Travel attorneys represent travel companies, travel agencies, and consumers in litigation against travel entities. They also work for trade associations, lobbying government or pressing suits on behalf of members.

Travel industry law entails labor relations, international law, contracts, property, liability – the standard fare of business law – but there are differences. The travel industry has rather unusual agent/client relationships that are only being established in precedent-setting consumer suits (such as one in which a travel agency was found liable for the murder by terrorists of an American passenger on the *Achille Lauro*).

Deregulation has raised new legal issues, particularly regarding antitrust. There are suits over rebates and competitive practices. Heightened merger and acquisitions activity has required assistance of attorneys with an understanding of the relative values of the businesses.

The field has emerged in only the past few years. Up until 10 years ago, few specialized in travel law. (Indeed, under bar association rules, lawyers are not allowed to "specialize"; they "emphasize.") Now, there is even an International Forum for Travel and Tourism Advocates, which includes professors who teach travel law. About 40 countries have members.

Alexander Anolik, U.S. delegate to the forum, has made a career of offering what he calls "preventive legal care" to the travel industry and representing its interests. And, he says, he feels as much a part of the travel industry as he does the law.

"We speak differently," Anolik observed, while attending the American Society of Travel Agents' World Congress in Rome. "We use different vocabulary. When you have litigation for the travel industry, we interpret and understand the travel industry issues and present them from a travel law standpoint." He estimated that perhaps only 30 to 50 attorneys deal with travel law more or less exclusively.

"You have to know the industry – the people, relationships," he said. "I can look at the same issue, such as banks in travel, and see what another lawyer cannot. I caught a bank giving illegal rebates."

Anolik has served as general counsel to some airlines (with the proviso that he not be involved in anti-travel-agent litigation). He has also represented a travel agency franchise, a consortium, some tour operators, and a hotel.

Anolik, who started out as a trial attorney working for other lawyers, reflected that the key difference in being a "travel attorney" is not the legal issues but the people themselves. "Travel people are a more enjoyable group – good people; they know how to enjoy themselves. Not the greatest business people, though – they need more preventive legal care."

The challenge for a travel attorney comes from being in a new field, where precedents are being set. Nonetheless, the law is the law. "You still have to be a good paper man, good antitrust."

There is something challenging about the cases, too, as indicated by the fact that 20 percent of Anolik's clients come via referrals from other lawyers who do not feel qualified. For these clients, a seemingly simple matter like a change in agency ownership is handled better when the lawyer is an expert in travel law.

The change in the regulatory environment has significant bearing on the travel law. "The laws we use need finessing. A good antitrust attorney can do a good job on antitrust, but a travel attorney can do the witnessing, ask the questions, take the depositions."

Travel law is a growing field. Besides the formation of an association, the International Bar Association has recently formed a committee on travel.

In preparing for the field, Anolik recommended studying contracts, antitrust, torts, and, given the present climate, bankruptcy law. If you plan to work with travel agencies, you should also study labor law. Then, get into the industry, affiliate with the trade associations, and go to industry functions. "Read the trade press, get to know the people, spend time with them, and learn what is bothering them," advised Anolik.

Anolik travels extensively, particularly as a speaker on the matter of preventive legal care for industry functions. He also writes articles for the trade press. Other individuals who specialize in travel law include Jeffrey Miller, of Ward, Klein & Miller, Gaithersburg, MD; Pestronk & Associates, Fairfax, VA; and Arthur Schiff, New York.

The "Gray Area"

A constant stream of innovative products, services, and companies is generated in response to changing market conditions and technology. A group of entrepreneurs who tread in the "gray area" between what is legal and what is not is likewise generated.

Off-Tariff Retailers

Deregulation, for example, allowed total pricing flexibility and generated a new market for "off-tariff" tickets (nonpublished or negotiated fares) and, with it, a new breed of entrepreneur. And, due to changing market and legal conditions, what may technically not be legal (like rebating) can become a perfectly acceptable part of business practice.

Various forms of off-tariff tickets include airline promotional fares, unused frequent flyer coupons, miscellaneous charge orders, bulk fares, and bartered trade-outs. The biggest chunk of this market is in the sale of frequent flyer coupons; about 45 companies (many of which advertise in the *Wall Street Journal* and *USA Today*) generate $75 million to $100 million from them. This business is extremely risky, and some of the pioneering companies have gone under by overextending. More significantly, the airlines have been successful in legally preventing companies from reselling frequent flyer coupons (which they claim undermines the whole point of the program), punctuating the point by confiscating tickets at the airport and denying boarding to the passenger (which often results in the broker's having to pay out refunds).

A newly formed trade association of coupon brokers, the American Association of Discount Travel Brokers, with about 14 members, is trying to force the Department of Transportation into requiring the airlines to allow free sale of the coupons by third parties.

Consolidators

Consolidators also tread in the "gray area." These companies enter into special contracts with airlines and cruiselines in order to sell tickets below published rates (a big issue in international tickets, which are still subject to governmental regulation). This is another borderline situation since these companies were designed to tap into ethnic markets and fill up seats that would have gone unsold, but they now sell their products to the public at large in direct competition with their airline sponsors. They also compete with travel agents, but, increasingly, travel agents buy the tickets for their clients in order to pass along savings (and in the process earn higher commissions). In effect, the consolidators function like an alternative distribution network. Among the largest and best-established consolidators is C.L. Thomson, San Francisco.

A host of companies have developed to capitalize on the essential fact of travel that unsold product is useless to a travel company. Moment's Notice, New York, for example, sells last-minute, distressed, unsold space to consumers. The clients are generally "fairly seasoned travelers" rather than first-timers, who are usually too timid to travel this way. Clients need to be able to pull up and go with only a few days or weeks or a "moment's" notice. Retirees are one group that generally has this flexibility. In exchange for the lack of advance planning and higher risk, travelers get discounts of 50 to 55 percent on most products, including cruises, tours, and airline tickets.

"We act as a safety valve for the travel industry," said a spokesperson. "We generate revenue on what would have been lost revenue. Travel is a completely perishable product."

A division of Matterhorn, Inc., which started out 28 years ago as a membership organization called the Matterhorn Sports Club, Moment's Notice also attaches a $35 membership fee. The company lists eight to ten "specials" on a tape-recorded message. The turnover in product is so fast that the company does not even publish a folder. The company already has 10,000 members nationwide and a host of suppliers (who preferred not to be named).

Travel Clubs

"America is a nation of joiners," said Patrick Gorman, chief executive officer of Encore Travel Club, Lanham, MD. This club, as others, maintains that they offer members discounts that they could not ordinarily obtain on their own, along with professional advice. Many clubs start locally, but a few like Encore market nationally, negotiating discounts based on the purchasing power of some 400,000 members. These clubs often publish their own magazine or newsletter. They employ people to negotiate with travel companies and reservationists to service members, as well as most of the other professionals of a tour wholesaler/travel agent.

Also on the list of "gray area" retailers are barter companies that negotiate deals involving an exchange of goods and services instead of cash for travel. This is another borderline industry.

Nontravel Services

The travel industry is so pervasive, incorporating so many services, products, and needs, that it draws many other companies into the industry that you might not even consider. For example, AT&T and MCI are in the travel business, as are most other major telecommunications companies, since the travel industry uses so much in the way of communications. AT&T employs travel industry specialists to market and sell its services.

Citicorp Diners' Club, American Express, Visa and MasterCard, and other travel and entertainment card companies are also very much in the travel business. So are insurance companies, like Travellers Insurance, Mutual of Omaha, and Travel Guard, which specialize in products that the travel agency industry offers their clients. Other insurance companies, like The Berkely Group, specialize in professional liability insurance for the travel industry.

There are visa agencies, such as Visa Advisors, Washington, D.C., that specialize in obtaining visas for individuals, companies, travel agencies, and tour operators. There are marketing companies and direct-mail houses, such as Todd Travel Promotion, Hauppauge, NY; representation companies, like Forster Associates Travel Marketing, Los Gatos, CA; and consultancies, like Douglas Thompson & Associates, San Francisco.

Finally, there are currency exchange companies that are actively promoting services for both the travelers and the travel companies, like Deak Perera, New York, and Reusch International, Washington, D.C. These companies not only service travelers with foreign currency and travelers checks but also have various financial instruments that travel companies use for their international payments and receipts.

Contacts and Sources

In the area of travel technology, contact:

Information Industry Association, 316 Pennsylvania Ave., SE, Ste. 400, Washington, D.C. 20003.

In the area of research and marketing, contact:

Travel and Tourism Research Association (TTRA), P.O. Box 8066, Foothill Station, Salt Lake City, UT 84108, tel. 801-581-3351.

In the area of advertising, consult Standard Rate and Data Services *Directory of Advertisers* and its *Directory of Advertising Agencies*. Also consult *Advertising Age* and *AdWeek*, the leading industry trade publications.

To find out which public relations agencies represent a good number of travel clients, talk to reporters on trade publications or check *Jack O'Dwyer's Newsletter* (it announces which public relations agencies landed which accounts). Also consult *P.R. Contacts* and *Media Notes*.

In the area of travel writing, apart from the major travel trade and consumer press publications, check *Writer's Market* (send query and self-addressed and stamped envelope for reply to the appropriate editor) and Standard Rate and Data Services directories for leads. Other sources include:

American Business Press, 205 E. 42nd St., New York, NY 10017.

Society of American Travel Writers (SATW), 1155 Connecticut Ave., NW, Ste. 500, Washington, D.C. 20036, tel. 202-429-6639.

In the area of guidebook writing, contact brand-name publishing companies such as Prentice-Hall, Houghton Mifflin, and John Wiley & Sons. Also check *Writer's Market* and *Publishers Weekly*.

In the area of travel photography, consult the *Yellow Pages* for names of stock houses. Also consult *Writer's Market* or *Photographer's Market* for leads.

In the area of education and training, check *A Guide to College Programs in Hospitality and Tourism* by the Council on Hotel, Restaurant, and Institutional Education, published by John Wiley & Sons. Other sources include:

Society of Travel and Tourism Educators, 19364 Woodcrest, Harper Woods, MI 48225, tel. 313-526-0710.

American Society of Travel Agents' Scholarship Foundation, 1101 King St., Alexandria, VA 22314; publishes a travel school directory.

National Tour Foundation (NTF), 546 E. Main St., Lexington, KY 40508; publishes a listing of 700 schools with tourism-related programs.

In the area of association work, for additional leads beyond those given in this chapter, contact the American Society of Association Executives and consult the *Directory of Associations*.

In the area of travel industry law, contact:

International Forum for Travel and Tourism Advocates, Alexander Anolik, U.S. delegate, Professional Law Corp., 693 Sutter St., San Francisco, CA 94102.

In the area of off-tariff retailers and barter companies, check with:

American Association of Discount Travel Brokers, 85 South Union Blvd., Ste. G300, Lakewood, CO 80228, tel. 303-969-9352.

International Reciprocal Trade Association, 4012 Moss Place, Alexandria, VA 22304.

Landing a Job

18

Breaking In

The Value of Travel Schools

The travel industry has had a tradition of on-the-job training, and sensational success stories of people rising through the ranks abound. However, this tradition has proved impractical in today's work environment. Reliance on specialized computer reservations systems, the incredibly fast pace, and vulnerability to consumer liability suits have all forced agencies and other travel companies to rely more heavily on a growing body of academic and vocational programs to provide them with their entry-level people.

Though few in the industry believe that the schools are capable of turning out graduates who can move right into a job, they are increasingly seeing the value of these programs: They weed out individuals who are looking for fun and glamour but who have little comprehension of what the real world of work will be like in the travel business; they demonstrate the commitment of the job candidate, which is important because an employer makes a substantial investment in new hires; they provide a foundation that makes the additional on-the-job training required much easier, particularly in geography and professional terms, and even better with regard to computer systems and how each of the various industry segments function together. The best programs are now being designed with input from industry professionals and include training on airline computer reservations systems, sales techniques, and industry ethics.

As yet, there are no industry-set standards (states bestow accreditation), though the American Society of Travel Agents has been seeking to impose standards and has formed an associate membership category for travel schools. Some programs are out-and-out rip-offs and offer little in the way of practical work experience. A rapidly increasing number, however, offer very solid programs and, perhaps even more importantly, more direct links to actual jobs through placement programs and industry alliances.

There has been a veritable explosion in travel schools and academic programs of two- and four-year colleges over the past decade, which in part is explained by the dramatic growth in the industry but more accurately can be attributed to the profits. Tuition ranges from under a hundred to several thousand dollars, with the greatest increase in schools on the higher-tuition side.

While only about 10 to 20 schools were dedicated to travel agency training a decade ago, the numbers have swelled to the hundreds. There are hundreds of schools that are affiliated with travel agencies and hundreds more at the college or university level.

Many of the travel-agency-affiliated schools are used as recruitment grounds for these agencies; they skim the "cream of the crop" off the top of the graduating classes. The schools are also becoming major profit centers for agencies. In some situations, the schools also are used as a source of free labor and new clients.

You must scrutinize the agency-affiliated as well as the academic programs. In the past, there was a fundamental difference in orientation. Colleges and universities emphasized generalism and had students think in terms of "life careers" rather than specific job skills. "The philosophy of the university is to teach people how to become well-rounded human beings, not to channel them into narrow areas," said Dr. Steve Ilum, former assistant professor of travel and tourism at the Institute of Travel–Transportation–Tourism at Niagara University, New York. Academia also tended to emphasize "socially motivated" public recreation and government policy areas, shunning the "profit-motivated" commercial recreation sector (where most travel industry jobs fall).

Universities and colleges have become more sensitive to the

issue of teaching skills that will lead to real jobs, and many of the programs have been revamped. Many curricula are actually based on the Institute of Certified Travel Agents' program or that of the National College, both of which are industry oriented.

You must be very discriminating when choosing a vocational school or college program. Though many suggest in their sales material that a degree is essential to getting a job or that it is in fact a ticket into a job, both suggestions are untrue.

You should be wary if a school does not try to discover your own motivations or expectations about the travel business. The best schools attempt to discourage people who have unrealistic expectations of salary, travel benefits, or work levels or who would simply be unsuited to a career in travel because they are not people oriented or detail oriented.

You should interview recent graduates about the quality of their education, its applicability to their work, and the effectiveness of their schools' placement offices. In considering a school, check the following:

- Faculty with industry experience
- Curriculum that reflects current needs and functions of the industry—particularly, the quality and quantity of computer reservations training (real computers, not generic dummies)
- Opportunity for hands-on experience, such as agency simulation and internships
- Background of the school—how long it has been in business, its relationship and reputation with the industry, whether it has any citations by the local Better Business Bureau
- Placement assistance and career guidance availability (some placement offices are very active in the process and have strong industry contacts)
- Licensing from the state education department
- Accreditation from appropriate agencies
- Tuition that is neither too low nor too high
- Recruitment, selection, grading procedures, attendance policies, and amount of hours devoted to each area

Remember that you are taking the program in order to get a job. The degree is only as valuable as the school's reputation. A prospective employer will not consider your degree valid if the school does not have a reputation for turning out skilled graduates. The degree is only helpful in landing your first job; it becomes less significant with each successive job.

A degree in a credible travel–tourism–transportation program is becoming more and more necessary in getting a first job. This is not to say that getting in is impossible without a degree, but having one just makes it a little easier. An educational background makes on-the-job training easier and faster and makes advancement possible more quickly. Starting salaries also tend to be higher for new hires who have a degree.

Several excellent directories to travel schools and academic programs are available:

Travel School Directory, ASTA Scholarship Foundation, 1101 King St., Alexandria, VA 22314.

A Guide to College Programs in Hospitality and Tourism, Council on Hotel, Restaurant, and Institutional Education, published by John Wiley & Sons, New York, NY 10158.

National Tour Foundation listing of 700 schools offering tourism-related programs (available for $10), 546 E. Main St., Lexington, KY 40508.

A Strategy for Success

John Crystal, an eminent career counselor, used to say that to get a job, you need the skills of a spy. It is more accurate to say you need the skills of a good investigative reporter. Finding a job is a matter of knowing where to find information and what questions to ask, targeting specific potential employers, and then assembling all the information into a convincing presentation.

The first questions to ask are whether you want to pursue a career in travel and tourism at all and whether you have what it takes to be successful in it. The industry is made up of about 500,000 separate businesses in some 15 different categories, with very disparate needs, problems, and approaches. Regardless of whether you target an airline, a car rental company, a hotel, or a travel agency, and regardless of whether you believe travel is a dream or a commodity, what each business sells is service.

The overriding quality that employers look for is not "love

people, love travel" but an ability to serve people selflessly. Travel and tourism goes on constantly; most industry jobs of any responsibility are not just weekdays 9 A.M. to 5 P.M. but require commitment and dedication.

"The world is so large, so complex, so vast, that the one thing human beings need more than anything else is one-on-one service that makes their world a little more orderly," stated Travis Tanner, senior vice president of Walt Disney Attractions Sales and former president of Ask Mr. Foster.

Another quality that employers look for is the ability to be very detail oriented. This business is one of minute detail and complicated logistics. Many jobs require someone who is organized and patient and who can handle the constant changes and hassles.

Many jobs, particularly at entry level, entail some sacrifice, especially in terms of income since the industry is low paying, and possibly the need to relocate. However, because the industry continues to expand, it affords excellent opportunities for rapid advancement into positions that do pay decently and that have considerable responsibility and prestige.

Know Thyself

Once you have decided that you have what it takes for a career in travel and tourism, the next task is to isolate where you want to focus your energies. The industry is so vast, so diversified; each segment manifests its own personality and style. Finding a job requires sorting through myriad choices so that you can focus your energies in one area.

Next, you have to establish priorities. What is important to you? Travel, money, power, influence? The chance to work with people, to help people, to make a mark on society? To create, to grow personally or intellectually, to submerge yourself in art, culture, science, or business? To have free time for other interests or for family? To work in a set routine or in a dynamic situation where nothing is predictable? What is your ultimate goal? Where do you think you want to be in 5, 10, or 20 years?

Recognizing that your priorities will change and that it is impossible to map out a career path precisely, make a list of your wants, desires, and needs on paper in order of their importance. Since few things in this world are perfect, any job you take will likely require some trade-offs. Determine what is vitally important to you and what you can compromise. If you can be flexible about where you want to live, for example, you will have a much easier time finding a job in travel and tourism. You will most likely have to weigh long-term benefits against short-term ones—higher pay against a learning experience, security against mobility, responsibility against free evenings and weekends to pursue outside interests.

Knowing who you are and what you really want can help expand your options. You may find that you can satisfy the same professional and personal objectives in a different industry segment from the one that first captured your imagination. For example, the field of tour operations is very limited, but you can be a tour planner in many different contexts, such as hotels, incentive houses, travel agencies, airlines, motorcoach operators, or even the railroad.

Once you have established your priorities, you can begin to focus in on potential employers. The approach you take depends upon your priorities. You can first decide what kind of professional you want to be—marketing, sales, public relations, administration, computer systems (positions that are common to most businesses)—and then zero in on what segment of the industry appeals to you most. Or, if getting into a particular segment of the industry—hotels, airlines, tour companies, travel agencies—is more important, then start there. If you have targeted a particular company, you will probably have to be a little more open-minded about what position you take. You can be very clear on a résumé about wanting a position in marketing, but many companies only fill these positions from within and you may have to start in some entry-level position.

Finding Leads

Once you have decided on an industry segment, consult trade journals (both the articles and the ads), trade associations (some have job banks, referral services, or internship programs), professional societies, newspapers (classifieds as well as the news items, particularly the financial section), employment agencies (some specialize in travel), and stock analyst reports about growth companies. Some references that are helpful are:

Standard and Poor's
Dun & Bradstreet Reference Book of Corporate Management
Moody's Industrial Manual
F&S Index of Corporations and Industries
Encyclopedia of Associations
Standard Directory of Advertisers
College Placement Annual
Sales & Marketing Management
Wall Street Journal
Business Week
Forbes
Fortune
Newsweek
Time

Trade journals include:

Travel Weekly
Tour & Travel News
Business Travel News
Travel Agent
Travel Management Daily
Travel Trade
Corporate Travel
Travel Life
ASTA Agency Management
Aviation Weekly
Meetings & Conventions
Successful Meetings
Hotel & Resort Industry
Lodgings

Be particularly alert to the names of new companies, formations of new divisions, corporate expansions, reorganizations, and new products or projects and trends that may suggest new endeavors. (The woman who landed the position of director of administration and personnel for the New York convention center had contacted the newly appointed chairman personally after reading about his appointment in the newspaper.) You might also try to attend vacation and travel expos and trade shows.

If you are restricted to finding a job within a geographical area, contact state travel offices, local convention and visitors bureaus, tourism information offices, or chambers of commerce to find out what travel companies might be potential employers.

If you have targeted specific companies, try to do some research about each company to find out what positions each is hiring for and then personalize your approach. You might start with the human resources department, just to get an idea of what openings are available before you make a formal introduction. It is best, however, to try to contact people in specific departments.

Networking

Getting into the travel industry with no prior experience requires creative approaches designed to personalize your application. Once you have isolated the names of the companies where you want to apply, one technique is to find out the name of someone who will allow you to come in and conduct an "information interview." The purpose of the information interview is to find out as much as possible about the organization–job titles, background, how people apply–and, with luck, to get a personal introduction to the person who does the hiring.

Another technique is networking, which can make the real difference for a person coming in from outside the industry with no prior experience working in it. As many of the human resources professionals interviewed in this book noted, much depends on who you know. "We get thousands of unsolicited résumés from people with marketing degrees," said the manager of central employment for TWA, "but there is a lot of networking going on."

How do you get into the network from outside? First, you ask every friend and relative, and friend of a friend or relative, whether they know anyone in the target company or industry, even if that person is not in a hiring capacity. Being able to telephone someone and say, "So-and-so asked that I call," or, better, being introduced by an associate, makes a big difference. You have to realize that no matter how terrific your résumé looks, it is only one of hundreds or thousands that a personnel office has to consider.

Be Selective

You should try to be selective about the company you work for, but if this is not possible, take any job just to get inside and have a travel company on your résumé. If you can afford to be selective, the kinds of questions you should research are: How large or small is the company? How new or old? What position does the company hold in its field? What is its reputation? How progressive, innovative, or conservative is the company? How many people are employed and in what kind of organization? What are the company's human resources policies and what kind of working environment does it offer? What has the company's record been during industry downturns; is turnover particularly high or low? Is it affiliated with trade associations? What kinds of products and services does it offer and who are its customers? Try to get a sense of what your own advancement prospects will be like by looking at the ages of your superiors and what turnover rates are like.

There are advantages and disadvantages of working at both large and small companies. The largest organizations generally have the most entry-level positions and better training and management programs (and usually but not always are better paying with better benefits). But they are also deluged by thousands of résumés and generally can afford the best schooled or trained or experienced people. Working in the largest organizations tends to be more specialized and advancement tends to be slower, though there are usually higher positions to advance into because there are more management tiers. Smaller organizations can also be training grounds because they tend to pay less and thus cannot afford the more skilled individuals. The working environment may be more cramped, but you are apt to get a more generalized education and greater responsibility more rapidly than in a larger organization. Frequently, smaller companies are used as steppingstones to larger ones, but they can also provide a more close-knit and comfortable atmosphere.

Getting In

To get a job, you have to see yourself as an entrepreneur; you must find a need and fill it. Frequently, this means creating your own position.

Do not regard yourself as a novice looking to break into the industry. The travel and tourism industry draws on every professional background. From reading the chapters in this book on the specific industry segments, you should have a better sense of how you can present your own work or life experience as an asset in a position in a travel entity, even if you are just graduating from school. If you are trying to change careers, it may be necessary to move into a parallel function in travel, even if you would really prefer to leave as far behind as possible what you were doing before (say, accounting, teaching, or clerical work). Those who are returning to the work force after raising a family should recognize their assets as managers and also realize that many organizations appreciate the maturity gained by this experience.

No matter where you are coming from or what your prior experience, your strategy should be to just get into the organization because, once inside the company and the industry, you can move within it or to another company much more easily. Getting in is the hard part; once over this hurdle, you can go as far as your abilities and ambition let you.

Given the fact that deregulation, automation, and growing professionalism are probably the most significant developments underway in the industry, the greatest opportunities for new hires are in marketing and research, sales, computer services, information management, telecommunications, training and development, quality control and customer service, and operations.

The Résumé

The résumé is a necessary document, but it will not be what gets you a job (it could even lose a job for you). The objective of the résumé and its accompanying cover letter is to get you an interview. A résumé should be neatly presented, with absolutely no spelling mistakes or typos, preferably word-processed or offset but definitely typed on a quality white or off-white paper (not blue or gray), and should not be longer than two pages. It should state your name, address, and telephone number. If you are cold-canvassing, the résumé should also specify a job objective, which can be as specific as "salesperson" or "travel counselor" or as open as "a marketing position in which I can use my knowledge and contacts in the travel agency industry." The objective should *not* read: "a rewarding career in travel."

The organization of the résumé varies, but, depending upon what arrangement best presents your case, it should contain your work experience, listing dates, employer, title, and a brief description of your duties, responsibilities, and any major accomplishments. The kinds of details you should mention are the number of staff managed, how sales grew during your tenure, and any new program or innovation you created or implemented. Example: "During my tenure, sales increased 50 percent; opened new territory; won company's top sales award; introduced new product; market share improved." Use active words and do not keep repeating the same ones. Examples: managed, directed, oversaw, initiated, created, conceived, designed. Always specify whether you managed people (how many), called upon clients (corporations, travel agencies, church groups), made presentations, and/or wrote proposals. The point is: show results.

You should list your educational background, including dates of graduation, degree, name of school, and any special awards or honors you received. (If you are a recent graduate, emphasize your educational background and stress any internships or summer employment.) You might include a list of extracurricular activities.

The résumé should also include any military experience. You should list any memberships in professional or community organizations, awards, honors, distinctions, any published works, job-related activities, certificates or licenses (pilot's, driver's), and special skills (computer, foreign language, photography) or assets (extensive travel; lived abroad).

Instead of ignoring what might be perceived as a negative (hoping that the employer will not notice), turn a negative into a positive. For example, some employers are skittish when they see that someone has changed jobs every two years. You need to note that you had a rapid advance with a steady increase in responsibility. Explain that you were contracted for a one-year project, recruited by the president for a one-year project, or recruited by a client. Express the fact that the position was moved to Minneapolis and you chose not to move with it, or that the company was merged or went out of business. Since potential employers will generally ask why you left the last job, have a good answer planned. (You do not have to say you were "fired." You could say instead that there was a wave of layoffs when the company was forced to cut costs.) Never lie; just choose your wording strategically.

Remember the key themes and try to weave them into your résumé and cover letter. Travel companies look for people who are *service oriented, people oriented,* and *detail oriented,* and who have *good communications skills.* If you have broad experience, say so; if you are a specialist, say so.

Do not assume that the person reading your résumé is going to understand how your experience applies to his or her organization. Explain how your experience is relevant. If you are coming from outside the travel industry, you can use a summary of job expertise – sales and marketing, operations, public relations, calls on corporations, made presentations – all of which are directly applicable to travel. Use the fact that you bring experience from outside the industry to your advantage. For example, you can speak the language of another industry and have wide contacts in order to better sell corporate clients on your travel services.

Ideally, it is best to tailor the résumé to specific companies and positions, which is not so difficult if you have a word processor. If this is not practical, you can get around this issue by writing a convincing sales presentation in your cover letter.

The Cover Letter

If you are approaching a company cold, the cover letter ideally should start off with, "So-and-so suggested I contact you directly about a position . . . , given my interest and experience." Try to be specific and to the point. You might want to mention any outstanding qualifications for the job in the cover letter rather than depending upon the résumé alone. The cover letter should be designed to get you an appointment for an interview; rather than asking for an interview, suggest a time and state that you will call to confirm the date. Be aggressive but not pushy. Be respectful and polite.

If you know of a specific position you want to go after, try to learn as much as possible about the company – its corporate philosophy, its human resources philosophy, its plans to expand into new products or markets – and weave these concepts into your letter. Example: "Knowing that your company is diversifying into . . . expanding into . . . opening . . . , I wanted to contact you concerning how I might contribute directly to your company's success."

The Interview

Prepare yourself for the interview by learning as much as possible about the company. Prepare questions you might have about the company and the job position for which you are interviewing. This will go far to set you apart from other candidates; it will impress the interviewer that you are serious and committed, as well as demonstrate the skills that you can bring to the job.

There is a great difference in whether the interviewer is a professional personnel officer or the owner or manager of the firm or department head for whom you would be working. Personnel officers are trained to reject; they will pose questions to determine whether you are who you say you are and whether your credentials fit the bill. Frequently, they do not have actual knowledge of the position but only a listing of criteria to match against. They may use open-ended questions, which require straightforward answers. There are no right answers or wrong answers; in fact, it may not be the answer that is important at all, but what is not said or the manner in which you answer.

In contrast, department heads more likely direct questions to gauge your knowledge, experience, and, perhaps even more important, whether you have the right personality to fit into the organization. Many do not even put much stock in prior experience or knowledge but prefer to train people in their own methods. They are more interested in your intelligence, willingness to learn, and energy level.

What people look for is highly subjective. Nonetheless, essentially they look for "people-orientation" (the ability to work with people and serve others), good communications skills (the ability to organize thoughts and express them clearly in speaking or in writing), willingness to accept responsibility, energy, motivation, commitment, flexibility, and experience. A knowledge of geography and typing skills are very desirable for travel positions. You will probably also be rated on personal appearance, manners, social amenities, leadership potential, and maturity.

Try to counter negatives or objections. One interviewee, undeterred by her lack of specific product experience, rejoined, "What can I do to change your mind?"

The Follow Up

The follow-up is critical. After an interview, you should follow up with a note, thanking the interviewer for spending the time with you and summarizing the key selling points (your assets) for the job. Example: "Based on how you described the position, I know I have the qualifications you seek. I am skilled at meeting planning, I have a sales background, I have excellent communications skills, and I can represent the company in a professional manner. I am a go-getter who can spot new business opportunities. I very much want to be a part of a people-oriented, growth-oriented leader in the travel industry such as your company."

Such a letter gives you the opportunity to make your last sales pitch, shows that you care about getting the job, helps you stand out from the crowd, refreshes the interviewer's memory (the interviewer might have also seen dozens of other people for the same job), and, perhaps most importantly, corrects any misunderstandings or false impressions. Do not assume that the interviewer heard, understood correctly, or remembered. (One applicant was almost rejected because the interviewer understood him to say that he did not know a particular reservations system when, in fact, he did.)

You should not feel discouraged or rejected if you do not get a job. Frustration is an inevitable part of the process. Timing has much to do with it. Be persistent. (Dick Sundby of Tauck Tours had to try four times before landing a job as a tour escort—and that was nearly 20 years ago.) Be creative; be enterprising.

Getting Ahead

You are likely to stay in your first job in the travel industry only two or three years. How far and how fast you progress depend largely on the company or entity you are working for as well as on your own ability and aggressiveness. "Make yourself indispensable," advised Trudy Baron, who started her career in travel as a secretary and rose to become a vice president of a major international hotel company.

Do not just settle for the job description; go beyond it. Grow your own job, or grow yourself into one. (The public relations manager of one prominent New York City hotel began to create packages for the hotel with the aim of working into a position that reflected her expanded role.) Do not be locked into preconceived roles or plans; be flexible. Join trade organizations. Network. Read the trade press for your own field as well as other travel segments; read beyond the headlines and between the lines. If necessary, take additional training or schooling. (The Institute of Certified Travel Agents' CTC is one of the most coveted designations in the industry.)

In travel, especially, it is impossible to plot out a career path. You should have a plan for yourself—plotting your next move and where you want to be in 5 years and in 15 years—but be ready to change it. There are countless examples of people who began in one area and moved on to another like Robert Coffey, vice president of market planning for Alamo Rent A Car, who started in the airlines; Richard Valerio, president of American Sightseeing International, who also started in the airlines; and Colin Marshall, chief executive of British Airways, who was recruited from Avis Rent A Car before. There are also countless examples of people rising up like Gideon Spitz, president of Golden-Tulip Hotels, who started in public relations; and Pat Foley, chairman of Hyatt Hotels, who started out as a front-office supervisor nearly 30 years ago. The industry lore is full of sensational success stories of people attaining the heights of their profession without great wealth or educational background. There will continue to be such amazing successes because the industry is still growing and innovating. However, it is likely that, in the future, people in the top positions will be required to have more education and professionalism than they did in the past.

Indeed, the whole concept of "career" in the travel industry has changed. Not too long ago, people tended to spend their entire careers in a single segment, such as with airlines or hotels, and even in a single company; their career paths were vertical. Now, there is much greater integration of the elements, and career paths tend to be horizontal and diagonal, from segment to segment.

People frequently attribute their success to "being in the right place at the right time." On closer inspection, however, in most instances success is a matter of perceiving an opportunity or making an opportunity happen.

Where Dreams Come True

You spend most of your waking life in a job; it should be something that is satisfying and fulfilling. So many people fall into a career or fit themselves into some slot where they feel stifled and frustrated because their natural abilities are not given expression. The travel industry utilizes so many different professional skills and personal talents; it offers a dream come true not only for those who seek to travel but also for those who seek other forms of creative or professional expression.

It used to be said that travel was a dream of a lifetime, and people who worked in the industry, when asked what they enjoyed most about their jobs, would frequently reply that they "fulfilled dreams." For all those, however, who seek to work at something that is personally satisfying and for all who started at the lowest rung of a career ladder and rose to top management, being a part of the travel industry has been the means to fulfilling a personal dream. It can be for you.

Index